The New Music

The Avant-garde since 1945

REGINALD SMITH BRINDLE

LONDON/NEW YORK/TORONTO
Oxford University Press
1975

Oxford University Press, Ely House, London W1

GLASGOW NEW YORK TORONTO MELBOURNE WELLINGTON CAPE TOWN
IBADAN NAIROBI DAR ES SALAAM LUSAKA ADDIS ABABA DELHI
BOMBAY CALCUTTA MADRAS KARACHI LAHORE DACCA
KUALA LUMPUR SINGAPORE HONG KONG TOKYO

ISBN 0 19 315424 2

Printed in Great Britain
by W & J Mackay Limited, Chatham

Contents

Preface

The purpose of this book is to give a concise picture of the more adventurous evolutions of music since 1945. There is no mention therefore of many major composers such as Britten, Carter, Copland, Walton, and even Stravinsky, for their work hardly enters my picture. There is also little biographical detail, and I have made no attempt to discuss the complete works of any one composer.

My approach has been highly selective, picking out only those salient features which marked the paths of avant-garde development. This has sometimes meant the study of a relatively slight work like Feldman's *Projection 1*, while such an important large-scale composition as Penderecki's *St. Luke Passion* is hardly mentioned. Moreover, the book is made up of personal musical experiences and judgements. Thus it may well omit composers or works which others may regard as significant.

If these omissions require an apology, I apologize. But for a book of this sort they are necessary, and I do not regret them.

To my old friends of the Florentine 'Scuola Dodecafonica'—Bruno Bartolozzi, Arrigo Benvenuti, Sylvano Bussotti, Alvaro Company, and Carlo Prosperi.

Acknowledgements

Grateful acknowledgements are due to the following for permission to quote from the works cited.

Universal Edition

Webern: String Quartet, Op.28. Concerto, Op.24. Variations for Piano, Op.27. Variations for Orchestra, Op.30

Schoenberg: Five Piano Pieces, Op.23

Stockhausen: Kontra-Punkte. Zeitmasse. Mixtur. Klavierstück XI. Zyklus. Prozession Kontakte. Aus den Siebe Tagen. Stimmung

Boulez: Structures. Improvisation sur Mallarmé. Le Marteau sans maître

Bo Nilsson: Quantitäten

Bussotti: Sette Foglie

Bedford: Music for Albion Moonlight

Berio: Circles. Sequenzas III & V. Passaggio. Sincronie

Haubenstock-Ramati: Mobile for Shakespeare

Earle Brown: String Quartet. Corroboree

Cardew: Solo with accompaniment

Logothetis: Agglomeration

Also various quotations from Die Reihe

Ars Viva Verlag, Mainz (Schott & Co)

Nono: Polifonica-Monodia-Ritmica. Il Canto Sospeso. La Terra e la Compagna

Durand & Cie

Messiaen: Mode de Valeurs et d'Intensités.

Colfranc Music Publishing Co.

Varèse: Integrales

Boosey & Hawkes

Maxwell Davies: Antechrist

Schott & Co.

Donatoni: Composition in Four Movements

Suvini Zerboni

Camillo Togni: Tre Capricci

Pousseur: Quintette. Exercices pour piano

Berio: Serenata I. Sequenza.

Donatoni: Black and White. Etwas Ruhiger im Ausdruck

Levine: Parentheses

Buonomo: Percussion time

Kayn: Signals

Bartolozzi: Concertazione a Quattro. Concertazione per Oboe

Ricordi

Bussotti: Pieces de Chair II. Piano Piece for David Tudor 4. La Passion selon Sade

ACKNOWLEDGEMENTS

Renosto: Players
Associated Music Publishers
Brown: Available Forms 2. Folio
PMW- Music Publications Krakow
Dobrowolski: Music for Magnetic Tape No. 1
Bruzzichelli
Barraqué: Sequence
Bussotti: Siciliano
Maderna: Oboe Concerto
Leduc
Messiaen: Chronochromie
Peters Edition
Feldman: Projection I. Intersection No. 1. Atlantis. Christian Wolff in Cambridge. Durations 2.
Ligeti: Volumina. Aventures. Lux Aeterna
Cage: Piano Concerto. Amores. Water Music. Music of Changes II
Englert: Aria for Timpani
Smith Brindle: Three Dimensions. The Death of Antigone
Berberian: Stripsody
Globokar: Voie
Kagel: Sonant (1960/. . . .)

1

The Historical Background

Music is the child of its social environment, which in its turn is moulded by the major events of world history. Very seldom has music *formed* its environment. The flames of patriotic fervour which led to the Italian Wars of Independence were certainly fanned by Verdi's *Sicilian Vespers* and *Nabucco*, but they were not lit by them. The more sensual brands of pop music may incite today's youth to what would once have been called loose moral standards, but it is not the prime cause of even the least degree of immorality.

Music has always reflected the outside world and sublimated it, breathing the mysticism of the medieval epoch, the poetry and finesse of the Elizabethan court, the superficial charms and graces of the rococo period, and so on. In this century its progress follows the history of peoples and societies as never before, and this close association of music and society is particularly evident since the Second World War. So before any study of the more progressive music of the period can begin, it is necessary to give a glance, however brief, at world history since 1945. And it is 'world' history that matters, for with the enormous development of communications the world has become small, and what happens in the most remote corner of our planet one day can affect the rest of humanity the next.

Since 1945, two events have occurred which are more significant for mankind than anything since the birth of Christ. Firstly, atomic bombs were dropped on Hiroshima and Nagasaki. Secondly, man has walked on the Moon. The first means that man can destroy mankind in one great holocaust, the second that we are no longer chained to this earth until its extinction, but can set off into space on a journey without end.

Inevitably, the discovery of the atomic bomb has had the most immediately far-reaching consequences. Due to a state of 'cold war' between the great powers, atomic weapons have proliferated so that the whole human race lives under the threat of annihilation. To add to the state of unease, the world has lived in a constant condition of minor war. Israel is besieged by the Arab

States; in Korea and Vietnam the U.S.A. was at war for twenty years; in Latin America and Africa, brief conflicts flare up and are extinguished at frequent intervals. There have been over fifty wars in the quarter-century following 1945, though the actual war zones have fortunately remained small.

Further, there are internal divisions within the Eastern and Western blocks. The different communist ideals of Russia, China, Yugoslavia, and Albania produce discords between themselves and their satellites; the Western democracies have political ideologies which are virtually incompatible. Every nation has its internal conflicts too, of race, religion, class, or age-group.

These events and facts may seem to have little to do with music, but in reality have gone far towards dictating its developments. The psychological adjustments we have had to make to live with the atomic bomb are beyond measure. Peace is not in our souls, and many of us have had to learn to overcome varying degrees of neurosis. Some seek relief in protest and violence, others withdraw into anti-establishment groups of a more pacifist nature. Some reject society completely and acknowledge no responsibility towards it. All these facts of life are reflected in our music, and as we shall see, make it what it is, for good or ill.

There is one last historical observation to make. In the distant past, history moved relatively slowly, and there was only a slow rhythm of change. But the speed of change has gradually accelerated during the last thousand years, and there has been a correspondingly increased pace of musical development. Change in this century has continued to accelerate so that since the Second World War, successive events of world-wide importance are continually thrust on us. So music too has changed at a vertiginous speed, and no sooner has one trend been established than a new development has superseded it.

We have also to consider the social conditions of our times. This is a mechanistic age in which technology is rocketing ahead, leaving a wake of social ills and spiritual disorders. Man, in his real essence, is hardly better off than the cave dwellers of 40,000 years ago, in spite of all his technological benefits. Nevertheless, though we may protest, this is the life we all live. The sound of machines is part of our existence, and inevitably the same kind of sound has become an integral part of our music.

This, then, is the background to all that has happened in music since 1945. Yet it must be confessed that the relationship of some musical events to world history is still by no means clear, for we are far too near our subject-matter in time to see things in their true perspective.

2

The Post-War Years

Inevitably the Second World War disrupted musical activity, and even the years which led up to it were troubled ones for many composers. After Hitler came into power in 1933, many composers fled into exile or withdrew into artistic seclusion, some to live in extreme poverty (Webern and Bartók), most of them to encounter a severe setback in their fortunes. The end of the war therefore promised the beginning of a new golden era.

After 1945, German composers favoured by the Nazis became discredited, and though the same discredit did not fall on Italian composers of the Fascist period (the proscription of Italian composers by the Fascists having been most moderate) a great wave of revulsion for the art of the totalitarian period swept both countries and a search began for artistic renewal. This movement quickly spread through all Western Europe, to the U.S.A., and eventually even as far as Japan.

But though, with the discrediting of the 'idols of the Nazi cave' and the desire for artistic renewal, a revision of aesthetic ideals and technical resources was clearly inevitable, it was by no means clear how and where to begin again. As the radios of Western Europe began to broadcast the wealth of neglected works by Bartók, Stravinsky, Hindemith, Berg, and Schoenberg, it became evident not only that the available styles, aesthetics, and techniques were considerable, but that these were in considerable contrast with each other.

If music had had to 'begin again' at any previous moment in musical history, there could hardly have been such a wealth of alternatives, or so many contrasting and irreconcilable factors, as in the late Forties. Generally speaking, composers were attracted by the works of Bartók, Stravinsky, or Hindemith and imitated one or other of their styles; works such as Stravinsky's *Symphony of Psalms* and Bartók's *Music for Strings, Percussion, and Celesta* were frequently imitated during this period. Though in some contrast, the works of these three composers are not in strong conflict and may be regarded as a continuation of the style of the Twenties and Thirties. If they had stood alone, the idioms of

Stravinsky, Bartók, and Hindemith could have been amalgamated in a general post-war technique of composition of some stability and durability.

But with the circulation of Schoenberg's serial music, a seriously disruptive element was injected into the post-war scene and all chance of stylistic and technical stability was lost. Serialism proposed such radical changes in the traditional concepts of musical structure (and particularly in form, melody, and harmony) that it was completely irreconcilable with the works of Bartók, Hindemith, and the then Stravinsky. And so a conflict sprang up between serialism and the rest.

This splitting of the musical world into serialists and non-serialists during the first post-war decade was absolute and lasted for some considerable time, even after Stravinsky himself became a confirmed serialist during the early Fifties. Particularly in Western Europe, composers, critics, and performers had to become partisans of one camp or the other; to have a foot in both worlds was almost an impossibility. To one faction, serialism itself was a virtue, the mechanisms of which could lead only to perfection and high artistic merit. To the other faction, the use of Schoenberg's series could only produce non-music. Naturally, the polemics of this period are often blind to what really matters—true artistic value—and many gallons of ink were wasted on vitriolic, highly biased nonsense. I would like to make public confession that at one time my own music criticism treated modern non-serial works in very intolerant fashion. Such prejudice can be excused only on one ground. At that time, such blasts of uninformed criticism were aimed *against* serialism, that one was led to counter them by any means, fair or foul. Good criticism—impartial and constructive—was almost impossible in such circumstances.

But this straightforward confrontation of serialism and non-serialism was soon to become further complicated by divisions among the serialists. Some, striving towards a more ascetic, less emotional language than Schoenberg's high-pressure expressionism, seized on Webern's slender, intellectual conceptions as the basis for a new musical language. This so-called 'Post-Webern' school will be treated in the next chapter. Others preferred to eschew Schoenberg in favour of a milder, Bergian form of serialism, and sought to unify the new compositional method with tradition.

This bridging of the gap between atonality and tonality, between dodecaphony[1] (as serialism was sometimes loosely called) and tradition, once seemed

[1] 'Dodecaphony' is a term which has often been used to denote serial music. 'Twelve-note', or in America 'twelve-tone', have been similarly used. Strictly speaking these three terms should refer to music which uses the total-chromatic (of twelve chromatic notes contained within the octave) consistently and in a free manner, without serial organization. To make sure, however, that serialism is not intended, it has become customary to refer to 'free' twelve-note

very important. To many composers of the post-war period it appeared that between the more conventional musical languages and serialism lay an immense field which must be well explored and made familiar before music could again move forward. Particularly critical seemed such factors as harmony, melody, and form. Serialism had changed these so radically, had challenged traditional concepts so brusquely, that it seemed necessary to spend a long period reconciling the new language with more orthodox conventions. In fact, whether they intended it or not, composers of a whole generation dedicated their efforts in one way or another to the exploration of the field between tonality and atonality,[1] and to the integration of serialism into a more accessible musical language. To name but a few, Fortner and Henze in Germany, Searle and Seiber in England, Vogel and Liebermann in Switzerland, Dallapiccola, Peragallo, Riccardo Malipiero, R. Nielsen, and Vlad in Italy—these and many more sought to blend some facet of serialism with traditional idioms. For some time it did seem as if a new great extension of the traditional, so-called 'classical' dialectic was emerging, as if the old language had been given a new lease of life. But, too soon, it was all over.

By the early Fifties this phase of recuperation was coming to an end. It was already clear that there was not going to be a long period of fusion of serial and traditional elements, of exploration of the vast terrain supposedly lying between the tonal and atonal worlds. Music was passing on. It was not that the Schoenbergian language was already exhausted, nor that attempts to fuse the serial and tonal worlds did not bear good fruit. The truth is that the intellectual climate of the atomic age demanded to be expressed through sounds completely different in nature. And these new sounds were characterized by the omission of traditional elements and Schoenberg's modification of them, rather than by their inclusion.

The new sound of the Fifties aimed towards no mellifluous melodies (however brief), no coherent harmonies and clear-cut forms. In fact, at the time it

---

music. This is particularly necessary when referring to post-serial music (as opposed to the 'free-atonalism' of early Schoenbergian dodecaphony).

[1] The word 'atonal' was first used early in the twentieth century as a derogatory term, meaning not only 'non-tonal', but 'non-musical'. It was often applied to music which, far from being 'atonal', was merely obscure in its harmonic aspects but did not belong clearly to traditional key systems and so perplexed and offended the listeners of that time. In strict logic, 'atonality' is a mistaken term, for whenever two or more sounds are combined, harmonic relationships are formed. These relationships may be extremely complicated, but the music will not be completely non-tonal. By now, the meaning of 'atonality' has changed considerably and is today accepted as signifying not non-tonality, but an all-inclusive tonality which includes all possible harmonic products of the total chromatic space enclosed by the twelve semitones within the octave.

was not clear what kind of sound was being searched for, only what was to be avoided. Composers talked of 'beginning again' with a 'tabula rasa'. Every element of the musical language had to be subjected to reappraisal and examination before it could be made part of the new art, which aimed at eradicating any suggestion of past musical languages.

But in reality the new sound of the Fifties had already been anticipated in one way and another for some considerable time. Luigi Russolo's *Arte dei Rumori* ('Art of Noises') dates from as far back as 1913 and certainly anticipates to a considerable degree the more percussive, mechanistic music of later days and even the 'musique concrète' of our own time. Pratella's *Manifesto of Futurist Musicians* (1912) and his *Technical Manifesto*, as well as preaching a music of the machine age, advocated the use of several technical features, such as atonality, microintervals, and complex rhythmic figurations, which are typical of more recent music. Edgard Varèse, in such pieces as *Ionisation* (1931), and John Cage, in *First Construction in Metal* (1939), had already exploited the percussion ensemble and shown how fascinating music could be when written without reliance on pitched sounds and the melodies and harmonies that go with them.

These composers, and many others, had already expressed the sounds of a mechanistic age long before the Fifties. But though the introduction of 'noise' elements into music has been gradually accepted by composers and public alike, and has become a characteristic feature of post-war music, the greatest influence in the 'beginning again' was from another source—Anton Webern, who had been creating his enigmatic, almost passionless art during the previous four decades. In these four decades his quiet voice was seldom heard. But, as we shall see, in the years that followed his music became exalted and glorified almost beyond measure.

3

The Webern Cult

Nobody would have been more astonished than Webern if he could have seen how his name was revered by a new generation of composers only ten years after his death. Withdrawn, diffident, and modest, resigned to artistic obscurity and embittered by the apparent failure of his life's work, he would have been overwhelmed to find his name already a legend and his works regarded as jewels of perfection.

That he should so rapidly have become the idol of a cult is difficult to explain. His music was not easy to obtain after the war (indeed many of the works on which his reputation rests were not published until the later Fifties); nor were performances frequent. At the main platform for the Webern revival—the Darmstadt Kranichstein Summer School—no Webern was performed until the Piano Variations Op. 27 in 1948 and some early songs Op. 4 in 1949. Only in 1953, to mark his seventieth birthday, was any quantity of Webern's music played—seven pieces.

Gramophone records were scarcer still. Until the mid-fifties, the only Webern record available in England comprised the Trio Op. 20 and his orchestration of Schubert's *German Dances*. In the U.S.A. Dial records had eight pieces on issue in 1954, though these were not obtainable in Europe.[1] On the Continent, only a single piece was issued, the Symphony Op. 21.

It was not until 1957, when Columbia issued Robert Craft's complete recordings of Webern's music (excluding a number of works without opus numbers, and transcriptions), that his work could be widely known. Even so this album could only be obtained in Europe with difficulty. Everything therefore seemed to militate against a rapid diffusion of his works. Yet the Webern cult grew apace. Perhaps the very difficulty in hearing his music (or even seeing his scores) gave it a magic aura, and lent a certain mythological quality to his name.

Much of the early information about Webern has come from René Leibowitz's three books *Schoenberg et son école*, *Qu'est-ce que la musique de douze*

[1] 'Dollar restrictions' made it difficult to obtain American records until the late Fifties.

sons ?, and *Introduction à la musique de douze sons* published in France between 1947 and 1949.[1] As a pupil of Webern, few were more qualified than Leibowitz to discuss his master's works when he taught at Darmstadt in 1948, though it is highly probable (if his books are any guide) that his teaching concentrated largely on Schoenberg's serial methods, with little mention of Webern's 'preformed' concepts which later became so important for the younger generation. But in 1949 Olivier Messiaen taught at Darmstadt, and as he was just then evolving a system of a 'preformed' nature analogous to that which Webern partly aimed towards in his later works, it is probable that Messiaen highlighted Webern's models in his teaching.

Both Messiaen and Leibowitz lived in Paris, and as teachers of some of the most important figures of the new generation (such as Boulez, Henze, and Stockhausen) they obviously had great influence in post-war events. But it would be mistaken to attribute the 'Webern myth' to them alone. It would be more accurate to record that Webern and what he stood for was 'in the air'. His restraint, lack of bombast, brevity, and intellectual quality made much appeal, an appeal given all the more allure because one could so seldom hear his music.

Serialism, particularly in Germany where it had for so long been banned, became a symbol in the post-war years of spiritual and intellectual freedom and renewal. But if knowledge of Schoenberg had to come first, it became evident that the younger generation showed distaste for his music, regarding it as heavily burdened with late romantic expressionism, shackled by traditional melodic and rhythmic elements, and unsuitable for beginning a new musical language. Webern's work, instead, had the great appeal of being rational yet pointing the way to still further rationalization. Above all, it made the kind of sound composers were looking for and which was so representative of the new times. Inevitably, enthusiasm for Webern often went too far. His music was perhaps overrated and he was credited with more radical innovations than he actually accomplished. But before debating these questions it is best to discuss briefly what Webern's innovations really were, and to what ends they were designed.

Webern's musical language is carefully circumscribed. He did not aim at a richly varied idiom, full of colourful contrasts, suited to the expression of a wide gamut of emotions. On the contrary, his music deliberately covers a limited emotive field and therefore the technical means used are not widely varied. Moreover, he tended more and more to limit his working material only to those elements which would best serve his expressive needs, and it was his endeavour to 'preform' these elements (so that an entire work could be derived from a

[1] Published respectively in Paris 1947, Liège 1948, and Paris 1949.

minimum of material) which so appealed to the young post-war generation. To them, this 'preforming' represented the quintessence of Webern's work.

Webern's circumscription of his musical material was designed to achieve coherence and homogeneity, to obtain the greatest possible unity. His endeavour was to create as many relationships as possible, so that the totality of any work was built up of interrelated factors which could ideally be reduced to an absolute minimum of initial material. I shall briefly summarize Webern's methods, and his main compositional characteristics, as they often form the basis of much of the music which was to follow.

He actually wrote very few serial works, and it is striking how the series he used tended to become more and more similar in construction. In all his series he used a preponderance of semitones, interspersed usually by thirds. In its most rational application, this material would be arranged in symmetrical patterns so that one group of notes would form the basis for the remainder of the series:

Webern: Series *Concerto,* Op. 24

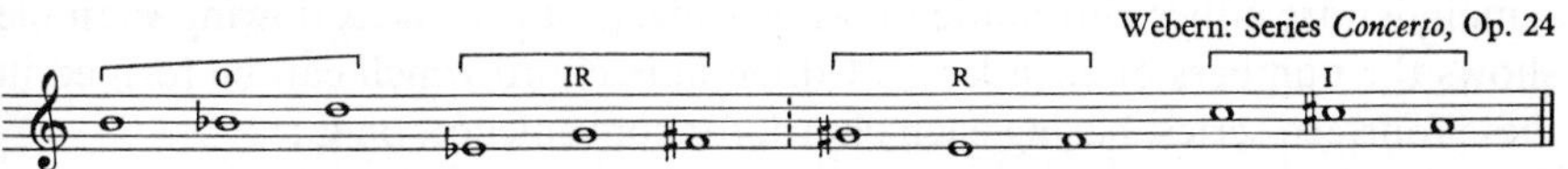

The first three-note group ('O') is a basic shape or cell on which the other groups are based. The second group ('RI') is a retrograde inverted of the original cell, the third group a retrograde ('R'), and the final group an inversion ('I').

Other series have even more relationships between various note-groups built in:

Webern: Series *Variations for Orchestra,* Op. 30,

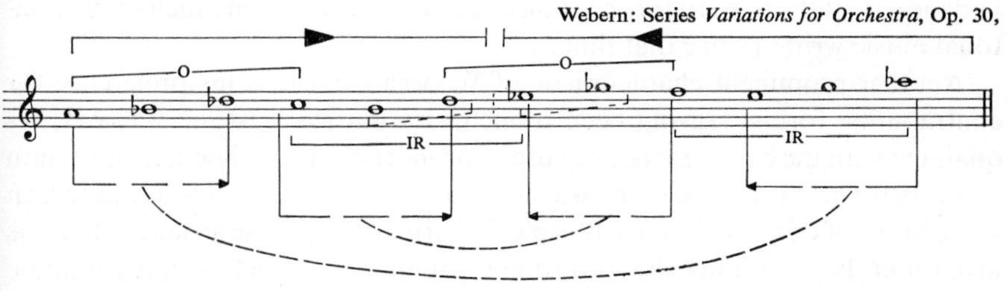

The inter-relationships here of various two-, three-, four-, and six-note groups are obviously so profuse that it would be tedious indeed to put them into words. What is significant is that it was towards such symmetry and cross-relationships that Webern's serial formations increasingly tended.

This grouping of the series into similar cells had inevitable consequences on the horizontal (melodic) and vertical (harmonic) products of such works. For example, in his Concerto Op. 24, the two- and three-note melodic fragments which make up all three movements of the entire work use only the semitone and third (and their inversions) which make up the series. Harmonically, too, in the Concerto, Webern never steps outside the limits of the same material. Two-note chords are always formed from either semitones or thirds (or their inversions), three-note chords are always made up of a semitone and a third, and so on. Inevitably, this usage gives great melodic and harmonic unity, but not variety.

Finally, it is worth mentioning that Webern's series always gave harmonic results which avoided all triad chords, scale formations, or 'cadential bass' successions (fourths and fifths). In addition, whole-tone groupings were kept to a minimum. On examining fourteen of Webern's series from Op. 17 onwards it will be found that of the 140 three-note chords which can be formed, ninety-four comprise a semitone and a major or minor third in one way or another. The remainder are either chromatic or whole-tone groups. The following example shows the numbers of each kind of three-note chord which can be formed in these fourteen series, basing each chord, for convenience, on C:

This kind of note grouping was to become characteristic of Webern's followers, and indeed set the pattern for the choice of note successions in much of the non-tonal music written since that time.

Another prominent characteristic of Webern's music is his preference for contrapuntal forms. Having been trained as a musicologist, he was well acquainted with the early renaissance use of proportionalisms, hocket, and canon in all their various forms. Consequently many of his movements are based on successions of canonic designs. It is particularly in the phrase structure that his love for early polyphony shows through—in his use of brief, simple rhythmic cells derived from number proportions. For example, the following section from the String Quartet Op. 28 is based entirely on the proportion 2:1. Roughly, this is a double canon, with semitones as basic intervallic units expanded to major sevenths and minor ninths. The beginning of this section is omitted as it overlaps previous bars of different material:

Webern: *String Quartet*, Op. 28

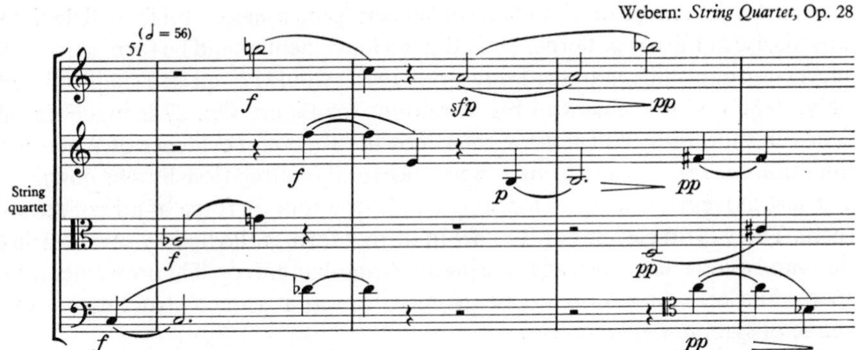

As will be seen, 𝅗𝅥 and ♩ are the smallest time units to which the proportions 2:1 are applied so the element of change is small. But elsewhere, by varying the duration of the basic unit more frequently, Webern often turns the simplest material into a surprisingly complex aural result. In the following, the proportions 1:1:1 are used with four different time values to exciting effect:

Webern: *Concerto*, Op. 24

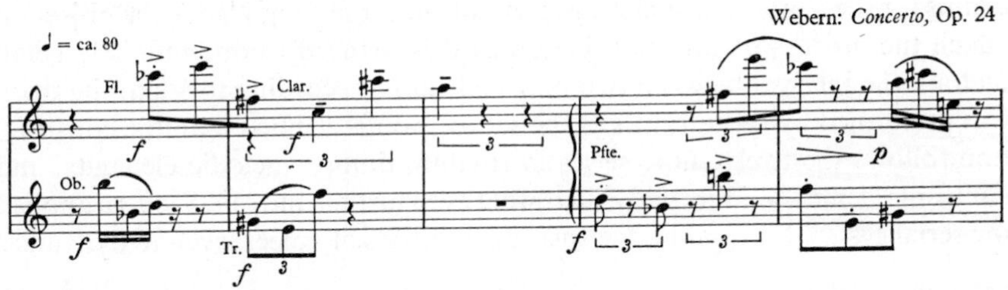

As well as the proportionalisms so characteristic of his canonic structures, Webern sometimes used a further kind of 'precomposition': throughout a passage or canon the octave position of certain notes was always fixed. For example, the first movement of the Symphony Op. 21 is made up of three canons, and in each canon the octave for each note is fixed. To add further to the symmetry, the notes are positioned so as to form a regular pattern around a central pitch. The following example shows the disposition of all notes in the first (double) canon (bars 1 to 26):

Webern: *Symphony*, Op. 21

Apart from his use of canon, one of Webern's most successful formal devices was his use of mirror patterns. Sometimes a movement would be formed from a succession of small mirror sections, sometimes it would comprise a single mirror only.[1] The first movement of his Variations for Piano, Op. 27 is made up of fourteen short mirror structures, each showing abundant evidence of Webern's intention to create as many correspondences and interrelationships as possible. The last movement of the Symphony Op. 21 is a tour de force of mirror structures. There is an eleven-bar 'theme' in mirror form, followed by seven variations and a coda, each part again being an eleven-bar mirror. This movement, so sparse and economical, is one of the most closely reasoned structures in the whole of symphonic literature.

This reasoned construction of Webern's music, this maximum of organization, seemed to be about to reach its culmination in his penultimate work, the Variations for Orchestra, Op. 30. During the composition of this work in 1941, he wrote a letter to Willi Reich[2] which later led many to believe that the work was a fully-fledged example of integral serialism. His statement that the work is 'preformed' in the first few bars led many enthusiasts in the Fifties to make wild claims for the Variations which are certainly not true. For Vlad,[3] 'the object on which the process of variation is exercised is reduced to one infinitely small factor—the interval between two notes'. That is, according to Vlad, the work was preformed by the intervals of the series. Nono[4] claimed that 'the construction follows the twelve-note series in rhythm, timbre, melodic elements, and harmonic elements'. Winfried Zillig[5] went even further and said Webern applied the serial system 'to rhythm, the successive entries of voices, even to dynamics,

[1] Note the rhythmic mirror already quoted in Ex. 5.

[2] The best translation available seems to be that by Humphrey Searle in Walter Kolneder's *Anton Webern*, though unfortunately it omits a vital final sentence. He says: 'Everything in the piece is derived from the two phrases stated in the first two bars by double bass and oboe! But this is still further reduced, as the second phrase, in the oboe, is already retrograde in itself: the second two notes are the cancrizans of the first two, but in augmentation rhythmically. Then the first (double bass) phrase follows again in the trombone, but in diminution! And in cancrizans as to motifs and intervals. That's how my series is built up, formed from these three groups of four notes. But the succession of the motifs joins in this retrograde effect, though using augmentations and diminutions! These two kinds of variation lead almost exclusively to the ideas of the different variations: this means, motivic alteration only takes place within these limits, if at all. But by changing the centre of gravity in all possible ways within these two phrases something new in time-signature, character, etc. keeps on appearing.' Finally, the important last sentence taken from another source: 'The entire development of the piece is already present in the row of the first few bars: Preformed.' (Quoted from *Anton von Webern: Perspectives*, edited by Demar Irvine.)

[3] Roman Vlad, *Storia della Dodecafonia* (Milan, 1958).

[4] *Die Entstehung der Reihentechnik* (Darmstädter Beiträge, 1958/25).

[5] *Variationen über neue Musik* (Munich, 1959).

the tone-colour, and even the expression of each individual note'. In other words, the series determined just about everything.

This is not the place for an extended investigation of this matter which, though so important in the Fifties, is now past history. We can, however, take a brief look at the music:

As will be seen, the double-bass motif uses the proportions 2:2:1:2, which are reflected in retrograde and in diminution by the trombone (2:1:2:2). The oboe motif uses the proportions 3:1 together with its retrograde in augmentation. At the same time, these phrases feature alternations of close and expanded forms of the semitone and major third (a 'wide' form is followed by a close one and vice versa). These two constructive principles—proportionalisms and interval alteration—are certainly prominent throughout the Variations, but there is no indication whatever that they govern the successive entry of voices, dynamics, tone-colour, and expression. There is indeed much else in the Variations which cannot be explained away by the preformed principles outlined in Webern's letter (such as the 3:1:2:4 proportions of the viola part shown in Ex. 7, the overall structure which demands 113 changes of metre in only 180 bars, etc.), but these should be evident to those who read the score.

What really matters, historically, is that the preformed structure of the Variations became a significant aspect of the Webern myth. Before the work even appeared in print, its structural processes (as known from Webern's letters)[1] were already part of the influences pushing composers towards the goal of integral serialism. For the many followers of Webern, his cerebralism was yet another inducement to follow his example. In fact, Webern's proportionalisms appealed much more widely than to the limited field of the more advanced younger composers. They began to feature prominently in the works of such established composers as Dallapiccola from the early Fifties onwards, and even Stravinsky soon afterwards.

The tenuous, abstract, timeless, almost supernatural music of Webern had

[1] Soon after Webern wrote to Reich, he wrote also to Hildegard Jone with a strangely different explanation of his structuring.

therefore not only a strong appeal as sound, it also had an intellectual attraction particularly suited to the inclinations of the post-war generation of composers. But though Webern's influence has lasted long, his musical language, so deliberately limited in emotive scope and already so perfect as to be unsurpassable, has inevitably given way to the different, more forceful needs of others. For those who were to come—the 'Post-Webern' school, or the 'avant-garde'—Webern's music was not so much a model to be copied, as an art form to be expanded into a widely different language, a language at times so complex that its Webernian origins are hardly discernible.

4

The Avant-Garde—Pointillism

History is said to repeat itself. The same situations are gradually created and resolved time and time again. This is because, though circumstances and times change, man remains immutable. But musical history, on the surface, does not seem to repeat itself. Music changes substantially from one age to another. It becomes more complex too, so that we have been led to talk of its 'development' and 'progress', as if it were improving and growing in stature, almost implying that development means greater artistic qualities and refinements. But beneath the surface, things may remain unchanged. What really matters is what music says to the hearts of men; in themselves development and progress may be worthless and to give them undue intrinsic value is only to deceive ourselves.

The belief that music must progress is perhaps not new. In 1868 Rossini wrote: 'I am obliged to admit that when I read big, ugly words such as *Progress*, *Decadence*, *Future*, *Past*, *Present*, *Convention*, etc., my stomach heaves with a motion I find extremely difficult to repress.' What provoked his outburst was the 'Music of the Future' movement led by Liszt and Wagner—a movement which has some analogies with music after 1945. Bizet perhaps had the real answer: 'It is not the "music of the future"—that means nothing—but . . . it is the *music of all time*, because it is admirable.'

But this 'towards the future' mentality has been all too evident since the Fifties. The 'avant-garde'[1] has looked forward, leading the way towards an obscure and still indiscernible goal, blazing new paths with great vigour and resource, though changing course so often that the musical public has been left bewildered. Eimert[2] wrote arrogantly in 1957 'today, either music exists as it is in the vanguard, or it does not exist at all'. Which is of course ridiculous: to look forward gives no guarantee of aesthetic quality. At times indeed we have seen

[1] The term 'avant-garde' used of an artistic movement is by no means recent. It can be traced back for some considerable period, but really came into prominence in France a hundred years ago to designate the rebel impressionist movement.

[2] Herbert Eimert, 'The Composer's Freedom of Choice', in *Die Reihe* 3 (Vienna, 1957).

the avant-garde fall into some disrepute, for though it has always included hard-working, talented musicians, there have been ample opportunities for unscrupulous charlatans whose abilities lie in self-publicity rather than musicianship. Yet, despite this, something great has been accomplished. A musical language has emerged which is the quintessence of the spirit of our age, which succeeds in expressing our most intimate feelings and, it is to be hoped, will speak with equal significance to men in the distant future.

In retrospect, it is now easy to see why the Webern cult was necessary, and how, becoming merged into a 'Post-Webern' school, it crystallized into a cult of the Avant-Garde. (Though there has always been an 'avant-garde' in music, and always will be, the term was seized on in the Fifties by the progressives as a new emblem, signifying their separateness from all else, which, by implication, was retrogressive.) Cults are necessary to artists, writers, and composers for their own protection and to create a feeling of artistic security. To be alone is distressing to all but the greatest few, the prime movers. To others it is a psychological and artistic necessity to belong to some movement, some cult which is a protective umbrella against outside dangers. The cult, too, can offer a certain measure of success. As a simple example, writers of popular music who belong to either a pop, folk, trad, or rock cult have a consumer market ready to absorb their output, while to be outside one of these trends is to invite failure and isolation. The avant-garde has therefore been necessary as a cult, even though the title once meant one thing (following Webern) and by now can mean almost anything else (sham oriental rites, group happenings, audience hypnosis, way-out jazz, etc.).

'Belonging' to the avant-garde has meant a certain amount of imitation of the most successful models. Of course this is no unusual situation in music. Imitation has been the way composers have learned their trade for thousands of years. But this question of imitation posed a problem for many of the early members of the avant-garde. For, being by nature revolutionaries, breaking away from the more conventional paths of post-war music, their first instinct was for change, not imitation. As a result, their music was made to conform to a general *style*, but composers gave their inventive faculties no boundaries of variety in *method*.

An exhaustive study of the period would have to investigate a mass of different compositional techniques, each the more or less personal product of a particular composer. Fortunately, this will not be necessary here: so many individual methods are derived from the same basic principles that it will be possible to demonstrate only the foundation techniques and ignore more personal applications.

Before going on to investigate the beginnings of integral serialism,[1] it would be preferable to dwell for a moment on the characteristics of earlier works (written around the early Fifties) which, though belonging to the post-Webern movement, were still not conceived with all-pervading structuralism in mind. These interregnum works often have very sparse textures, brief phrases tracing stark, angular melodic outlines, and as often as not very subdued dynamics. This almost single-note texture, with widely scattered, almost disconnected sounds and uniformly subdued emotive undertones, came to be called the 'pointillist' style[2]—a not inappropriate description. As works of the following period of integral serialism at first continued the same kind of sound texture, the term pointillist continued to be used almost throughout the Fifties, until music changed its character to such a degree that the term was no longer appropriate and fell into disuse. Some have said that pointillist music should comprise only isolated sounds—that each 'point' is a separate sound entity, not to be associated with what has gone before or with what follows. This extreme view has never been realized in European pointillist music. Just as the eye, in pointillist paintings, assembles all the points of colour into overall shapes, so the ear relates isolated sounds and interprets them as linear communication. (Only in the music of John Cage are sounds sometimes separated by so much silence that they can no longer be connected with each other. For example, Cage's *Piano Music No. 3* comprises only seven widely-separated notes.)

A typical example of the pointillist style of the early Fifties is the opening section of Luigi Nono's *Polifonica—Monodia—Ritmica* for chamber orchestra, written about 1951. The first movement is mostly pianissimo, beginning with touches of cymbal sounds and then whispered pitched notes in relative isolation:

[1] Other terms such as 'total serialism', 'total organization', and 'predetermined composition' have also been used to indicate music which has been written with a high degree of organization. Their usage has not always been strictly accurate, but being accepted terms they are used in this text where appropriate.

[2] The term 'pointillism' is derived from an impressionist style of painting initiated by Georges Seurat in the 1880's. Though he preferred the name 'divisionism', the word pointillist aptly describes his method of painting with masses of dots of primary colours which the eye is able to assemble into colour mixtures and figurative shapes.

At first each instrument emits single points of sound, but gradually these move into note groups of two and then three sounds, and eventually these note cells combine in various ways (eg. 1.3.2.1 : 1.2.3.1 : 2.2.3, etc.) to give a more complex contrapuntal texture with an even flow and (in spite of the restlessly leaping melodic fragments) almost static atmosphere:

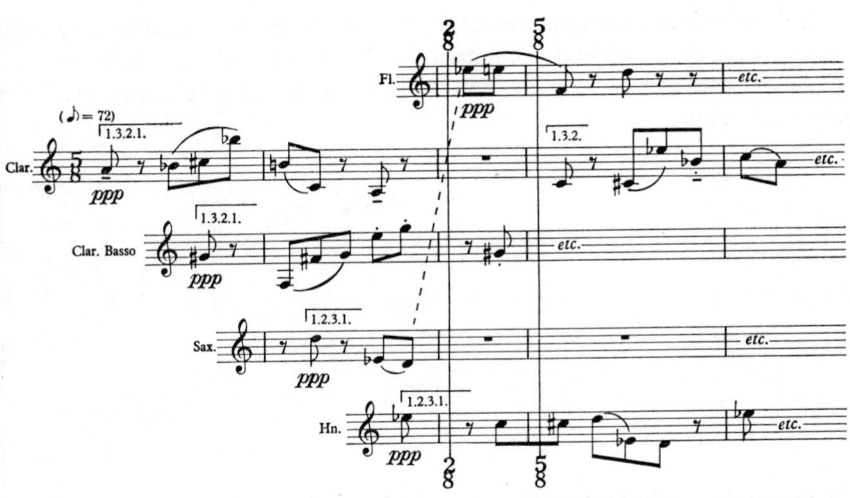

Pointillist compositions may have large zones of isolated sounds, but inevitably, because of the European composer's instinct to create emotive change, these precipitate into denser note groups, which may eventually disperse so that the whole process may begin again. This alternation of rarefaction and condensation is strongly featured in Stockhausen's *Kontra-Punkte* for ten instruments, where the composer's aim was 'the idea of resolving the antitheses of a many-faceted musical world of individual notes and temporal relationships to the point where a situation is reached in which only the homogeneous and the immutable is audible'. In other words, the music begins with widely spaced instrumental sounds of contrasting timbre, and ends with the uniform colour of the piano in 'a two-part, monochrome counterpoint wrested from the antitheses between vertical and horizontal tonal relationships'.[1]

[1] Karl H. Wörner, *Stockhausen: Life and Work* (London, 1973).

This work is notable not so much for its pointillist style, as for the way some passages foreshadow the coming period of integral serialism, with impetuous jagged phrases of a new kind, which at that time were almost beyond the limits of performance:

These flamboyantly contoured phrases and their forward-propelling power are quite unlike Webern and the music of his close followers. In fact they were virtually unique in music at that time, foreshadowing the even more irregular kinds of phrase structures which integral serialism was just about to introduce.

Certain aspects of *Kontra-Punkte* have been claimed to be predetermined, such as the 'Limitations and articulations of the time-space and time-flow' in 'macro-regions' and 'micro-regions', while there is said to be some relationship between the tempi used and the ratios of the frequencies of the first seven pitches,[1] but these structural devices seem to have no perceivable musical significance. Yet in the music which was to come, structure was to become so obsessively important that to some composers it became an end in itself—so that poetry could be abandoned in favour of the beauty of mathematics.

[1] cf. Dieter Schnebel's analysis of this work in *Die Reihe* 4.

5

Integral Serialism

The reasons for the beginnings of such a radically new, dynamic movement as integral serialism have been much debated and never satisfactorily clarified, perhaps because the reasons are many, perhaps because there has been much obscure thinking and partisan propaganda. In the early years, adverse critics would say that such structuralism was a legacy from the excessive regimentation of Nazi and Fascist politics. (Incredibly, this theory still exists, and as recently as 1971 one authority told me that the decline of total serialism was due to the gradual forgetting of Nazi disciplines by central European composers!) Obviously, post-war composers did not care for such accusations. In 1957, Eimert wrote emphatically:

> At present it is the fashion for empty-headed critics to make out that the systematic 'management' of musical material is identical with the terrorist rule of force in totalitarian political systems . . . one such 'social critic' of music has in fact attributed to the twelve-tone system the power to produce detailed programme music, whose only suitable counterparts would be concentration camps, machine shops, and the world of Kafka . . . To listen to music in which there is systematic order, and to hear in it the counterpart to political totalitarianism, is just as witless as to appeal to 'Nature' when what one really means is textbook harmony.[1]

A composer of communist sympathies such as Nono refused equally to identify the 'constraints and limitations' of total serialism with totalitarian politics:

> Comparisons of so-called 'totally organized' methods of composition . . . with totalitarian political systems are . . . a pathetic attempt to influence the intellect which understands freedom as anything rather than the surrender of the free will. The introduction of superficial ideas of liberty and constraint into the creative process is nothing but a childish attempt to terrify others . . . to cast doubt on the very existence of spiritual order, creative discipline, and clarity of thought.[2]

[1] Herbert Eimert, 'The Composer's Freedom of Choice', in *Die Reihe* 3.
[2] Luigi Nono, 'The Historical Reality of Music Today', *The Score* (London, July 1960).

If we can put aside the 'totalitarian' theory for the genesis of integral serialism (with the proviso that there is a grain of truth in most cock-and-bull stories), there are a number of other influences to consider. Firstly, there had been a tendency for a more rational, even mathematical approach to the arts for some time. Painting had long since seen cubism flourish, followed by geometric and almost mechanically conceived graphic styles. In music, Messiaen had already indicated certain mathematical applications to musical elements in his *Technique de mon langage musical*, written as early as 1942; as we shall see, these principles were furthered and put into concrete form in his *Mode de valeurs et d'intensités* composed in 1949. Another composer-scientist had however already gone to much greater lengths in associating music and mathematics. Joseph Schillinger published *Electricity, a liberator of music* as early as 1932, and when he died in New York in 1943, left two important works: *The Schillinger System of Musical Composition* and his great *The Mathematical Basis of the Arts*. These works, published after his death, are of major importance, the latter having a wide influence on creative art in general. The following sums up his views on art produced by scientific synthesis:

> If art implies selectivity, skill, and organization, ascertainable principles must underlie it. Once such principles are discovered and formulated, works of art may be produced by scientific synthesis. There is a common misunderstanding about the freedom of the artist as it relates to self-expression. No artist is really free. He is subjected to the influences of his immediate surroundings . . . he speaks only the language of his immediate geographical and historical boundaries. There is no artist known who, being born in Paris, can express himself spontaneously in the medium of Chinese 4th Century A.D. . . . The key to real freedom and emancipation from local dependence is through scientific method.[1]

Here is not the place and time to discuss the pros and cons of Schillinger's theories. It is sufficient to record that already in the Forties mathematical and scientific lines of thought were invading the realms of music. And the moment was ripe, for with the advent of electronic music in the early Fifties, not only did music and technology join hands as never before, but control of the electronic medium was at first based largely on a mathematical approach. Inevitably, such an approach to electronic music's basic 'parameters', or elements, induced similar methods in conventional composition. Thus integral serialism and electronic music composition were in a way complementary to each other.

There is one final and decisive reason for the genesis of total serialism, a reason which has never been made clear despite the avant-garde composer's natural tendency to theorize. In the post-war years, one of the most difficult obstacles to

[1] Joseph Schillinger, *The Mathematical Basis of the Arts* (New York, 1948).

our 'beginning again' was our own musical memories. Our minds normally create only out of what memory suggests. Thinking subjectively, we tend to reassemble familiar musical patterns. To avoid this needs deliberately objective reasoning and the use of thought-processes into which memory cannot obtrude. This was precisely the main reason for the flourishing of integral serialism. It was, in theory at least, a system of composition which obliged composers to think objectively and eliminate memory, so that the musical heritage of the past was blotted out and a completely new music created. Few composers did work completely objectively; they used a system to eliminate musical memory, but often kept some 'parameters' free so that they could adjust the composition into a satisfyingly musical end-product. In reality, therefore, musical memory, instinct, or 'inspiration' was only shelved at one stage of composition, to be reintroduced later (though few composers would have been ready to admit this).

In conversation with Italian composers who adopted total serialism in the early Fifties such as Nono, Maderna, and Donatoni, I was left in no doubt that the main reason for the use of predetermined principles was to obliterate memory. Total organization was, at that time, the only way to create the *tabula rasa* on which completely new edifices could be constructed. Furthermore, it was always evident that what troubled these composers most was their fear of conventional *rhythmic* configurations. Familiar rhythmic shapes are the most difficult of all to root out of our subconscious memories, but unless completely unorthodox rhythmic designs can be created, the new music is still not truly new. Therefore, since total serialism (or total organization) throws up of its own accord rhythmic designs which never belonged to music before, it seemed the most suitable mechanism for creating the new music of the Fifties.

The first European work to be written with total organization in view was Messiaen's *Mode de valeurs et d'intensités* for piano, written in 1949, being part of the group *Quatre études de rythme*. Milton Babbitt is said to have used similar procedures in his *Three Compositions for Piano* in 1948, so it would be unjust not to record his work here, but unfortunately it remained unknown in Europe until comparatively recently. Though written in 1949, Messiaen's *Mode de valeurs* can be seen as the fruit of years of development, certain aspects of the work's organization appearing as early as 1940 in his *Liturgie de Cristal* from the *Quatuor pour le fin du temps* and later in his *Technique de mon langage musical* written in 1942.

Messiaen's *Mode de valeurs* is not serial music at all in the Schoenbergian sense, as the work is not based on a single twelve-note series, but on a 'mode' which comprises three 'divisions' of twelve notes which can be *freely ordered.* The three voices which make up the piano part throughout are based on these 'divisions' in which the octave register, duration, dynamics, and mode of attack are predetermined for every note. In each of the three divisions, notes of the same name always have different octave registers, durations, and intensities as follows:

The upper division (corresponding to the upper piano part) has durations based on 1×𝅘𝅥𝅰 increasing to 12×𝅘𝅥𝅰. The middle part similarly has durations based on from 1 to 12 multiples of 𝅘𝅥𝅯, while the lower part is based on similar multiples of 𝅘𝅥𝅮. Messiaen also used twelve modes of attack, and seven degrees of volume, but it would seem that these were used rather unevenly and distributed without any specific method except that notes of the same name have different dynamics and attacks in each division. For example, certain dynamics are omitted from each division, while though twelve modes of attack are laid down, they are not fully used (the middle voice in particular being limited in variety as to dynamics and attack). The music begins as follows:

As can be seen, Messiaen at first retains the original note order to some extent in the two upper divisions, and one is led to expect music in the serial manner. But his mode is really based on a free ordering of the sounds in each division and as the piece progresses the original 'falling' note order disappears. Messiaen's method here produced music which was somewhat out of the mainstream of his music, even taking into account the other three pieces of *Quatre études de rythme* and others which have since been written according to structural principles. Strangely enough, too, the *Mode de valeurs* has remained comparatively unknown and little performed, and its status as the prototype of European total serialism has gone almost unrecognized.

It is ironic that the renown which *Mode de valeurs* failed to achieve was abundantly won not only by a pupil of Messiaen, but by a work which carried exactly the same principles further and was based on exactly the same note order as Messiaen's upper 'division'. This work was the first book of *Structures* for two pianos by Pierre Boulez (b. 1925), who had been a pupil of Messiaen since 1943 and obviously knew *Mode de valeurs* intimately. The first book of *Structures*, written from 1952 on (Boulez sometimes revises and amplifies his music over a lengthy period), is a work of considerable complexity. It is therefore not easy to analyse, but as it set the pattern which others followed or modified, it is necessary to sketch out the main constructive aspects of at least the first part (*Structure Ia*) of this three-part work.[1]

[1] I hope to be forgiven for going over material which has already been so well presented by

As we have already observed, *Structures* is based on a twelve-note series derived from Division 1 of Messiaen's *Mode de valeurs*:

In *Structure Ia*, all twelve transpositions of the series and their derived forms (inversions, retrogrades, and inverted retrogrades) are used once each, in a specific order to be described later. From the original and inverted series Boulez prepared two tables or matrices of numbers which govern the construction of many details of the music. The number matrices were obtained by numbering each note of the original series (1 to 12) and then forming the first matrix from all transpositions of the original series, beginning on each note in turn. Thus, the following two series begin respectively on the second and third notes of the original, and produce the number series shown:

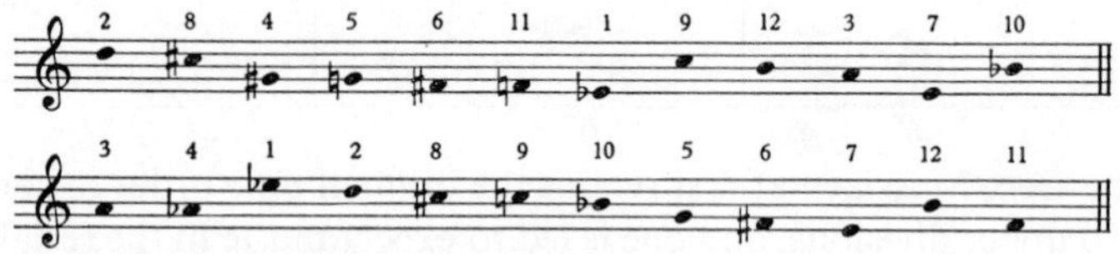

The original and eleven transpositions of the series make up the 'original' ('O') matrix as follows (reading left to right):

'O' matrix

1	2	3	4	5	6	7	8	9	10	11	12
2	8	4	5	6	11	1	9	12	3	7	10
3	4	1	2	8	9	10	5	6	7	12	11
4	5	2	8	9	12	3	6	11	1	10	7
5	6	8	9	12	10	4	11	7	2	3	1
6	11	9	12	10	3	5	7	1	8	4	2
7	1	10	3	4	5	11	2	8	12	6	9
8	9	5	6	11	7	2	12	10	4	1	3
9	12	6	11	7	1	8	10	3	5	2	4
10	3	7	1	2	8	12	4	5	11	9	6
11	7	12	10	3	4	6	1	2	9	5	8
12	10	11	7	1	2	9	3	4	6	8	5

Ligeti in *Die Reihe* 4 (and by Eimert in a German publication), but as the analysis of precisely this work so powerfully influenced a whole generation of composers, it seems right to use again what, after all, has been so highly regarded.

Obviously, this matrix can serve for retrogrades of the original series, by reading from right to left (e.g. retrograde of series O^5 is 1.3.2.7.11 . . . 5)

Similarly, the inversion of the original series is as follows and produces the number orders shown:

A second 'inversion' matrix is then formed by all transpositions of the inversion, beginning on each note in turn, i.e. 1.7.3.10.12.9. etc. The 'inversion' (I) matrix is therefore as follows (reading left to right):

'I' matrix

1	7	3	10	12	9	2	11	6	4	8	5
7	11	10	12	9	8	1	6	5	3	2	4
3	10	1	7	11	6	4	12	9	2	5	8
10	12	7	11	6	5	3	9	8	1	4	2
12	9	11	6	5	4	10	8	2	7	3	1
9	8	6	5	4	3	12	2	1	11	10	7
2	1	4	3	10	12	8	7	11	5	9	6
11	6	12	9	8	2	7	5	4	10	1	3
6	5	9	8	2	1	11	4	3	12	7	10
4	3	2	1	7	11	5	10	12	8	6	9
8	2	5	4	3	10	9	1	7	6	12	11
5	4	8	2	1	7	6	3	10	9	11	12

Again, by reading from right to left, retrogrades of the inversions can be obtained.

Having obtained the 'O' and 'I' number matrices, these are used to determine all note durations, dynamics, and modes of attack, as well as to govern the order in which the note series are used, and also to form an overall plan for note durations. These may be explained briefly as follows:

Note durations. Throughout *Structure Ia*, there is a basic time unit of a demisemiquaver multiplied by the numbers in each row of the 'O' or 'I' matrices, or the retrogrades of these ('R' and 'RI'). For instance, the piece begins by Piano I playing note durations of the series RI^5 (12.11.9.10.3.6.7.1.2.8.4.5). This produces a succession of durations as follows:

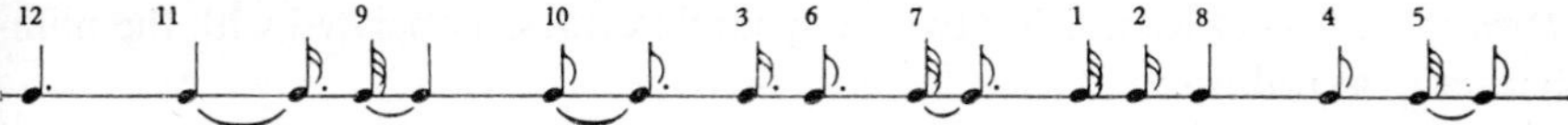

At the same time Piano II plays note durations of the series R^{12} (5.8.6.4.3.9.2.1.7.11.10.12). As Piano I plays the original version of the series and Piano II its inversion, the result is as follows:

(This forms a complete section of the work, which in all comprises fourteen sections and sub-sections, the distribution of which will be described later).

Dynamics. Boulez establishes twelve dynamic values, associated with the number series as follows:

1	2	3	4	5	6	7	8	9	10	11	12
pppp	*ppp*	*pp*	*p*	*quasi p*	*mp*	*mf*	*quasi f*	*f*	*ff*	*fff*	*ffff*

These are then applied to number successions derived from diagonals of the 'O' and 'I' matrices as follows:

Piano I

O

						7					12
							9			7	
								6	7		
								11	1		
							11			3	
						5					2
7					5						
	9			11							
		6	11								
		7	1								
	7			3							
12					2						

Piano II

I

						2					5
							6			2	
								9	2		
								8	1		
							8			3	
						12					7
2					12						
	6			8							
		9	8								
		2	1								
	2			3							
5					7						

The diagonals of the 'O' matrix then determine the dynamics of the entire *Structure* for Piano I and those of the 'I' matrix for Piano II. The dynamics for Piano I would be as follows:

12	7	7	11	11	5	5	11	11	7	7	12
ffff	*mf*	*mf*	*fff*	*fff*	*quasi p*	*quasi p*	*fff*	*fff*	*mf*	*mf*	*ffff*
2	3	1	6	9	7	7	9	6	1	3	2
ppp	*pp*	*pppp*	*mp*	*f*	*mf*	*mf*	*f*	*mp*	*pppp*	*pp*	*ppp*

Each of these 24 dynamics is applied in turn to each of the 24 note-series which make up the part of Piano I. Piano II has similarly 24 dynamic values, one for each of its twenty-four note-series. It will be noticed that as numbers 4, 8, and 10 do not occur in the 'O' diagonal number series, *p*, *quasi f*, and *ff* do not occur in the whole of Piano I. 4 and 10 are also not present in the 'I' diagonals for Piano II. These discrepancies caused Boulez to make several deviations from his scheme, which are however not sufficiently important to mention here.

Modes of Attack. Ten modes of attack are assigned:

1	2	3	5	6	7	8	9	11	12
>	>̣	.	normal	⌒̣	▾	*sfz* ^	> ▾	−̣	⌒

These are associated with the ten numbers occurring in the following diagonals (which are the 'opposites' of those used for dynamics, and again omit 4 and 10):

Piano I

O

1					6						
	8			6							
		1	2								
		2	8								
	6			12							
6					3						
						11					9
							12			1	
								3	5		
								5	11		
							1			5	
						9					5

Piano II

I

1					9						
	11			9							
		1	7								
		7	11								
	9			5							
9					3						
						8					6
							5			1	
								3	12		
								12	8		
							1			12	
						6					12

Again the 'O' diagonals determine dynamics for Piano I throughout the *Structure* and the 'I' diagonals those for Piano II, though there are many irregularities. In general, one mode of attack only is used throughout each twelve-note series.

Ordering of the Note Series. The two number matrices are used to determine the order of the twelve-note series. All forty-eight versions of the series are used, twenty-four to each piano. *Structure Ia* is divided into two main parts, A and B, and in each part twelve series are used by each instrument according to the following master plan:

Note Orders

	Part A	Part B
Piano I	All 'O' series in order I^1	All 'RI' series in order RI^1
Piano II	All 'I' series in order O^1	All 'R' series in order R^1

Ordering of the Duration Series. Similarly, each of the forty-eight twelve-note series has duration successions derived from the number matrices according to the following plan:

Duration Orders

	Part A	Part B
Piano I	All 'RI' series in order RI[1]	All 'I' series in order R[1]
Piano II	All 'R' series in order R[1]	All 'O' series in order RI[1]

So much for elements of the composition which have been derived more or less directly from the two number matrices (which in turn were derived from the twelve-notes series). Many other compositional factors still remain, some being conceived according to specific plans, others resulting from free choice:

Overall Form. As already mentioned, *Structure Ia* comprises exactly the forty-eight versions of the twelve-note series, subdivided so that each piano plays all twelve of a certain form of the series ('O', 'I', 'R', or 'RI') in both parts A and B. Each series forms a 'strand' which lasts exactly one section or subsection, which is always the same length: 1+2+3. . . . +12 = 78 demisemiquavers. Part A comprises more sections than Part B, in the proportion 8:6, though in Part A some sections are made up of two or three fast subsections (see below). Each instrument contributes one, two, or three strands (i.e. complete twelve-note series) in each section or subsection, and remains silent once in the *Structure*, according to the following plan:

	Part A								Part B					
Section	1	2a	2b	2c	3	4a	4b	5	6	7	8	9	10	11
No. of Strands														
Piano 1	1	2	2		3	1	2	1	3	1	2	2	1	3
Piano 2	1	2	1	1	3	1	3		2	2	2	2	1	3
Total Strands	2	4	3	1	6	2	5	1	5	3	4	4	2	6
	24								24					

The density of the whole of the *Structures Ia* can better be represented in the following diagram, which reveals the contrast of thick and thin textures adopted in Part A, and the more massive density used in the shorter Part B:

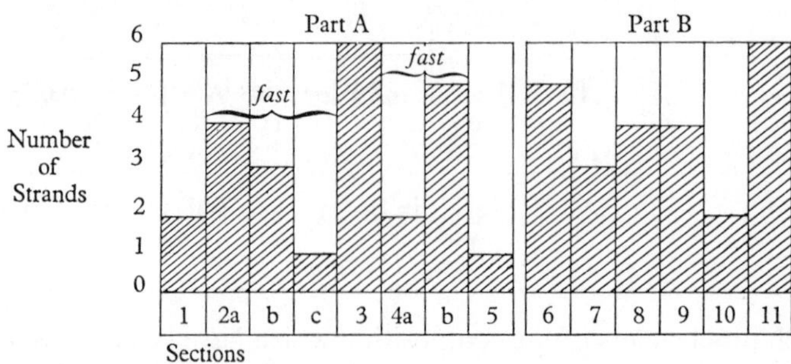

It will be noted, however, that the overall formal structure is really a *free* conception. The only formal relationship with the twelve-note series (or with the number matrix) is that each section or sub-section is 78 × 𝅘𝅥𝅰 in duration, which of course would apply equally to any twelve-note series. So the particular series used does not govern the form in any way.

Tempi. The speed of each section or group of sections is either 'lent', 'très modéré', or 'modéré, presque vif'. Representing these by S, M, and F, (Slow, Moderate, and Fast), Part A has tempi in the symmetrical order:

M : F : S : F : M

The fast sections (2 and 4) are those with subsections, as one would expect. Part B, however, has a less symmetrical order of tempi:

S : F : M : F : S : M

At this point, it would seem that we have come to an end of the predetermined elements in the composition. Several other factors remain:

Octave Register. The octave register used for each note is quite arbitrary except for two principles: (1) in general, successions of notes in each part are spread over wide areas and (2) whenever the same note occurs in two or more strands, it is played at the unison. Octaves are therefore avoided. (Note in Ex. 17 how E♭ and C♯ are unisons, while other notes which sound close together such as A and F♯ are also kept in the same register.)

Rests. Very frequently in staccato passages the note is shown as 𝅘𝅥𝅰 or 𝅘𝅥𝅯 and the remainder of its duration is filled out by rests. This seems to apply to all sections where the six modes of attack . -̣ ' >' poco sfz ^ and sfz ^ are used. No other rest signs are used, except occasionally to clarify the part writing.

Metre. Changes of metre are frequent but conform to no plan. A sense of metre is so conspicuously absent from this music that its only function is 'on paper' as an aid to performers.

To sum up, *Structures Ia* has been composed with devices which ensure that a twelve-note series not only determines all the note-successions of the music but also the duration of every note. Furthermore, the series itself determines not only the order in which the forty-eight serial variants are used but also the order of duration-series derived from them. The dynamics and modes of attack have also been devised from the same sources. In all other parameters the composer had freedom of choice, to varying degrees, though he adopted (perhaps deliberately) abstract plans which limited his scope for free action.

In reality the note-series in *Structures Ia* does not directly determine note durations. It only does this at second-hand, through the number matrix, which though derived from one form of the series, can then be applied to any other form of the same series, or indeed to any other series whatsoever. So in reality number and pitch are not completely integrated, and to a considerable degree the composition is a numerical abstraction.

A much closer association of pitch and duration was sought by many composers, the ideal being that each note in a series should have a duration derived from its special position in the note-row. One of the simplest and most-used solutions has been that each note should be proportional to the size of the interval which separates it from the next note. For instance, if 𝅘𝅥𝅯 = a semitone, then a tone = 𝅘𝅥𝅮, a minor third = 𝅘𝅥𝅮. and so on. In the following symmetrical series of Camillo Togni, for example, each note is given a duration proportional to the interval which follows it (𝅘𝅥𝅯 = a semitone):

The following example of (mostly) two-part writing, shows the rather free manner in which Togni used this system. The 'theoretical' duration of sounds is shown in numbers, but the real duration is often something slightly different. Sometimes the rests which follow a note are included in its theoretical duration, sometimes not. At other points, chords usually have durations equal to the sum of the note-durations they comprise, but not always. This practice of 'bending' the system to produce better artistic results is common to most composers, as also is Togni's obviously free treatment of most other factors such as dynamics, octave registers, attack characteristics, formation of chords, and so on:

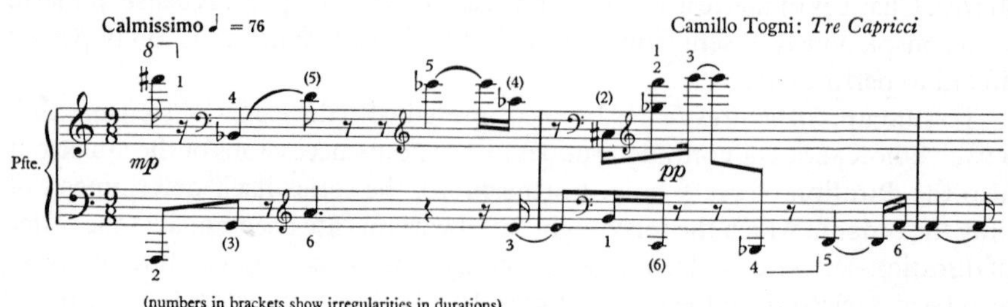

(numbers in brackets show irregularities in durations)

One defect in this system is that all transpositions and inversions of a series (and, with symmetrical series, also all 'R' and 'RI' forms) will produce the same rhythmic pattern. For example in Ex. 19 the note-durations always increase from 1 to 6 and then decrease again. There are ways of overcoming this difficulty, many indeed, but the easiest way to produce variety in durations has been to use permutations of a series: that is, to alter the note-order by some logical process. (Why logical? For no reason at all, except that our brains prefer order to chaos.) It would be tedious to go into permutations at this point (this delight will be deferred for a more mathematical chapter). It is sufficient to say that almost 500 million permutations of a series are possible, so that there is ample material for variety, in durations or any other related factor.

In Togni's *Capriccio No. 2*, quoted above, the semitone is equal to a semiquaver, so the music always moves at an even pace. But by varying the basic duration wide contrasts of speed can be produced, as well as periods of growing tension and relaxation. For instance, if the basic duration is gradually decreased from ♪ through ⌐3¬ ♪ and 𝅘𝅥𝅯 to 𝅘𝅥𝅰, the music will move faster and faster (creating tension), whereas if it is gradually lengthened (𝅘𝅥𝅯, ⌐3¬ ♩, ♩, ♩., ⌐3¬ 𝅗𝅥)) the music slows down and becomes relaxed. Of course various strata can be formed, moving at different speeds, to give great variety of effect.

Some composers use diabolically inconvenient basic time durations, such as semitone = ⌐5:4¬ 𝅘𝅥𝅯 or ⌐7:8¬ ♪, which when combined also with ⌐3¬ 𝅘𝅥𝅯 produces music which is not only difficult to play, but of a rhythmic complexity which is metrically self-destructive:

Pousseur: Quintet
(♩ = 48)
187
Cl.
Cl. b.
Pfte.
Vn.
Vc.
arco
sul La

Though the above Quintet by Henri Pousseur (1955) is written in $\frac{2}{4}$ metre throughout, the phrase articulations are completely fugitive, giving an impression of random rhythmic shapes rather than mathematically precise configurations. This enigmatic, almost 'undefined', quality of such highly predetermined compositions is characteristic of much music in the style of total serialism, and will be further discussed later.

In the last three compositions discussed, the composers endeavoured to derive the rhythmic articulation of their music from the twelve-note series. The music determined its own shapes from 'within', as it were. But other composers worked in an opposite way. The rhythmic configurations were imposed on the sounds (normally of the twelve-note series) from the 'outside'—that is, they established rhythmic designs to which the note series had to conform. The rhythmic shapes (and perhaps other parameters) usually had some form of serial principle as their basis, and even if this had nothing to do with the twelve-note series being used one can still loosely call it 'integral serialism' or 'total serialism'. However, when different series are used for different parameters, or the work is organized by other logical processes, it would be more accurate to refer to 'predetermined composition', or to works which are 'totally organized'.

Composers have always 'predetermined' their compositions to a considerable extent, otherwise they would have been stumbling in chaos from one bar to another. A good fugue can only be written if its subject has been preconstructed to allow a variety of strettos, diminutions, and augmentations, or to invert well, or to furnish material for interesting episodes. Unfortunately, today's composers feel they have to make explicit what used to be taken for granted, so that they have to decide on the 'limitations and articulation of the time space in Microregions and Macroregions', and discuss group aggregates, chronometric densities, morphological behaviour, sound-rhythm complexes, etc. (This arduous terminology often refers to quite simple things like tempo, loudness, chords, and so on, things we used to predetermine without a lot of fuss.) However, we must bear in mind that everything is relative. There are various degrees of serialization and organization, and no successful piece of music is totally one thing or another. If music is totally organized and the systems have done their work unmolested by the composer's fantasy, it is almost certainly sterile and fruitless.

Predetermined or serial systems which establish the rhythmic shape of the music from 'without' (i.e. not using the twelve-note series) are legion. Webern's use of rhythmic proportionalisms was an example, and many systems stemmed from such simple beginnings. Composers devised highly sophisticated ways of preparing rhythmic schemes which could preform the whole composition. Some schemes are highly complex, embracing higher mathematics. Others are quite simple. Fortunately, as artistic quality does not depend on complexity, it will be sufficient to illustrate this system with one or two very simple examples.

Franco Donatoni's *Composition in Four Movements* (1955) for piano is based on permutations of various rhythms. In the first movement four rhythms are used, (A) (B) (C) and (D) , which have no retrograde possibilities,[1] nor are they used in augmented or diminished forms. These four rhythms occur in perpetually varied order by using permutations. In all, twenty-four different orders are possible, and these are arranged in various 'squares' such as:

	↓			
	A	B	C	D
(1) →	B	C	D	A ←
	C	D	A	B
	D	A	B	C
	↑			

	↓			
	D	C	B	A
(2) →	C	B	A	D ←
	B	A	D	C
	A	D	C	B
	↑			

Each square can be read off in four directions (though this duplicates the available orderings), and as this music aims at the maximum of rhythmic variation, the order of permutations used must obviously avoid monotony and repetition. In the following example, the permutations D C B A and C B A D have been used:

The composer has used the scheme freely. Sometimes rhythms are almost superimposed one on another; he forms chords at strategic points; and all factors such as dynamics, note register, rests, etc. are quite free. This produces a dynamic, decisive piece of music which is remarkably varied, given that Donatoni's rhythmic material is so limited.

[1] The rhythms belong to the 'nonretrogradable' variety discussed in Messiaen's *Mon langage musical*, Ch. V.

The fact that in this piece all rhythms are nonretrogradable and are always played at the same speed is very limiting. It is usual, therefore, when using this rhythmic 'cell' principle, to exploit the greater variety of retrogradable rhythms, and to vary their basic duration values (i.e. move faster or slower) according to the mood of the music, and create tension and relaxation both in each structure and in the overall design.

A simple extension of the principle of using rhythmic cells is to establish the rhythmic patterns of the music through a set (or sets) of number proportions. This will be further elaborated later. For the time being we will use a very simple example, showing how Luigi Nono uses the numbers 2, 3, 5, 8, 12, and 17 to construct part of his *Canto Sospeso*. At the beginning of section No. 6b of the work these numbers are associated with semiquaver quintuplets (5) and quaver triplets (3) in the following order:

17	12	8	5	3	2	‖	2	3	5	8	12	17
3	3	3	5	5	5	‖	3	5	3	5	3	5

As will be seen, in the first half 17, 12, and 8 are used with 3 and 5, 3, and 2 with 5. In the second half, this plan is changed so that 3 and 5 alternate. These numerical duration values are laid out initially in the following way:

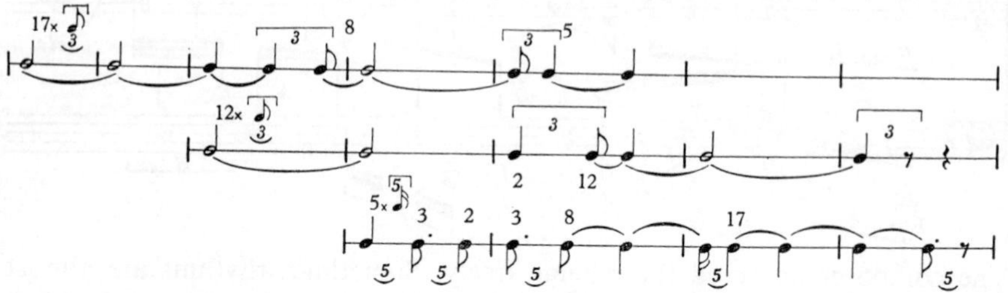

Once having designed this rhythmic basis, the notes of the series are then applied in turn as follows:

After this preliminary draft is arrived at, the notes are then spread among various voice and string parts, in different registers, and dynamics are allotted according to some subsidiary scheme. This section is for full chorus and strings, but parts which are silent during these bars are omitted:

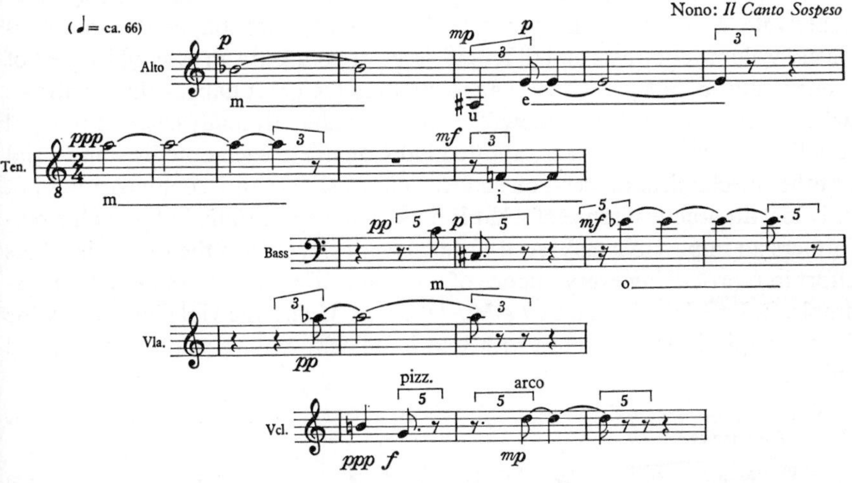

As will be seen, this scheme creates a gradual increase of movement in the first three bars, and then a decrease. An ebb and flow of tension is thus established which characterizes the whole movement, constructed as it is by similar means throughout. The number orders are retained throughout this fifty-bar piece, but a speeding-up of the pace of the music is achieved by increasing the use of ⌐5¬𝅘𝅥𝅯 and decreasing ⌐3¬♪ in some parts, producing an intensification of the tragic emotive undertones of this music. The note-series is used ten times, and is never transposed; in fact most of *Il Canto Sospeso* seems to have been written with only the original form of the series, without recourse to variants or transpositions. The scheme of number proportions outlined above is used throughout *Il Canto Sospeso*, and though more complex variations on the principles involved are used to a considerable extent, the whole of this fine, grandiose work is derived from very little basic material indeed. (While this work was in progress, I had occasion to see Nono at work. Plans of number sequences and combinations, note-durations, dynamic-value orders, and so on were prepared beforehand on large sheets and pinned to the study walls. Then the composer set to work and laid out the music rigorously according to his predetermined schemes. It seemed that Nono was intent on observing the rules of the game, not giving way to his own musical inclinations. Yet *Il Canto Sospeso* has such drama and poetry that he must have steered the results into a more musical channel than could ever have been achieved by constructivism alone.)

One important feature of integral serialism which has so far not been adequately illustrated is the insistence, to the point of obsession, on dynamic contrasts. Volume contrasts and different forms of attack are an essential aspect of modern music, but perpetual change involves the great danger that contrasts will go unnoticed, and will therefore have no value. In many cases of integral serialism, where dynamics are allotted individually to each note by some serial or other mechanical process, one has the impression that the composer has not only lost all practical sense of what is musically appropriate, but gives the performers an impossible task. And if the player *can* perform the music, is all his effort in reproducing every nuance of volume really worth the candle? For example, in Part IV of Boulez's *Le Marteau sans Maître* the viola has to play the following pizzicato, in contest with xylorimba, vibraphone, small cymbals, and guitar:

Boulez: *Le Marteau sans Maître*

Every note or chord has a different dynamic indication, accents and sforzandi abound, and the first chord is even split into *mf* and *ff* notes. And all this is 'assez rapide'! (I recall one very experienced flute player who found the dynamics in *Le Marteau* so difficult to deal with that he ringed every forte in his part red, every piano green, every mezzo-forte blue, and so on. The result was brilliant!)

There is no doubt that integral serialism produced much music that bristled with difficulties, partly because the mechanisms threw up results which no performer could ever have met before. Most classical music, however difficult, has a certain predictable quality, and once played the music is easily remembered. It is already partly familiar. But the music of total serialism was unpredictable; performers had to struggle through it note by note, and memory was slow to come to grips with such unfamiliar material. Fortunately time passes and to the players of today the language of yesterday is already half-familiar, so that the difficulties of the Fifties are now becoming normalities.

To conclude this brief survey of 'integral serialism', I would like to quote what Luciano Berio wrote as early as 1956:

> Today, for the first time we have the curiosity of composers whom even our fathers would not have hesitated to call 'antimusical'. It is disconcerting to see how the possibility of writing music without being personally involved . . . has already become part of the 'history' of music.[1]

Certainly it is possible to write music through cerebral devices, without getting emotively involved or even attempting to mould it into more artistic form. But is this really art? Berio and all the others were under an illusion if they thought their mechanisms produced the greatest music of the period. On the contrary, it was only when the composer became master of his system and made the mechanisms work towards fruitful ends that real creative art came about. But this is surely what has always happened. All art has its formal schemes, which in the hands of some give only meagre fruit, while others reap a rich and abundant harvest.

[1] Luciano Berio: '*Aspetti* di Arti*gianato Formale*, in *Incontri Musicali*', No. 1, (Milan, 1956).

6

Numbers

This chapter may need an apology. To some it may seem superfluous, to others not thorough enough. I am no mathematician, and find figures tedious, but I recognize that in music there is more than a mythical magic of numbers. Mathematics is the basis of sound.[1] Perhaps mistakenly, the ancient Greeks attributed to the association of music and numbers a predominant place in the philosophy of the cosmos. Perhaps equally mistakenly, some composers of the Forties and Fifties tried to build music entirely by numbers. But regardless of the rights and wrongs of such beliefs, there are incontrovertible mathematical facts which must be outlined, however briefly. Other numerical data less closely associated with musical reality, but forming a basis for modern composition, are also worth some mention, even though they only demonstrate man's subconscious awareness that there is beauty in numbers, and that they in turn can make beauty out of chaos.

The ancient Egyptians and Mesopotamians are known to have studied the mathematical principles of sound, and even in prehistory such instruments as the ground zither must have made man aware of the proportional relationship (in string lengths) of one pitch with another. But it was only with Pythagoras (sixth century B.C.) that a school of researchers set about codifying the mathematics of music and teaching its principles as part of a philosophical moral code. The musical scale was conceived as a structural element of the harmonious cosmos, and tonal space was subdivided in such a way as to reflect this harmony. They devised mathematical descriptions for all the intervals now known in Western music (including quarter-tones) and a coherent explanation of harmonic phenomena.

[1] Some would regard this as an overstatement, preferring to say that while all sounds can be analysed in mathematical terms, sound itself is part of physical reality, whereas mathematics is only a man-made artefact. This would seem to imply that if man had not discovered mathematics, the mathematics of sound would not exist. But in fact the nature of sound depends on mathematical principles, whether man is able to deduce them or not, and therefore there is a mathematical reality which is just as actual and absolute as physical reality.

Nature is amazingly mathematical. Sound itself in its musical aspects, whether of scale formations, harmonic series, or harmony, exhibits a remarkable array of number proportions. The harmonic series (on which depends not only the timbre of a sound, but much of conventional harmonic theory) is built on a rational set of proportions. For example, the following fundamental, G, has a large number of overtones or harmonics, all of which have a simple arithmetical relationship with the fundamental:

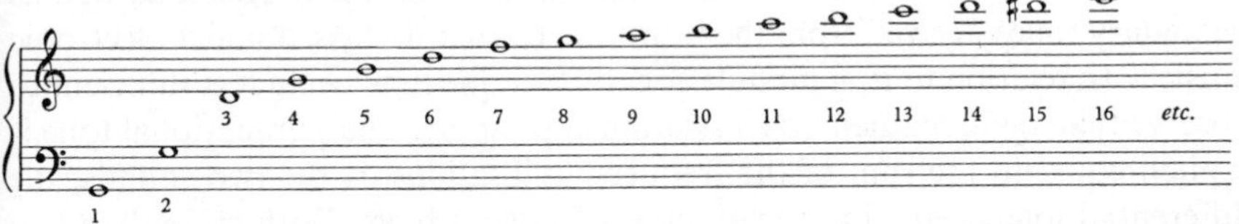

The above shows only the first sixteen harmonics of a sound, the fundamental being called the first harmonic. The number below each note indicates not only the order of the harmonic series, but also how any harmonic is a multiple of the frequency of the fundamental tone. Supposing, for example, the fundamental G corresponds to a hundred vibrations a second (it is in fact 97·99 in the equi-tempered scale), the second harmonic would be 2×100, the third 3×100, and so on, while the top G would be 1600 vibrations. Similarly, a plucked string will give the same harmonic series if it vibrates in all its length (the fundamental) or if it is touched lightly so as to divide it successively into halves, thirds, quarters, fifths, etc. (Not all notes of the harmonic series are completely in tune with modern scales; in fact, some are seriously divergent. In many cases the modern equi-tempered scale is a compromise.)

Similar proportional principles apply to the ratio of frequencies in intervals:

Interval	*Ratio of Frequencies*
Unison	1:1
Octave	2:1
Twelfth	3:1
Double Octave	4:1
Fifth	3:2
Tenth	5:2
Fourth	4:3
Major Sixth	5:3
Major Third	5:4
Minor Third	6:5
Minor Sixth	8:5

Also, the frequencies of all notes of the diatonic scale have fractional relationships with the tonic (though small adjustments are necessary to conform with mean-tone temperament, equal temperament, etc.):

C	D	E	F	G	A	B	c
1	9/8	5/4	4/3	3/2	5/3	15/8	2

When two notes are sounded together, other less audible tones are produced as well—the 'summational' tone and the 'differential' tone. These, as well as secondary tones derived from them, will be further discussed under electronic music with relation to ring modulation, but for the time being it is sufficient to observe that again mathematical relationships apply. The summational tone is a pitch equal to the sum of the frequency vibrations of the two sounds, the differential tone is equal to the difference between them. With more than two sounds, these Pythagorean phenomena still apply in ever more complex ways, as will be seen later.

This is all relatively simple information. If we were to go further, into more complex realms of acoustics such as the principles of sound diffusion and reflection, wave formations, sound absorption, architectural acoustics, electro-acoustics, etc., we would continue to find that all factors depend on mathematical bases. In fact without adequate mathematical knowledge a full understanding of the subject is impossible.[1] But enough proof should already have been furnished to show how sound, music, and numbers are inextricably entwined. Remarkably, even such apparently 'dehumanized' sounds as electronic tones seem to conform with 'nature' if they can. For example, in a voltage controlled studio, sounds can be set up in mobile form, with movement in staircase or cascade fashion, or even various combinations of mobility can be created. In such situations, with many sounds in movement, it would seem that when they can the sounds 'lock on' to some succession of natural intervals, scale patterns, etc. For instance, if one oscillator locks on to rising and falling over wide areas in minor thirds, arpeggios of diminished seventh chords result—which may hardly be welcome! However, the point is that this locking on to natural phenomena is almost certainly due to the predominance of some mathematical fraction, which tends to put all else into a seemingly natural order.

Permutations have already had a preliminary mention in the previous chapter. Permutation means the variation of the order of a series (of any numbers,

[1] I am aware of having over-simplified the basic acoustics, in the interests of a clear exposition of the subject. For those who prefer to go further, I recommend C. A. Taylor's *The Physics of Musical Sounds* (London, 1965), which through its musicianly approach is a particularly suitable publication.

notes, etc.), but usually implies rational and not haphazard variation. Permutation is resorted to in ordeı to create variety and extra resources. Chinese restaurants may have remarkably extensive menus, but on examination the basic ingredients can be seen to be very few, while it is the permutations which are many. The possible number of permutations grows astronomically according to the number of ingredients. Two ingredients have two permutations, three have six, four have twenty-four, while five have no less than 120 permutations ($1 \times 2 \times 3 \times 4 \times 5 = 120$). Composers who use permutations of the twelve-note series only scratch the surface of its possible orderings. If a composer used different permutations of twelve notes at the rate of a hundred each week, it would take him almost 100,000 years to exhaust the 479,001,600 possibilities.

Permutations are usually arrived at by some logical process such as Boulez used in forming the two matrices used in *Structures Ia* (see pp. 26 & 27). Some of the first methods of twelve-note permutation were devised by Berg in his opera *Lulu*, to create special melodies as leitmotifs. New series were derived from his basic series as follows:

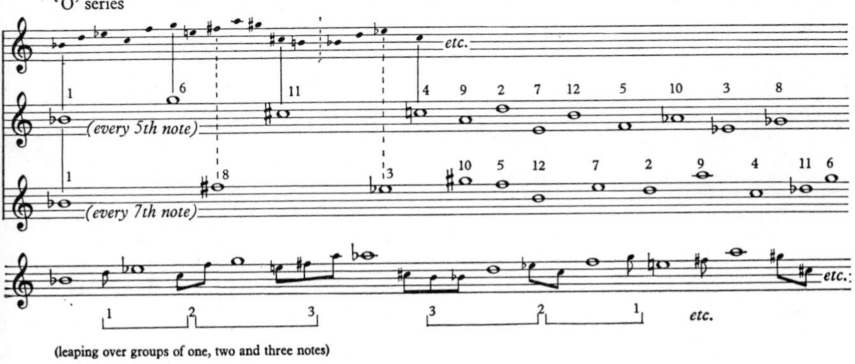

(leaping over groups of one, two and three notes)

As will be seen, new series are formed by using every fifth note of a repeating series, or every seventh note, or as in the last example, by 'leaping over' first one note, then two, then three, and then reversing the process. Berg must have investigated this system of permutation very thoroughly, because only one other variant would have been possible with such a system, that obtained by using every eleventh number.

Similarly, one could form new series by writing down odd numbers followed by even numbers: 1.3.5.7.9.11.2.4.6.8.10.12. This 'every second number' process can be repeated again and again until the system repeats itself after the ninth variant:

(a)	1	3	5	7	9	11	2	4	6	8	10	12
(b)	1	5	9	2	6	10	3	7	11	4	8	12
(c)	1	9	6	3	11	8	5	2	10	7	4	12
(d)	1	6	11	5	10	4	9	3	8	2	7	12
(e)	1	11	10	9	8	7	6	5	4	3	2	12
(f)	1	10	8	6	4	2	11	9	7	5	3	12
(g)	1	8	4	11	7	3	10	6	2	9	5	12
(h)	1	4	7	10	2	5	8	11	3	6	9	12
(i)	1	7	2	8	3	9	4	10	5	11	6	12
	1	2	3	4	5	6	etc.					

Similar permutations can be formed by using every third, fourth, or sixth number, though these have only a limited number of variants (eight) and all have a special limitation in that the first and last numbers are always the same.

Of course one of the most obvious ways of forming permutations is by simple transpositions of numbers which can be carried out in many logical ways. The following number-transpositions are elementary, and need no explanation:

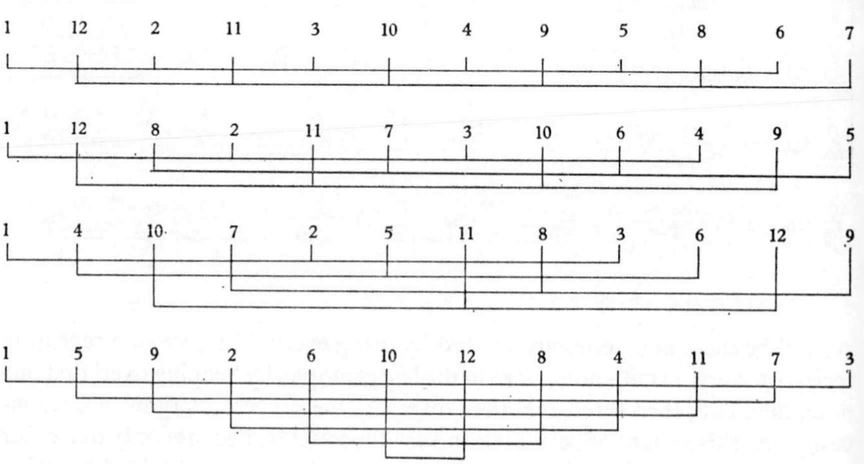

So far I have demonstrated several simple means of permutation. More complex and abundant results can now be obtained by permuting one system with another, and cross-permuting yet again with a third system, and so on. Already, by these simple means, hundreds of different permutations could be formed.

But are they necessary? It is impossible to imagine a situation where a vast number of permutations are really needed. If they are used to obtain variants of a twelve-note series, as soon as permutation begins, any memorable thematic 'unity' of a note-series flies with the wind. If instead the purpose of permutations is to avoid thematic unity (or monotony of note successions), then this can be just as easily done with few variants as with many. The same is true of permutations of numbers for application to parameters such as note durations, etc. As the mind cannot grasp infinite change, or even remember more than a modicum of variety, few permutations are just as good as many.

A further application of mathematics to music has come about through various composers' attempts to find what we could call a musical Golden Section. Since the early days of Greek art and architecture, man has been aware that beautiful proportions obey fixed rules, and that the most perfect beauty is attained when a great artist's intuition leads him to vary only very slightly something which is mathematically or geometrically perfect. The Greeks devised the geometrical proportion known as the Golden Section[1] which was regarded as the key to the mystery of art for many centuries, and has been abandoned only in more recent times when symmetry and classical proportions are sometimes deliberately shunned.[2] In music, particularly where the composer has adopted a more rational approach, it would seem that some kind of 'Golden Section' has been the foundation of creative thought. Perhaps, subconsciously, man needs to work in orderly patterns or proportions, and perhaps in sound as well as vision these proportions are determining factors in the creation of perfect beauty.

The use of a 'Golden Section' is not limited to composers of the integral serialism period. As long ago as 1925, Alban Berg constructed his *Lyric Suite* around the composer's 'magic' number 23, a number which determined the length of movements, metronome markings, and even at some points the number of notes in chords.[3] Olivier Messiaen's *Technique de mon langage musical*

[1] In its most elementary form, the Golden Section is the division of a line so that the smaller segment is to the other as that is to the whole. This gives relationships of parts which, formed into rectangles etc., provide the overall proportions of architectural facades, their subdivisions, and smaller details such as doors, windows, decorations, etc. The Section was used in such a way that a harmonious unity of proportions ran through an entire structure and all its component parts, while avoiding that exact coincidence and similarity which only produced excessive formality and stiffness. The ratio approximates to 1:1.618 as in the Fibonacci Series.

[2] Note, however, that one of the most famous modern architects, Le Corbusier, has firmly sustained the use of the Golden Section. His book, *The Modulor*, contains some interesting comments on music and mathematics.

[3] cf. 'The Symbolism in Berg's "Lyric Suite" ', by Reginald Smith Brindle, *The Score*, No. 21 (Oct. 1957).

reveals a 'marked predilection for the rhythms of prime numbers' (five, seven, eleven, thirteen, etc.), and for the 'strange charm of impossibilities' which 'resides particularly in certain mathematical impossibilities of the modal and rhythmic domains'. It would seem too that Messiaen's preoccupations with proportions and number are only one aspect of his religious expression; they are not merely part of a musical language but an essential constituent of his theological thought. A striking similarity to the Greek Golden Section is found in John Cage's early works. Between the pre-war *Construction in Metal* and *Music of Changes* (1951) the structure of several works is based on a number of measures having a square root, so that the large lengths have the same relation within the whole as the small lengths have within the larger units.

In integral serialism, we have already seen how the rhythmic configuration of music was one of the greatest problems which composers had to solve. The discovery of new rhythmic shapes through mathematical devices was common enough, and some of these could be categorized as Golden Sections which became common property, and were adapted by composers to suit their own ideals. The Fibonacci Series, in which each term is the sum of the previous two terms (0, 1, 1, 2, 3, 5, 8, 13, 21, 34 . . . .), has been widely used to create sets of duration values, either in whole or in part. For instance, part of the series and its retrograde (1, 2, 3, 5, 8, 13, 13, 8, 5, 3, 2, 1) was used by Luigi Nono in most of *Il Canto Sospeso* (the slightly different number-set in Ex. 22 and 23 is not typical of the whole work). Stockhausen used the series also to establish the number of notes to be played in successive time-periods, especially where controlled improvisation was required (as in *Mixtur* and to a lesser extent in *Zyklus*).[1]

Other number-series have been derived from the various sequences of triangular numbers, of which the following shows a simple example:

1 3 6 10

Other number forms are assembled in the 'Triangle de Pascal', used by such composers as Iannis Xenakis, of which the following is only the first seven rows (the Pascal Triangle really being an *infinite* array):

[1] As noted previously, the Fibonacci Series is related to the Golden Section proportions, in that it moves progressively closer to the 1 : 1.618 ratio as the series increases. It may be regarded as a Golden Section series expressed in whole numbers, inaccurate at low values but becoming less so with higher figures.

1	1						
1	2	1					
1	3	3	1				
1	4	6	4	1			
1	5	10	10	5	1		
1	6	15	20	15	6	1	
1	7	21	35	35	21	7	1

Horizontally, each row corresponds to the coefficients in a binomial expansion. In practice, this portion of the Pascal Triangle, offering as it does seven different rows of numbers, gives a greater variety of material than a single series such as prime numbers (1, 3, 5, 7, 11, 13, 17, etc.) or the Fibonacci Series. It does not, however, offer the gradual growth of these latter series, and is therefore less suitable for determining such parameters as durations, etc.

Note-durations have sometimes been derived directly from pitch frequencies. In his article 'How time Passes',[1] Stockhausen elaborates at great length on a system whereby all note-durations can be in relationship to pitch frequencies (expressed as cycles per second (c.p.s.) or Hertz Frequencies (Hz)). In such a case, all durations should therefore logically be expressed in seconds, or fractions of seconds, because existing note durations can only indicate certain fractions of time and nothing between those fractions. For example, if a fundamental tone is represented as 1, with a notational equivalent of a semibreve, it would be quite easy to write note durations for some notes of the overtone series (for example, octave $= \frac{1}{2} =$ 𝅗𝅥, double octave $= \frac{1}{4} =$ ♩ etc.). But how is one to find equivalents for 1/13, 1/17, etc., or for notes less than an octave above the fundamental, which could only be expressed as such fractions as 9/13? Stockhausen certainly seems to do so, and even resolves far more knotty issues (but in such a complex way that his article had to be explained in a later edition of *Die Reihe*[2] by Gottfried Michael Koenig, without significant success). Stockhausen's system, however, works best in the electronic medium, where time durations are simply certain lengths of tape. Pitch frequency also has a direct relationship with tape length, so that the composer can think only in Hertz frequencies and centimetres of tape and forget notes, sharps, flats, semibreves, semiquavers, etc.

A similar attempt to relate note durations to complex numbers may be through the use of logarithmic series or square roots. For example, Giselher Klebe establishes note durations in his Piano Trio, Op. 22 by the square roots of numbers from 1 to 12, as follows:

[1] *Die Reihe* 3, p. 10. [2] 'Commentary': *Die Reihe* 8, p. 80.

Series	$\sqrt{12}$	$\sqrt{11}$	$\sqrt{10}$	$\sqrt{9}$	$\sqrt{8}$	$\sqrt{7}$	$\sqrt{6}$	$\sqrt{5}$	$\sqrt{4}$	$\sqrt{3}$	$\sqrt{2}$	$\sqrt{1}$
Values*	3·5	3·3	3·2	3·0	2·8	2·6	2·4	2·3 (2·23)	2·0	1·7	1·4	1·0
Time	𝅝‿𝅝‿♪.	𝅝‿𝅝‿𝅘𝅥𝅯	𝅝‿𝅝	𝅝‿𝅗𝅥.‿♪	𝅝‿𝅗𝅥.	𝅝‿𝅗𝅥‿♪	𝅝‿𝅗𝅥	𝅝‿♩‿♪.	𝅝‿♩	𝅝‿𝅘𝅥𝅯	𝅗𝅥.‿♪	𝅗𝅥‿♪

(Values × 10 semiquaver units.) *To nearest decimal place.

In the 'Time' sector the 'Values' have been multiplied by ten semiquavers, though other multiplications are used during the composition. The 'values' of the square roots are however not all accurate and it is hard to see any justification for adopting a mathematical system which requires great accuracy, only to abandon precise details and results.

Perhaps one of the most remarkable examples of a composer's trust in the magical application of mathematics to music is described by Gottfried Michael Koenig in an article on Bo Nilsson.[1] Relating how Nilsson sent his first electronic composition to Koenig for realization at the West German Radio electronic studio, Koenig explains that Nilsson could not have had much experience of electronic music, as he lived so far off in northern Sweden. So, in case his score proved impossible or inconvenient in 'particular manipulations', he suggested Koenig should use the following formula for 'aleatoric modulation':

$$(a+b)^n\,dx = \frac{(a+bx)^{n+1}}{(n+1)b} + C;\ n\infty-1$$

Such is the composer's faith in the Golden Section of his choice! But has all this mathematical application any real musical value? Is a composer's trust in the magic of numbers completely misplaced? The answer is not in the least clear. Regarding constructed music, Adorno said: 'Those moments in Webern where, in Schoenberg's words, a whole book is compressed to a sigh, do not allay the suspicions about highly constructed music which is essentially poor although giving the appearance of great concentration. Every composer today must ask himself about the actual substance of his constructions—and how much musical substance deteriorates through construction.'[2]

Many would cry out in contradiction. For the opposite—absence of construction—does not itself guarantee 'musical substance'. In great art, substance and construction are not only complementary to each other, but inseparable parts of a complete unity.

[1] 'Bo Nilsson' by G. M. Koenig, *Die Reihe* 4, 1958.

[2] 'Technique, technology and music today', by Theodor W. Adorno, published in English in *Ordini* (Rome, 1959).

Many composers would indeed regard music with a low constructed content as inferior to music which has been created by rational meditation. The very word composition implies deliberation, contemplation, the logical assembling together of various parts into a unity. Perhaps it would not be far wrong to regard the application of mathematics to music, or indeed any kind of constructivism, as a process which can stimulate the composer's talents. The words of one of the most mathematically minded composers, Iannis Xenakis, seem to suggest such a sublimation of creative thought through logic and reason by 'the effort to analyse certain sound sensations, dissect them, dominate them, and then use them in our own constructions; the effort to crystallize thought processes which create sounds and experiment with them in our own compositions . . . The effort to make art through "geometry", thereby giving it reasoned sustenance, which is less perishable than the impulse of the moment, and therefore more serious, more worthy of that struggle for higher things which exists in all domains of the human intelligence.'[1]

[1] Iannis Xenakis: *Musiques Formelles*, Paris. Note that Xenakis worked as an architect with Le Corbusier, previously mentioned with regard to the modern use of the Golden Section.

7

Free Twelve-Note Music

The Integral Serialism of the Fifties could hardly last for ever, though at the time it seemed to have qualities of permanence and durability which were beyond question. The methods of predeterminacy were so varied and yet so well defined that they seemed certain to determine the pattern of music for some considerable period. Yet well within a decade, in Europe at least, the system had already fallen into decline, and though its structures may still be used today, they have long ceased to be the mainstream technique they once were.[1]

Looking back, it now seems that integral serialism was bound to exhaust itself through sheer similarity of results. However the systems were evolved, permuted, and manipulated, the music always remained within the same limited confines. After a certain point, nothing strikingly different could emerge. Even such a die-hard integral serialist as Nono had worked himself out by *Intolleranza 1960* and then abandoned the medium for years. Integral serialism was also bound to reach a limit through sheer performance problems. No player could faithfully interpret all the diabolical contortions of mathematically contrived phrase structures, nor could he be expected to tolerate without complaint music which was so incredibly demanding, and yet to him seemed to have so little to give in reward. And so integral serialism quickly reached an impasse, through its own limitations and the burdens it laid on performers. But its importance, in both aesthetic and historical contexts, must not be denied. For it forged a completely new musical language, as different from anything that had gone before (except Webern) as chalk from cheese, and paved the way to a new, more spontaneous music which is still the most potent means of emotive expression today.

Once composers had assimilated the results of integral serialism, once the kind of sound, the phrase shapes, and note patterns became familiar to them,

[1] It would seem that in the U.S.A., however, under the influence of Milton Babbitt, integral serialism continues to flourish, in the East Coast universities and with composers of the middle generation.

the pendulum began to swing the other way. Rigid principles gave way to free invention, structuralism was abandoned for fantasy, complexity yielded to simplification. In short, a new, free music evolved, similar in many aspects to the products of integral serialism, but more varied and spontaneous, and with deeper emotive foundations. This music, which for want of a better term is loosely called 'free twelve-note music', has proved to be durable, and has continued to form the hard core of much of the avant-garde production of the last fifteen years. The break-away from the cerebralisms of total serialism in the later Fifties in fact went much further than the creation of a free twelve-note idiom. But the more extreme reactions (involving improvisation, graphic scores, etc.) will be discussed later, as they are outside the scope of this chapter.

From an historical point of view, free twelve-note music completes a full cycle spanning half a century, for in reality it is a logical continuation of the 'free atonalism' evolved in the years prior to the First World War. This free atonalism, first tentatively explored by Schoenberg and Webern around 1910, was finally rationalized by the introduction of serialism in 1923. After a period of interruption due to totalitarian rule and the Second World War, serialism was carried to a peak of rationalization in the Fifties. Then, as a reaction, liberalizing processes set in and created free twelve-note composition, reviving many aspects of the early 'free atonalism', but now in a fully evolved state and forming a completely mature musical language. The cycle was then complete and serialism had come and gone, but leaving decisive and lasting traces of its sojourn.

In free twelve-note music, the series is abandoned and note-orders are completely free. The total-chromatic of all twelve chromatic notes within the octave is used fairly consistently, but there is no rigid rule, as in serialism, whereby notes cannot be repeated until all the other eleven notes have been used. In fact composers seem to have used successions of notes freely according to the requirements of musical expression:

Berio: *Serenata I*

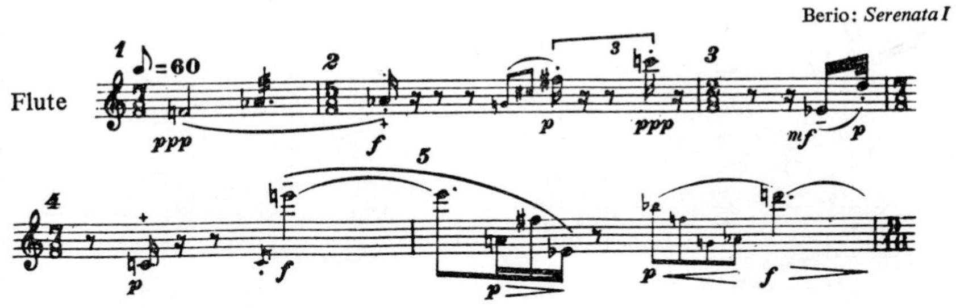

It will be noted in the above opening cadenza from Berio's *Serenata I* for flute and 14 instruments (1957) that note repetitions begin to recur from bar 4 onwards, and that the total-chromatic is not completely used until the G in bar 5. There are even tonal note groups and octave repetitions which would hardly be admitted in serialist circles. In the following example, indeed, from Boulez's first *Improvisation sur Mallarmé*, note repetition is an essential characteristic of the music, in fact there is an almost oriental insistence on one particular group of notes which runs through the whole of the first section of this piece:

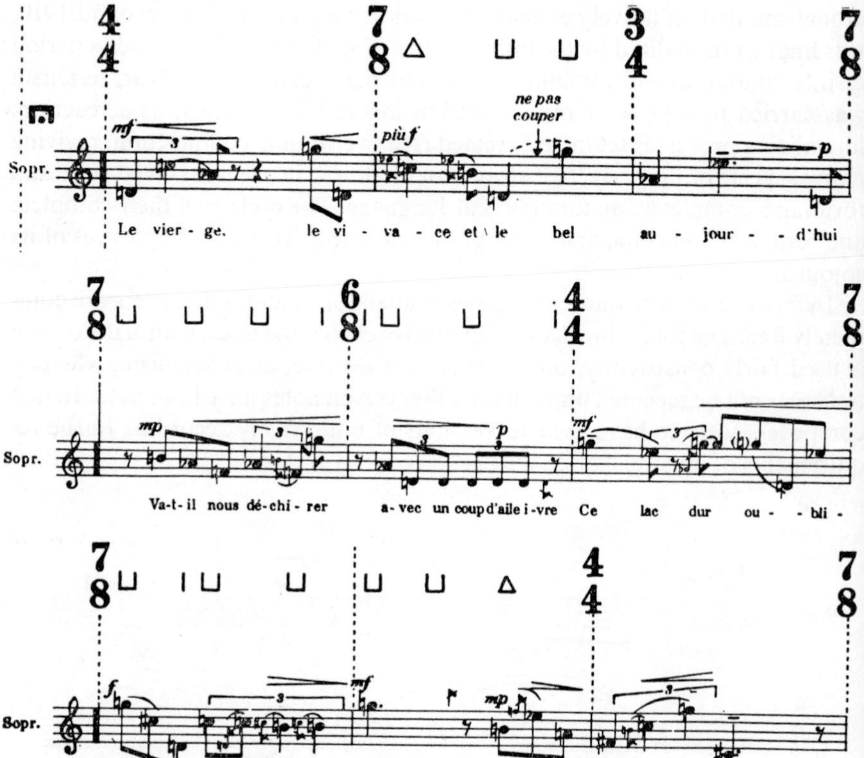

ne pas couper

Sopr.

Le vier - ge. le vi - va - ce et le bel au - jour - - d'hui

Sopr.

Va-t-il nous dé-chi - rer a-vec un coup d'aile i-vre Ce lac dur ou - - bli -

Sopr.

-é que han-te sous le - - gi - - vre Le trans-pa - rent gla - - - cier uch a degree of note repetition is however unusual in free twelve-note music, he general trend being rather to the contrary.

The rhythmic configuration of free twelve-note music often owes much to he irregular shapes thrown out by integral serialism. The 'feel' of metre is leliberately eradicated, often by asymmetrical proportions which performers an hardly be expected to play with complete accuracy:

Bo Nillson: *Quantitäten*

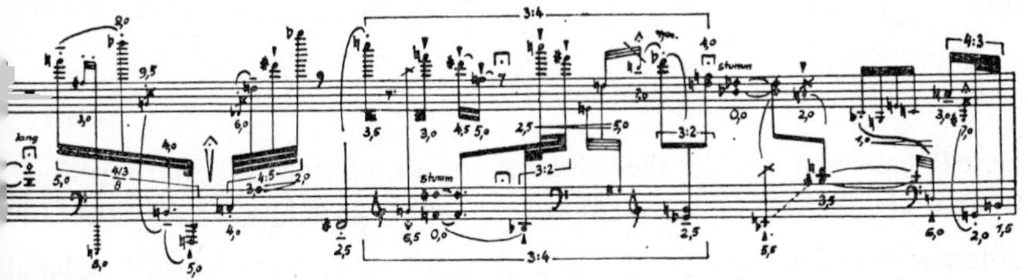

n this short space, phrases are formed by four notes in the time of three, four n the time of five, and three beats in the time of four (within which there are two roups of three notes in the time of two). The pauses, acciaccaturas, and ornanents make the exact interpretation of such finely graded durations beyond uman skill and perception. As the music has no indications of tempo or metre, t would seem that the performer has been given a deliberately impossible task, ike an explorer provided with great detail for a journey which has no point of leparture. Some composers, recognizing that to insist on such demanding hythmic designs is farcical (if they cannot be played accurately, nor heard to be ccurate), devised simpler solutions. This process of simplification led to the doption, in some cases, of graphic notations which (put loosely) merely suggest what the player should perform, leaving him to invent much of his material, while placing him under as few restrictions as possible. However, such solutions go beyond the confines of this chapter and will be discussed later. For the moment it is desirable to consider only the most conventional solutions, which generally retain many aspects of precise notation without using exact duration values, the performer relying very much on the general appearance of the music and the spatial disposition of the notes:

Pousseur: *Exercices pour Piano*

Here Pousseur has avoided the rigours of precise notation by the introduction of somewhat imprecise values for grace notes and silences (grace notes are of four different durations: ♪, ♪, ♪ + and ♪𝄐, while silences are similarly ordered: 𝄾, 𝄾, 𝄾 + and 𝄾𝄐 as well as short and long pauses: 𝄐 and ⊓). This system has almost substituted one complexity for another, but at least the music is not chained by notation to a metrical foundation which serves no audible purpose.

The following shows a much freer notation in which sounds have to be played according to their placing within the bar lines:

Kagel: *Sonant (1960/ . . . .)*

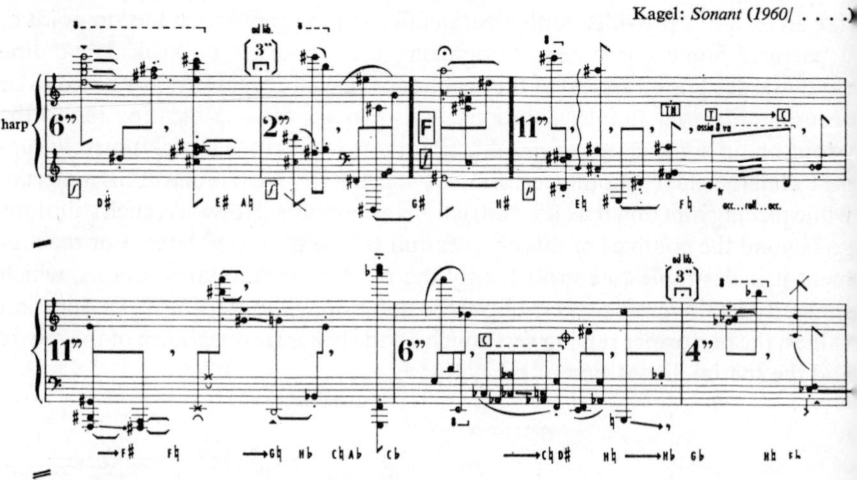

Each bar is given a specific duration, and as all instruments in the score (guitar, harp, double bass, and percussion) have bars of different length, the composer has obviously aimed at producing music of a somewhat indeterminate nature.

It will be noted that though most note values seem to be quavers, this is not really so. The horizontal line is merely a means of grouping sounds within each phrase.)

The following excerpt from Bussotti's *Pièces de Chair II* shows this process of free notation carried a step further. The duration of sounds depends only on the position of each note horizontally along the stave. As will be seen, the cardinal points in time are indicated by large notes, these being surrounded by groups of rapid ornaments written as small acciaccaturas:

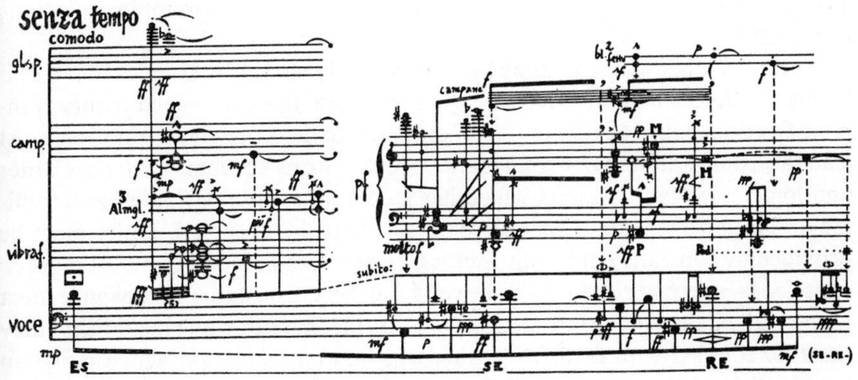

The whole passage is indicated to be played in free time, while vertical dotted lines are used to co-ordinate the parts. Presumably the total duration of the passage largely depends on the capacity of the singer's lungs!

Harmonically, free twelve-note music generally follows those principles of avoiding tonal associations which Webern had already explored before the First World War—the use of the total-chromatic, avoidance of any suggestion of triadic formations, and the contradiction (usually by semitone intervals) of tonal suggestions within any given note group. But whereas Webern's harmonic language was thin, free twelve-note music often has a much denser harmonic texture, with note agglomerations approaching cluster forms (in fact note clusters themselves are used frequently). Note, for example, how the Bussotti work quoted above begins with a multinote chord, how the piano part contains four clusters within such a short space of time, and every note combination comprises semitone contradictions (or inversions of semitones: major sevenths, minor ninths, etc.). The Pousseur work quoted above also reveals an abundance of similar half-tone contradictions designed to create an atonal norm; in fac there is hardly a single group of adjacent notes which does not have these semi tone conflicts. Finally, the main harmonic characteristic of such music is tha once having established a certain degree of non-tonal atmosphere, this is usuall maintained evenly throughout the work. In other words, harmony as a com positional device is virtually disregarded and is used mainly in a negative form

Conventional contrapuntal forms are also eradicated from free twelve-not music. Though a strong characteristic of this music is a play of instrumenta voices, there is very rarely any real imitation or use of canonic forms. In an case, melody is almost universally built of non-repetitive phrases where (excep as in the case of Boulez mentioned above) neither rhythms nor note-succession ever recur.

Formally, this music is difficult to classify. It would be simple to say tha forms are 'free' and conventional structures quite ignored, but in reality com plete freedom cannot exist, for it can only lead to disorder. The composer mus lead the listener along a coherent emotive path, through events which have orde and logic, and lead to a goal which has a complete sense of finality and fulfil ment. To do this, certain formal principles must be observed. Unity must b provided by constancy in certain factors, diversity and renewed interest must b supplied by adequate change and novelty in others. Constancy and change mus be carefully balanced if the music is not to be incoherent, while in addition they must be coupled with factors creating tension and relaxation which make up the emotive substructure. As all these various and complex elements are particular to each work, it is not possible or wise to draw precise conclusions, o make excessively definitive statements. This is especially true of the music o indeterminacy and those 'open-form' works which will be discussed later, and in which form may be deliberately left undefined at the composing stage.

Before leaving this brief chapter on free twelve-note music, it must be observed that, as the final product of the cycle embracing free atonalism, serialism, and integral serialism, it has proved a durable language, but not an all-embracing one. As will be seen, there have been many other developments since the Fifties, many of them including compositional methods where no actual musical notation is written at all. But very roughly, it can be said that where notation is used, the general norm is the free twelve-note language, while where notation is not used (in graphic scores, for example) still at some point the score has to be realized in sound, either by improvisation or in the player's own performing version, and again the same free twelve-note idiom would almost certainly be employed—unless the composer specified other means, which is extremely rare. In brief, the free twelve-note technique is the central core of a reat deal of the music of recent times. This may not always be apparent, especially where (as will be described later) composers have searched outwards and evised apparently new idioms, resurrected archaisms, or embraced orientalsms, jazz, etc. But in reality, beneath all the apparent novelty, the free twelveote technique remains a constant sheet-anchor, and this must be remembered n subsequent chapters.

8

Indeterminacy, Chance, and Aleatory Music

As we have already seen, integral serialism, while creating a new musical langu
age during the Fifties, contained within itself the seeds of self-destruction
Principally, it was excessively complex, creating performance problems whic
were rarely in proportion to the expressive returns. Secondly, the systems, how
ever diverse, tended to produce works of some uniformity. Free twelve-not
composition was evolved as an escape from the shackles of these cerebralisms
but in addition further means were employed which proved in the end to hav
even more extensive results. These means have been loosely called indetermin
acy, random or aleatory music, music of chance, or simply improvisation (total
controlled, or otherwise). It is hoped here to separate these concepts in a
orderly fashion, though it must be remembered that these terms have been use
very loosely. For instance, to one composer indeterminacy may mean com
pletely random operations, while to another it can apply to music which is wel
defined and may have some freedom only in one musical parameter.

Indeterminacy can in fact be partial or total; it can affect a small area of
composition only or the whole. For instance, the following example shows
work which is indeterminate in several parameters and precise in others. In thi
Projection I for solo cello by Morton Feldman, written as early as 1950, th
timbre is indicated (◇ = harmonic, P = pizzicato, and A = arco), and rela
tive pitch is shown as a square or oblong written within one of three boxes whicl
represent either high, medium, or low registers. Durations are indicated 'by th
amount of space taken up by the square or rectangle' within the dotted line
(¦ ¦), which represent four pulses at tempo 72 'or thereabouts'. Indeterminat
parameters are: (1) pitch within each of the three registers, (2) dynamics, an
(3) expression:

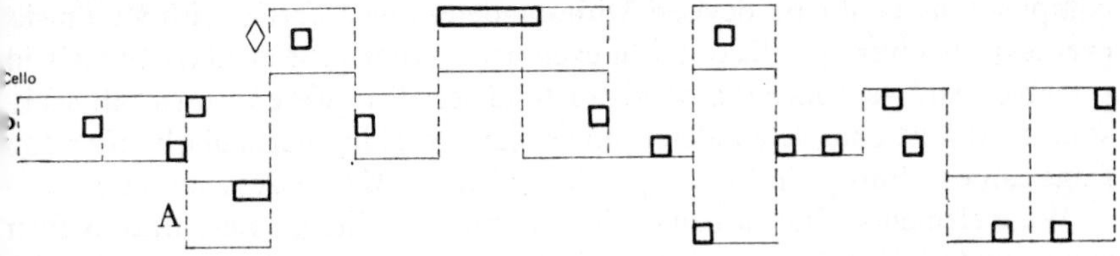

From the date of this piece it will be seen that in the U.S.A. indeterminacy egan at a time when European composers were just beginning to wrestle with ntegral serialism. In fact a whole group of American composers (including uch major figures as John Cage, Morton Feldman, Earle Brown, Harry Partch, nd Christian Wolff) circumnavigated integral serialism almost completely, ecause they were largely unaware of its existence, and in any case its mechanisms would have been completely contrary to their artistic creeds.

During the Fifties a considerable artistic void seems to have existed between he U.S.A. and Europe, at least as far as avant-garde music was concerned, and his produces a problem of exposition. We can either continue to trace the ath of European music towards indeterminacy, or turn back to before 1950 nd follow American indeterminacy through from its infancy to its maturity nd virtual abandonment by its originators. The choice is made even more ifficult by the fact that these two movements are quite opposite. The European novement is essentially one of simplification, the American one (in some comosers at least) proceeds from almost naïve and rudimentary concepts of ndeterminacy to greater musical definition and complexity.

Eventually these two movements converge and unite. But here and now it is mpossible to write about both movements simultaneously. I have decided, for he sake of logical continuity, to follow European music first, and to return to American music in a later chapter. To save duplication in musical examples, however, some quotations from American works will be included where ppropriate, while some side-tracking into the American scene will be inevitable n order to make some matters more explicit.

To return to European music in the Fifties. It is obvious that any composer using integral serialism should insist on complete definition in all musical parameters. He would write with precision down to the most microscopic detail, and xpect performances to be exact reproductions of his work. This absolute definition seemed to be the logical culmination of hundreds of years of growing compositional exactitude, from the looseness of Caccini's harmonic shorthand the 'continuo') to the precise detail of Webern's notation. To the integral erialist, therefore, the concept of indeterminacy was absolutely alien. That compositions could be devised without determined form, without music events being given specific order or even being notated, seemed completely in possible. And yet, once the bonds of total serialism were thrown off, such state of almost complete indeterminacy came rapidly, particularly after Joh Cage came to Europe in 1958 (a previous visit in 1954 was less notable).

What elements of music can be 'indeterminate'? Pitch, note-duration, form sound material, and expression (including dynamics, timbre, etc.). It will b seen on reflection that even indeterminacy in only one of these parameters ca have far-reaching effects. For instance, if everything in a composition excep pitch is defined, and players are left to choose notes freely, every performanc will produce different melodic, harmonic, and contrapuntal results. Similarly if players are given exact notes to play together with expressive indications, bu without precise durations, the vertical coincidence of sounds will be left t chance, and the harmony and general ethos will vary accordingly.

We will consider the various parameters of indeterminacy one by one, be ginning with its temporal applications. Perhaps the first instance of tim indeterminacy in Europe came from the arch-innovator Stockhausen, at moment when it seemed that the note durations thrown up by integral serialism could no longer be contained within time itself:

Stockhausen: *Zeitmass*

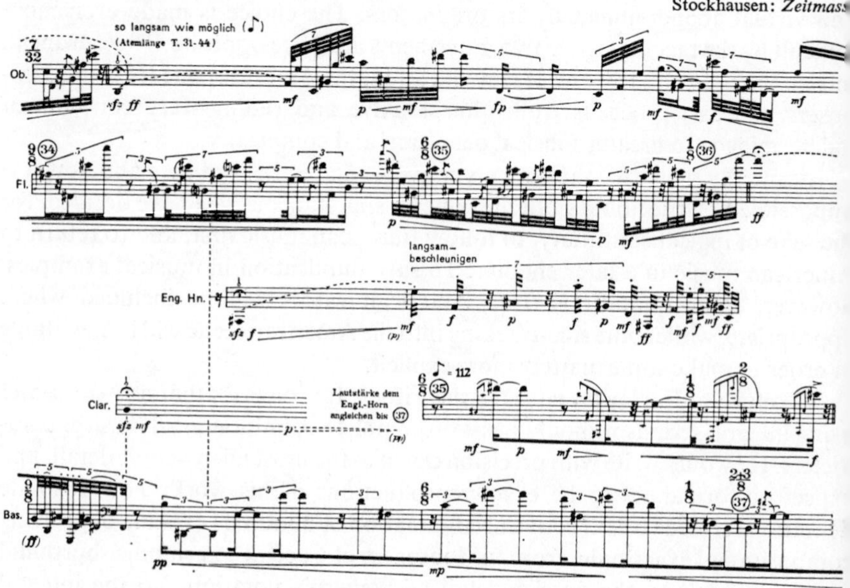

From this page of *Zeitmasse* (which signifies 'tempi') written for wind quintet in

956), we can see how flute and bassoon playing in exact time (♪ = 112) were et against the oboe playing 'as slow as possible', the English horn 'slow-uickening', and the clarinet beginning after a pause of imprecise duration. It vould seem that there is absolutely no possibility of this page ever being played n exactly the same way twice over. It is therefore indeterminate in time to some legree, yet it will always sound more or less the same, for 'chance' is not llowed much elbow room. Of course, the rhythmic configurations are diaboli-ally difficult and go beyond the bounds of reason (for instance, how can the English horn play seven and then five notes in the time of four while beginning lowly and getting faster?), so this page from *Zeitmasse* shows how illogical it ad become to use a complex conventional notation to produce results which ould only be approximate. But once the possibility of time indeterminacy was ccepted, even to only a limited degree, composers gradually discarded conven-ional notation in favour of more legible systems, often based on the spatial lisposition of the notes in the score. For instance, in the following example from Sylvano Bussotti's *Sette Foglie* (*Couple* for flute and piano), though the notes at irst appear to be semibreves, crochets, quavers, etc., in reality note-durations lepend on the space occupied on the written page:

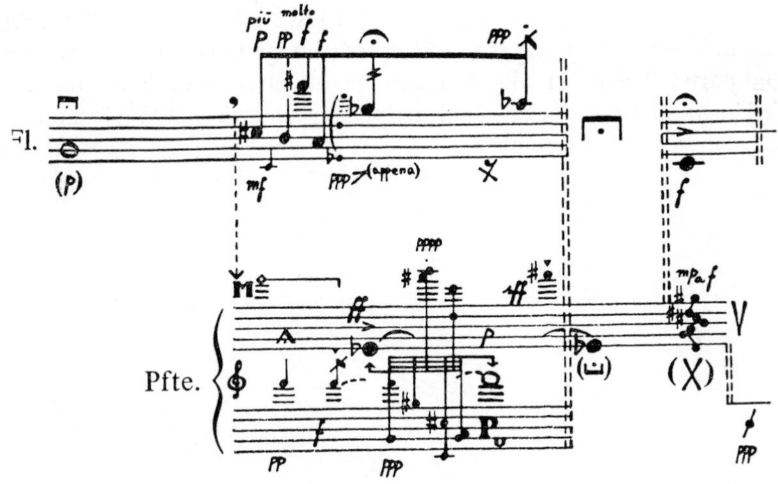

Though composers often continue to use conventional duration signs (𝅗𝅥., ♩., ♪, etc.) as means of indicating only approximate durations, certain forms of pro-portional notation have been in use for some considerable time, and some are very satisfactory. For example, the proportional notation used in Berio's

Sequenza (1958) for solo flute has been used (with various modifications) eve since. It is easy to play and represents the composer's requirements precisel (perhaps too precisely where real time indeterminacy is aimed at):

(Here Berio indicates that a space of about 3 cm. is equal to 70 M.M. Note indicated ♪ are separate sounds with their real duration governed by the mod of attack. Notes with stems joined are held until the next note is sounded. Legat slurs indicate sounds joined together.)

A much greater degree of time indeterminacy is shown in the following ex ample of a comparatively recent work by David Bedford. White notes indicat legato, black ones staccato. All pitches are given, but throughout this vocal pas sage (which lasts about half a minute altogether) each instrument plays six note in any order and time, using the signs written above each part in varied succes sion. All instruments play piano, except when '*f*' is written. Short glissandos ar indicated by ↗ and ↘; ◇ signifies harmonic and ≢ tremolo or flutter-tongue In reality, this music is very simple, comprising a 12-note chord throughout voice and instruments using the same notes (though G is omitted from instru mental parts). The effect will obviously be one of vocal declamation accom panied by a restless chord, each note being pinpointed in random fashion, wit varied emphasis and colour:

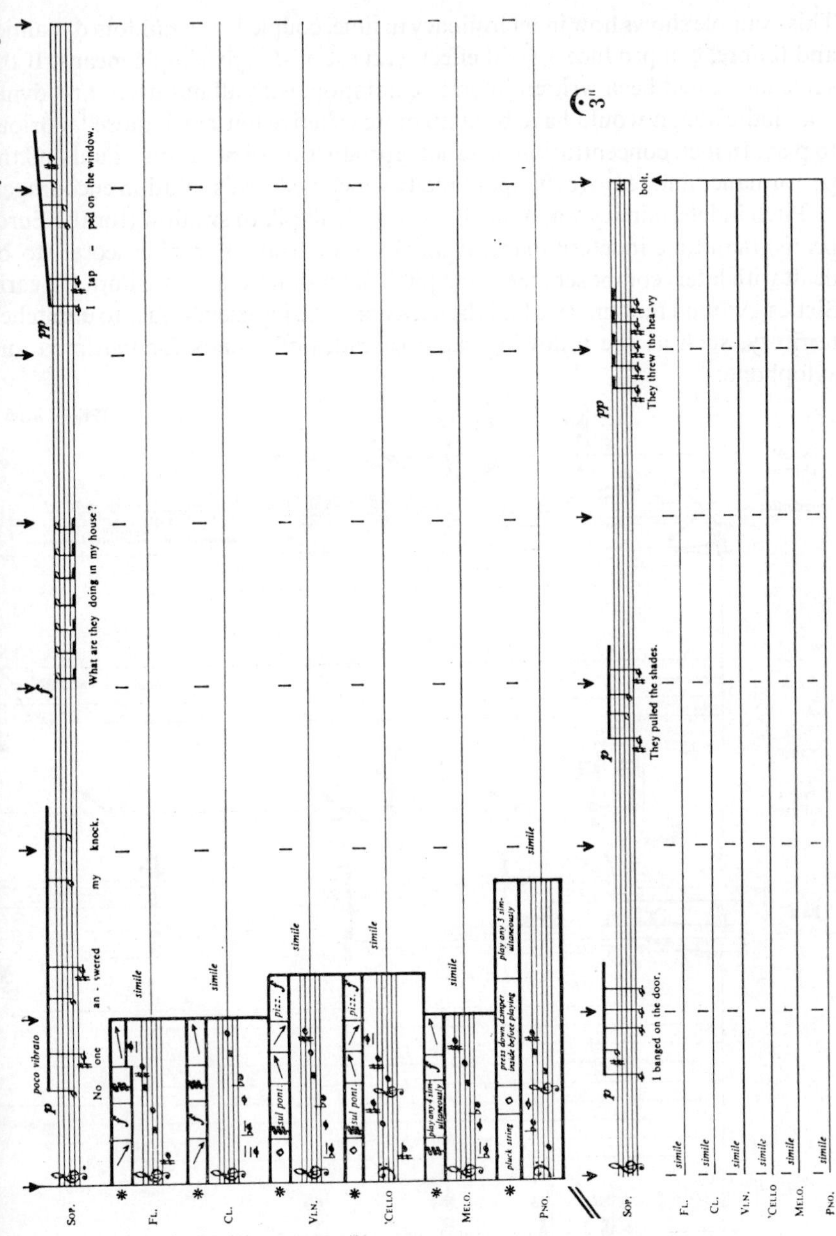
Bedford: Music for Albion Moonlight
Sop.
Fl.
Cl.
Vln.
'Cello
Melo.
Pno.
poco vibrato
p
No one an - swered my knock.
f
What are they doing in my house?
pp
I tap - ped on the window.
3"
sul pont.
pizz.
simile
play any 4 simultaneously
pluck string
press down damper inside before playing
play any 3 simultaneously
I banged on the door.
They pulled the shades.
They threw the hea-vy bolt.

This example shows how indeterminacy in time, coupled with random dynamics and timbre, can produce a vivid effect with astonishingly simple means. If the same music had been written in precise notation, with all durations and dynamics indicated, it would have been no more effective but much more laborious to play. In fact, concentration on exact reproduction of notation would dull the performance and remove the spontaneity which Bedford's solution encourages.

Pitch indeterminacy was a much more difficult pill to swallow (for the Europeans) than time indeterminacy. Apart from occasional graphic scores (to be dealt with later) composers regarded pitch definition as inviolate until the early Sixties. Around that time we find the occasional daring excursion into unpitched territory, such as the following rapid cascades of sounds for marimba and xylophone:

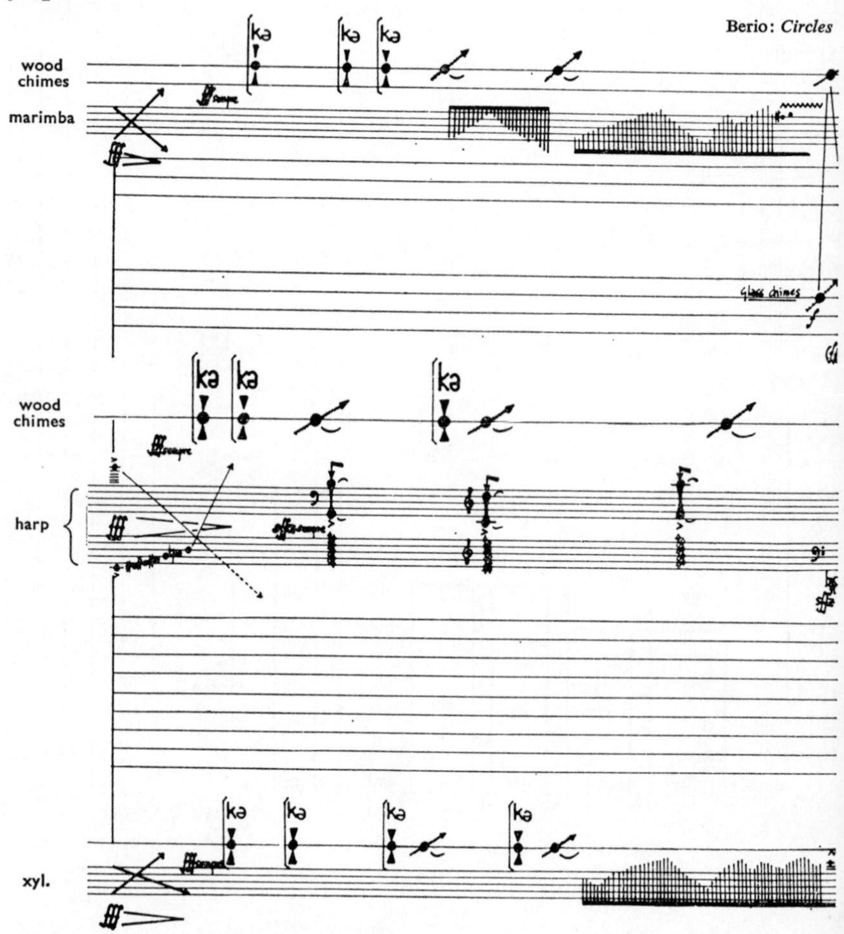

But of course this was written for instruments with fleeting sounds so that it was virtually a no-risk venture. Such evanescent sounds could hardly create the cacophony which European composers feared uncontrolled pitch would cause. And yet in 1951 Morton Feldman in the U.S.A. had already written for orchestra in the following extraordinary manner:

Feldman: *Intersection I*

In this fifteen-page score, there is not a single note of defined pitch. Instruments can play any note within the high, middle, and low ranges indicated. In fact Feldman's instructions are so refreshingly brief they can be quoted in full:

> The performer may make his entrance on or within each given time duration. Relative pitch (high, middle, low) is indicated: ⊤ High; ⊓ Middle; ⊥ Low. Any tone within the ranges indicated may be sounded. The limits of these ranges may be freely chosen by the performer. Duration is indicated by the amount of space taken up by the square or rectangle, each box (⁝ ⁝) being potentially 4 icti. The single ictus or pulse is at the tempo 72 or thereabouts. The dynamics are also freely chosen by all players, but once established, must be sustained at the same level to the end of the given time duration. A minimum of vibrato should be used throughout by all instruments.
>
> For strings: P = pont.; H = har.; Pz = pizz. The absence of any symbol means arco.

It will be seen that in *Intersection I* there are several other indeterminate parameters as well as pitch: players can choose their own dynamics as long as notes are sustained at the same volume, and may enter at any time during a given period. With pizzicato strings, especially, this is bound to create an effect of movement which is not apparent in the score. It seems obvious, however, that all fifteen pages of the score are bound to sound very much the same. Thus this music, in spite of its adventurous conception, offers little variety of sound texture, musical event, or emotive expression. (This lack of eventfulness was exactly what Feldman desired, and will be discussed later.)

What is more important to emphasize here is that European composers took a long time to accept the fact that a large mass of instruments can play random sounds of any pitch with a result that can still be termed 'music'. The whole European musical tradition has been built on the principle that music can only comprise precise sounds played at exactly defined moments, and that undefined sounds played at random can only produce non-music. For composers such as Stockhausen, Boulez, and Berio, brought up in the ultra-precision of integral serialism, it was particularly hard to digest the fact that all their exactitude could be abandoned—in fact Boulez has never accepted such a wild concept and Berio has hardly embraced it with open arms.

Stockhausen, however, took up pitch indeterminacy in the early Sixties, and it is interesting to compare his *Mixtur* for five orchestral groups with Feldman's *Intersection I* in the previous example—see opposite page.

Though *Mixtur* and *Intersection I* were written more than a decade apart, and though both composers were concerned only with relative pitch (high, medium, and low), these works betray the different mentalities of the two continents. For the European composer, music must have direction, moving in waves to emotive consummation. For the American (as exemplified by Feldman and his followers), music can be without the emotive surge; ideally it lulls the listener into a relaxed mental withdrawal. Decisive events are therefore to be avoided. Note by contrast the rhythmic precision and forward impetus of Stockhausen's first three bars, and how the remaining bars, filled with a scattering of pointillist sounds, grow in density and then thin out. (All the music is in tempo, the indications in the last three bars showing how many sounds occur during each beat, but omitting rhythmic designs. This score is written for five instrumental groups —percussion, woodwind, brass, plucked strings, and bowed strings—with electronic amplification and ring modulation.)

Pitch indeterminacy, as shown in the previous two scores, obviously produces note clusters (groups of sounds a semitone apart, or less)—the kind of sound we were already accustomed to in electronic music's filtered bands of white sound. This has had considerable attraction for orchestral composers. The Polish composer Krzystof Penderecki was one of the first to exploit such note clusters with intensely poetic effect in his *Threnody to the Victims of Hiroshima* for string orchestra. Some of his clusters are obtained by precise notation (the strings being so subdivided that each player knows exactly which note to play) while in other passages symbols indicate that each performer must play 'as high as possible' (▲), 'between the bridge and tailpiece' (⌒┼⌒), 'on the bridge' (☂), or using sharp or flat quarter-tones—all devices which produce clusters of the electronic white sound type already mentioned. In the example on p. 71 from György Ligeti's *Volumina* for organ both time and pitch indeterminacies are combined, the thickness of the clusters (for each hand and the pedals) being

Stockhausen: *Mixtur*

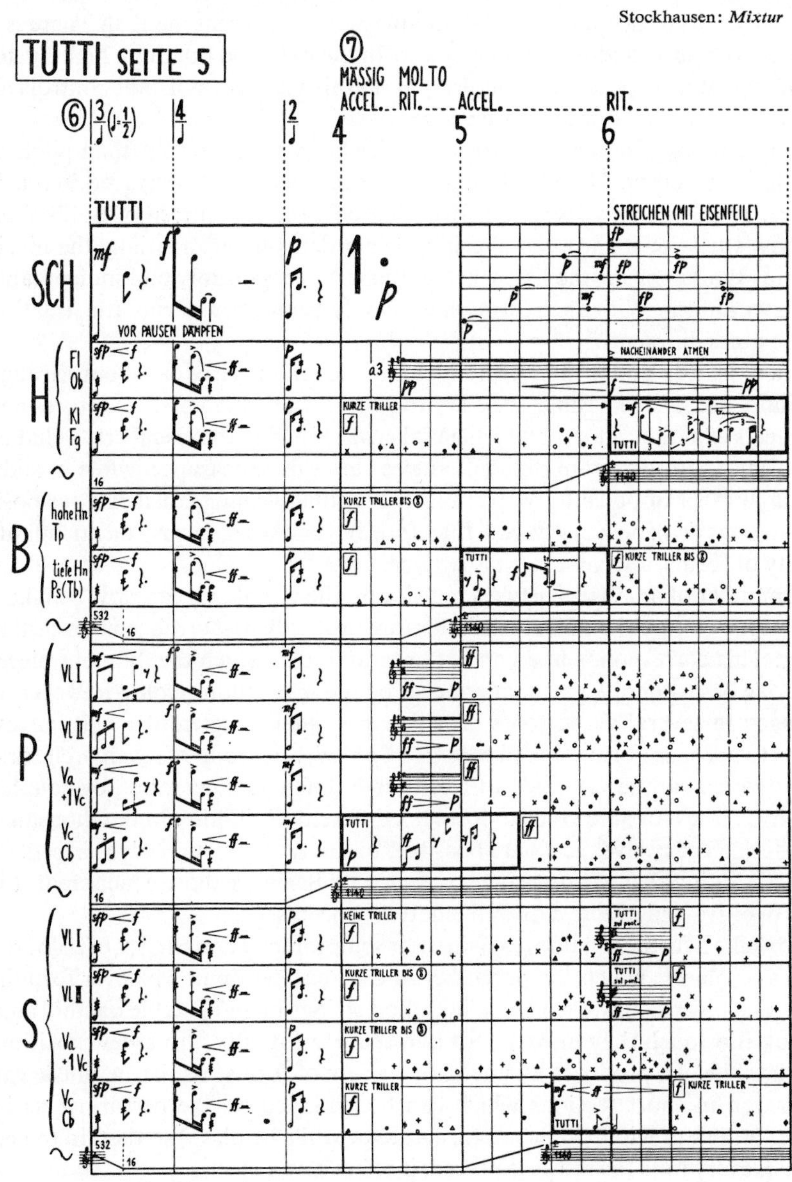

shown only approximately. The duration of the passage is not indicated,[1] nor is the registration, except that each hand plays on a different manual. There is a general crescendo and the passage ends with the left hand holding a high cluster on the 'great' organ with all couplers on (in this piece an assistant controls all stops and couplers)—see opposite page.

Indeterminacy in *form* has perhaps more far-reaching results than pitch or time indeterminacy. The resulting 'open forms' have rarely occurred in music before. True, one may feel like performing only the best fifteen of Bull's *Walsingham* variations, and even altering their order, but substantially the music remains the same. To the listener, the music is recognizably and indisputably Bull's variations. With open forms or even only 'semi-open' forms, the situation can be quite different.

There is little doubt that form indeterminacy in music came about through the influence of the visible arts. During the Fifties, painters, sculptors, and architects exploited a factor which has always existed in the visual arts—that is, an object when seen from different angles varies in appearance, while in addition, a number of objects grouped together actually change their relative positions. A work of visual art can therefore have several forms, or an infinite variety of forms, and yet remain the same.

A number of analogies between music and the visual arts can now be made. A group of pictures by different painters are probably best arranged in a certain order. This corresponds to a concert programme in which the different pieces have one best order. A group of pictures by the *same* author could however be arranged in several ways, some of which are equally preferable. This corresponds to an open-form work like Berio's *Epifanie*—a group of seven orchestral pieces which can be arranged to form three different 'Quaderni', or coupled with five pieces for solo voice to form ten different 'Epifanie'. Many thousands of orderings of twelve pieces are possible, but Berio indicates only thirteen. (It is worth noting that the orderings preferred by Berio are those which create the most decisive and effective overall emotive concepts.)

To make a further analogy, a painter or sculptor may design a set of coloured shapes or objects which the purchaser himself can set up in whatever form he likes. The objects may even be balanced on strings in an unstable equilibrium, so that at a touch they move about and settle eventually into a new position. This 'mobile' art produces an unending variety of forms. Similarly, music can be written in short sections which can be arranged by the performer as he desires (either previous to the performance or while he plays) so that, in theory at least, every time the music is played, it offers new aspects.

[1] Only the total duration of the work is given—sixteen minutes.

13

--- (sempre cresc.) --- cresc. molto --- fff

Tutti + General-kop.

Right Hand

(auf einem anderen Manual)

Keine Unterbrechung des Clusters!

--- (sempre cresc.) --- cresc. molto --- fff

Left Hand

Den Cluster auf dem Manual des Hauptwerkes allein weiterhalten.

--- (sempre cresc.) ---

Pedal

Some forms of architecture are based on prefabricated modules. Only a few different types of basic elements are required to complete a structure which, though admittedly of a primarily functional nature, such as the Italian Bortolaso System, has aesthetic value. For instance, though wall and window panels, entrance doors, etc., remain the same, these can be disposed so as to create buildings of widely different proportions, and of course the basis of architectural beauty is created by proportions—the balance of masses and their relative shapes and 'directions'. Similarly, some composers provide only a few basic elements indeed which, when differently massed together, form entirely different sound structures.

A final analogy of open forms with architecture: no building or group of buildings is ever seen in one way only. Even if an architect designs a whole town (such as a University City), like 'mobile' art it changes with the viewpoint. It may be first seen from the air at any angle, one may enter it by any sideroad, or even emerge into it at any point from a subway. Music may have the same ever-changing form. A work like John Cage's *Atlas Eclipticalis* has that bewildering unknown form one feels on entering a strange city, or (as the title suggests) as one explores the firmament with but few bearings to lead the way.

While such analogies between music and the visual arts can be used to justify and illustrate formal indeterminacy in music, we must not be deceived. Music is fugitive, intangible, while the visual arts are concrete and permanent. Music's forms are therefore difficult to perceive, in fact they cannot be observed at all except in retrospect, when memory is already beginning to fade, while the objects of the visual arts can be seen and reseen until every aspect is familiar. Now if one concedes that the language of contemporary music is itself largely enigmatic and particularly fugitive, it is obvious that to appreciate the many facets of open forms is beyond the means of any ordinary listener and possibly only of real significance to the composer himself. Form indeterminacy is therefore a phenomenon which has unsatisfactory aspects. But it must be admitted that with certain types of works, in the hands of some composers, open forms are indisputably valid.

It would be tedious to illustrate every type of formal indeterminacy, or to quote the lengthy expositions which so often preface these works. So the following outlines of a few of the main types of open forms are deliberately brief, illustrating the general structural concepts only.

One of the first pieces of European music in open form was Stockhausen's *Klavierstück XI* (1956). This comprises nineteen sections of music scattered over a large sheet, some sections being fairly long, others very brief, such as the following:

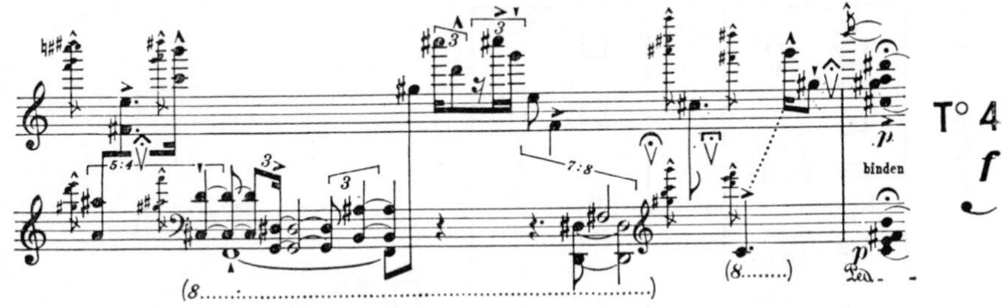

The player is directed to play any piece at random, choosing his own tempo, etc. On finishing that section he then reads the tempo, dynamics, and attack that follow, 'looks at random to any other group, which he then plays in accordance with the latter indications' (there are six types of tempo, dynamics, and attack). When groups are played a second time, octave transpositions are to be used. When 'arrived at for the third time, one possible realization of the piece is completed. This being so, it may come about that certain groups are played once only or not at all.'

Parts of Boulez's Third Piano Sonata are somewhat similarly conceived. In two sections—'Parenthèse' and 'Commentaire'—there are obligatory and optional structures, the latter being written in brackets and included or omitted as the performer fancies. The order of the sonata's four movements can also be varied. Stockhausen's *Zyklus* for percussion has similar bracketed parts and rectangular areas which contain 'reservoirs' of elements which may be included or excluded according to various rules. In addition, the score can be used upside down and the performer can begin on any page and then complete the rest in the given order—see next page.

In all these pieces, the notation, whether in obligatory or optional sections, is given with considerable exactitude, so that though the ordering and performance-style of sections may vary, the listener may well find recurring and recognizable elements in each performance. The situation is more enigmatic, however, when several players are involved with such open forms. For example, though each part in Arrigo Benvenuti's *Folía* for string quartet is written with absolute precision in tempo, pitch, etc., the work comprises five sections which the four players can each play in any order. There are therefore 120 possible orderings which could occur, but as any performance only comprises a limited, random choice of section orders, the result is unpredictable, even to the players themselves (if they really do choose at hazard).

This kind of music, where elements given with complete definition are put in chance combinations, perhaps comes nearest to what some of us mean by

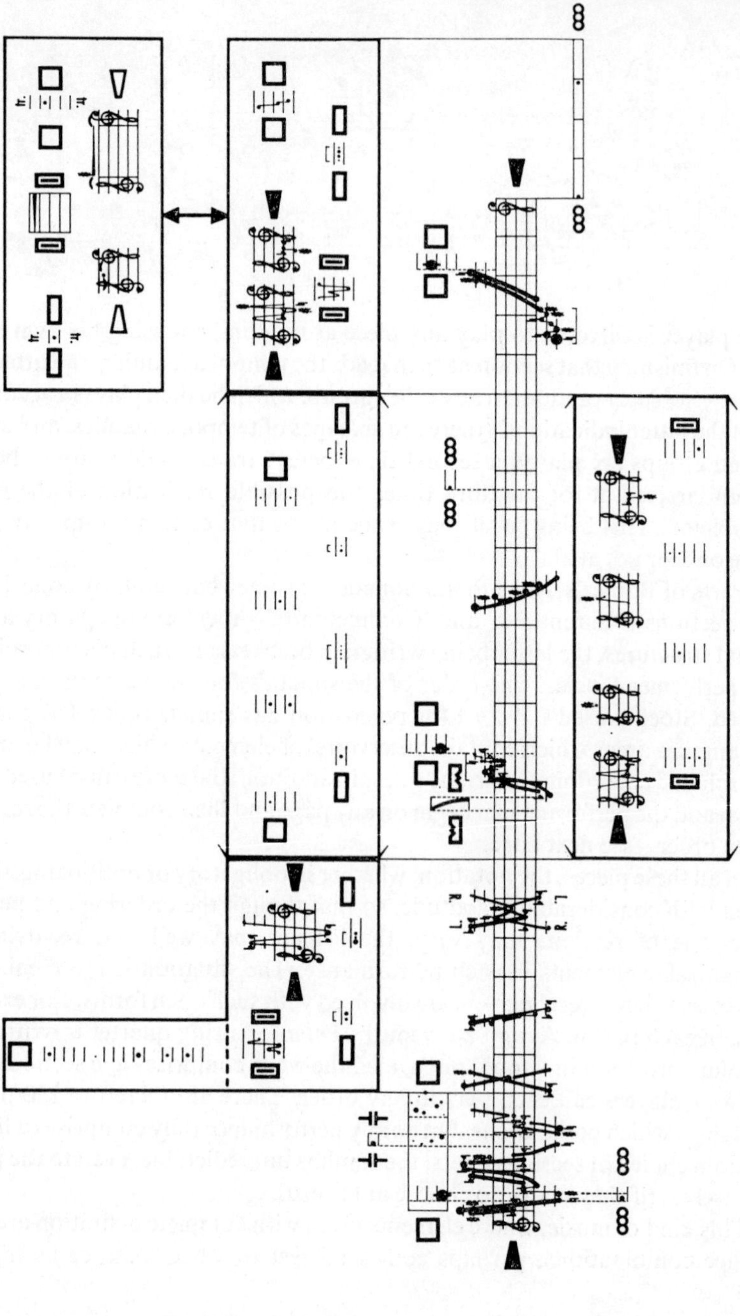

Stockhausen: *Zyklus*

'aleatory'.[1] Though this term is used to mean many things, from a small degree of indeterminacy to out-and-out improvisation, it would seem that its true application is only where musical elements are well defined, but used in chance combinations. If the musical elements themselves were random or undefined, they could not be put in 'aleatory' combinations. After all, one cannot play dice if the dice are not numbered, nor play cards if they do not all belong to conventional sets. On the other hand, to be strictly accurate, the term aleatory (or aleatoric, which seems equally admissible) first came into being early in the period of integral serialism when dice were actually used to determine note durations etc. This usage in itself probably followed John Cage's use of dice and 'chance' procedures culled from the Chinese *I-Ching* treatise. (This volume, often mentioned casually in avant-garde circles in a superficial way, is really such an extensive manual on the theory of probabilities that one could almost call it a philosophical treatise, the contents of which musicians (except Cage) have barely skimmed over. In any case, its real musical relevance is very limited indeed.)

A description of Cage's method of composition based on *I-Ching*, as applied in *Imaginary Landscape No. IV* and *Music of Changes*, is given in the article 'Composition' (1952) included in his book *Silence*. Basically, the system comprises the formation of hexagrams derived from the tossing of coins. He concludes:

> It is thus possible to make a musical composition the continuity of which is free of individual taste and memory (psychology) and also of the literature and 'traditions' of the art. The sounds enter the time-space centered within themselves, unimpeded by service to any abstraction, their 360 degrees of circumference free for an infinite play of interpenetration. Value judgements are not in the nature of this work as regards either composition, performance or listening. The idea of relation (the idea: 2) being absent, anything (the idea: 1) may happen. A 'mistake' is beside the point, for once anything happens it authentically is.

Obviously these results of aleatory methodology are far-reaching. On the one hand, the system seems to be as constructivist as integral serialism; on the other 'anything may happen'. In the end, therefore, it would seem necessary when referring to 'aleatory music' to specify what is really meant, if we mean anything precise at all!

Music which comes very close in form to *mobile art* is often conceived in a semi-graphic design, so that the performers follow certain paths at hazard. Roman Haubenstock-Ramati in particular specialized in this type of score, and his *Mobile for Shakespeare* (Sonnets 53 and 54) for voice and six players is an

[1] From the latin 'alea', meaning a game of dice, hence chance, risk, uncertainty.

ingenious example of this kind of conception. The score is on a single page and is divided into three areas:

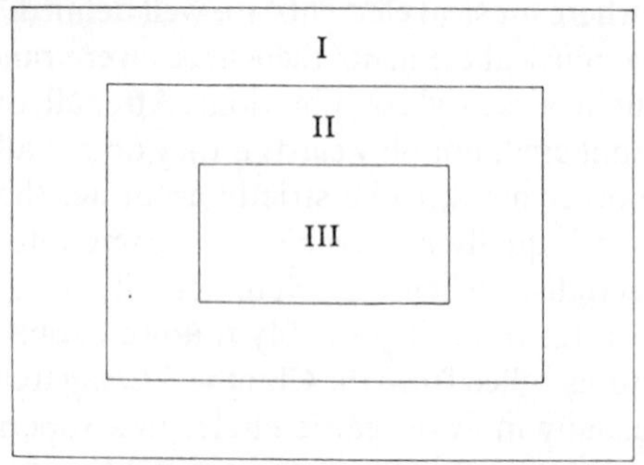

Area I contains twelve musical sections for soprano and percussion 3, area II comprises ten sections and is for piano and celesta, while area III is limited to only six sections, for percussion 1 and 2 and vibraphone or marimba. One quarter of the score (upper right corner) appears as follows:

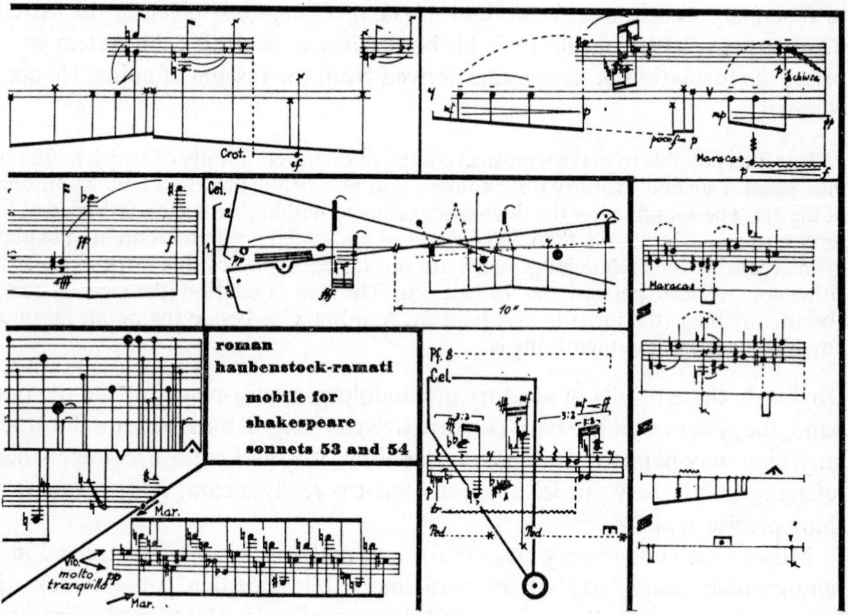

Each player can begin in any section of his total area and then read clockwise or anticlockwise in any tempo. As will be seen, the notation is in places quite specific, in others largely graphic. The soprano part in particular seems very sketchy, though there is a note in the score to the effect that 'a fixed voice version has been prepared by the composer and is available for performance of the work'.

The kind of musical construction which is analogous to architecture's prefabricated module structures usually comprises a number of brief segments which performers play in varied succession over a given time period. For example, the final section of Earle Brown's String Quartet (1965) comprises a small set of modules such as the following, which are found in similar form in all parts:

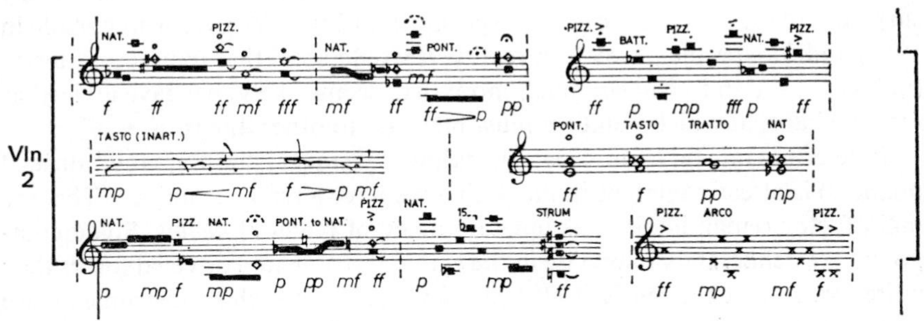

These eight modules are to be played for a total of between one and two minutes, the composer's instructions being:

> play events between dotted lines in any order independently (conscious of ensemble.) if played more than once vary the technique each time (or not) maintain basic rhythm & pitch, tempi: free. volume of total phrase may be raised or lowered proportionately.[1]

To complete this necessarily abbreviated picture of formal indeterminacy, brief mention must be made of schemes where the overall form of a work may be fairly defined, but the actual musical material taken from other sources. For example, in Stockhausen's *Prozession* the instrumentalists play events taken from his earlier compositions: 'the tamtam player draws from MIKROPHONIE I, viola from GESANG DER JÜNGLINGE, KONTAKTE, and MOMENTE, electronium from TELEMUSIK and SOLO, piano from KLAVIERSTÜCKE I–XI and KONTAKTE.' The instrumental parts contain only sequences of three signs (+, —, and =) which mean:

[1] In this and other quotations from American publications, the original punctuation and spelling are used.

+ higher OR louder OR longer OR more segments
− lower OR softer OR shorter OR fewer segments
= same (similar) register AND dynamics AND durations AND timbre AND number of segments

As an example of this skeleton score I quote the beginning of the piano part:

Stockhausen: *Prozession*

Obviously, this is not a score for every ensemble, particularly as (for example) there are no viola parts in any of the three works specified. In fact one has the suspicion that this was a work for a specific occasion (a Vox recording made in 1967) and for specific players. In reality, it would seem that in practical terms (unless +, −, and = mean much more than seems likely) we have arrived at formal chaos, at which point we must move on to other things.

Indeterminacy in *expression* (including dynamics, timbre, and musical nuances) is already implicit in much that we have already examined. The one main factor remaining is thus indeterminacy of material *means*. Some composers are deliberately imprecise in the actual instrumental or vocal forces they write for. In fact the music itself bears few clues as to which instruments are preferred. Opposite is a page from Paolo Renosto's *Players* which he says 'can be played by any instrument or small instrumental group. One or more female voices may be added'. It would seem, however, that the composer cares little for the final definitive version of his work, for he adds: 'the conductor is expected to prepare the instrumental score for each performance'. I have seen the actual parts used for some performances of this work and they bear no real relation to Renosto's score. In fact a good section of the parts contained one word: 'Bedlam'!

Indeterminacy of means is of course a prime characteristic of many works by Cage; here are a few (abbreviated) specifications: '*Variations III*, for one or any number of persons performing any actions'; '*34′ 46.776 for a Pianist*. To be used in whole or part to provide a solo or ensemble for any combination of pianists, string players, percussionists'; '*Atlas Eclipticalis*. Instrumental parts (86) to be played in whole or part, with or without *Winter Music*', '*Concert for Piano and Orchestra* ... to be performed in whole or part, any duration, any number of the above performers, as a solo, chamber ensemble, symphony, concert for Pf, and Orch., aria.'

Such deliberately indiscriminate performance specifications are unusual, because Cage himself is unusual. But his example has been followed by many

Renosto: *Players*

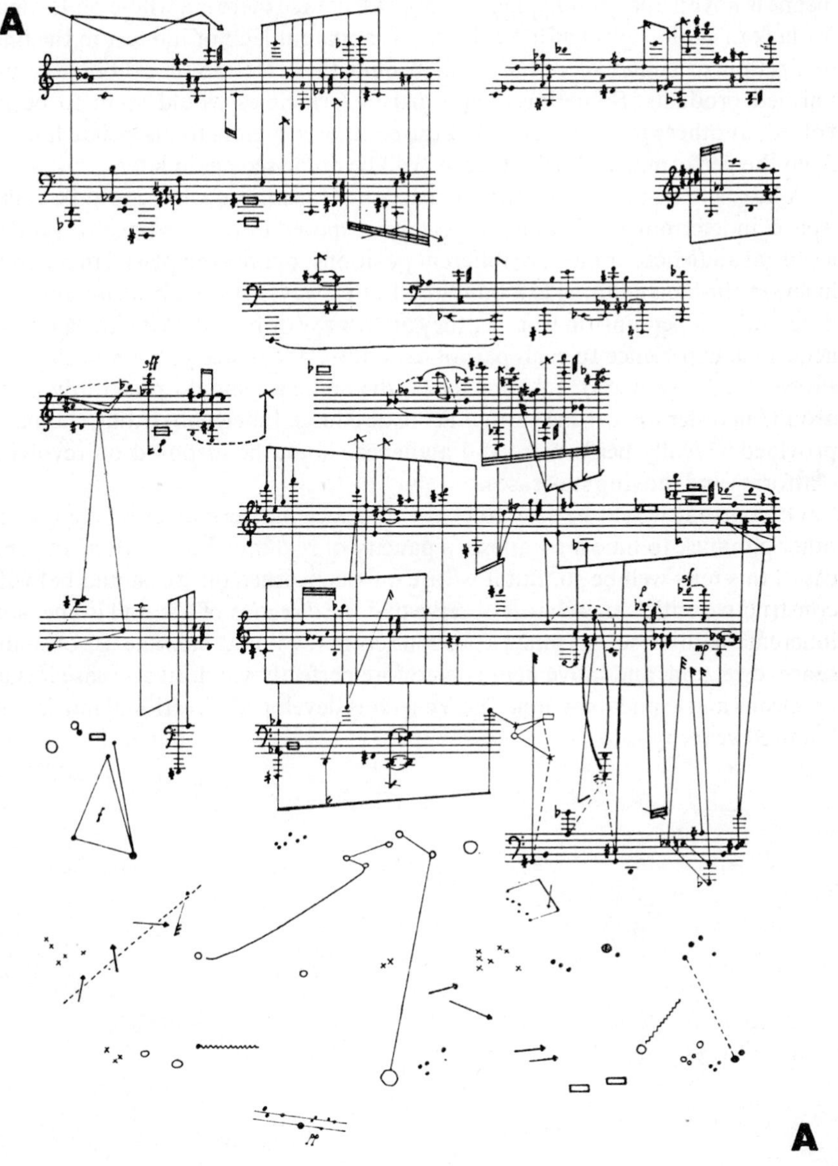

others, for various individual reasons, so that indeterminacy of performance means is not an uncommon phenomenon. Of course there is a whole philosophy (or lack of philosophy) of life behind this apparent lack of interest in the final realization in sound of one's work, behind this creation of deliberately unfinished products. Sometimes valid artistic principles would seem to be involved, at others it would seem that the composer prefers to dissociate himself from the performance. Such attitudes will be discussed again later.

A last factor in indeterminacy deserves brief mention, what could be called 'space' indeterminacy. That is, players are disposed in various positions round a central audience, or move to different positions, or are even placed in different locations inside and outside a building. In this way, listeners hear instruments differently, depending on whether they are nearby or far off, bringing 'a unique acoustical experience to each pair of ears' (as Cage writes in 'Composition as Process', *Silence* p. 53). In some cases, the audience should preferably move around in order to hear the various acoustic effects. Indeed no seating should be provided—ideally performers and audience should be disposed on revolving platforms and moving staircases.

Of course it would be easy to condemn space indeterminacy as merely another gimmick to hide a composer's paucity of real musical creation. In some cases, this may well be so. But if we are only concerned (as we should be) with constructive criticism, we must observe that the *direction* of a sound is one of its inherent qualities, just as much as its tone colour, volume, etc. The use of sound space, direction, and movement is therefore perfectly valid. In any case it is by no means a new phenomenon. The Venetians developed directional music four hundred years ago.

9

Improvisation—Graphic Scores—Text Scores

Improvisation, already implicit to varied extents in indeterminacy, music of chance, and aleatory music, is a term which needs some explanation and qualification. Improvisation (from the latin *ex improviso*—without preparation) used to mean an unprepared musical performance or 'extemporization' based either on precise themes or musical forms (fugue, theme and variations, passacaglia, etc.), or on the free development of musical ideas spontaneously suggested by the imagination, and resulting in a kaleidoscopic succession of events, often held together by only a tenuous thread.

Jazz improvisation, on the other hand, usually comprises the decoration of melodies (up to a point where the original theme is no longer recognizable) or inventions on set harmonic patterns. In both cases the basic harmony is always well evident. In more recent jazz, however, the harmonic-melodic foundation is abandoned, and except for the occasional quotation of prearranged musical ideas, players extemporize in a very free manner. This may feature some interaction between players and a loosely prearranged overall form.

Avant-garde improvisation spreads over a similarly wide area, varying from situations in which the performer is given only a limited degree of freedom, to schemes which indicate only skeleton details which must be considerably elaborated. More rarely, there are even occasions when the performer is virtually composer, as the score may contain such minimal information that almost complete improvisation is the only solution. (One must bear in mind that players are responsible for the success of their programmes, and inevitably have to present music in the best possible way. This means that improvised passages must be well prepared, and as no risk can be taken performers may write out their own 'version'. They may therefore well contribute more than the composer.)

To illustrate a few examples involving semi-improvisation:

Beno: *Circles*

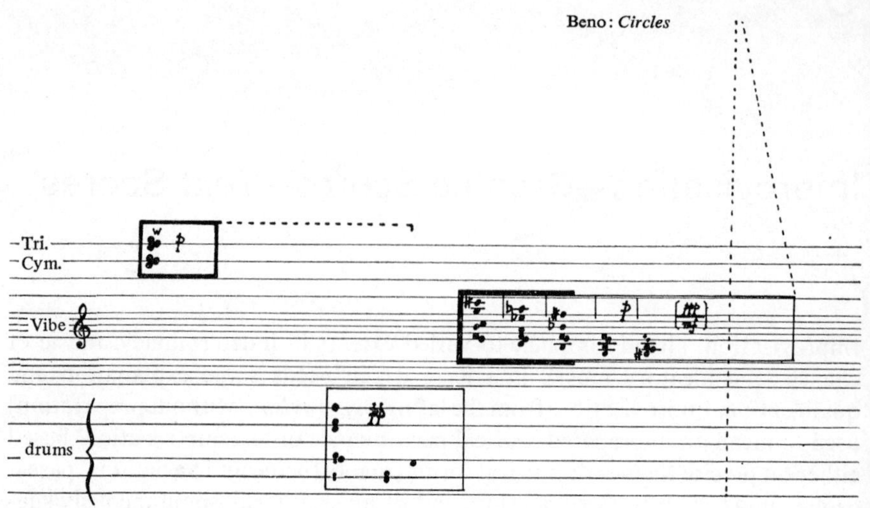

Cage: *Concert for Piano and Orchestra*

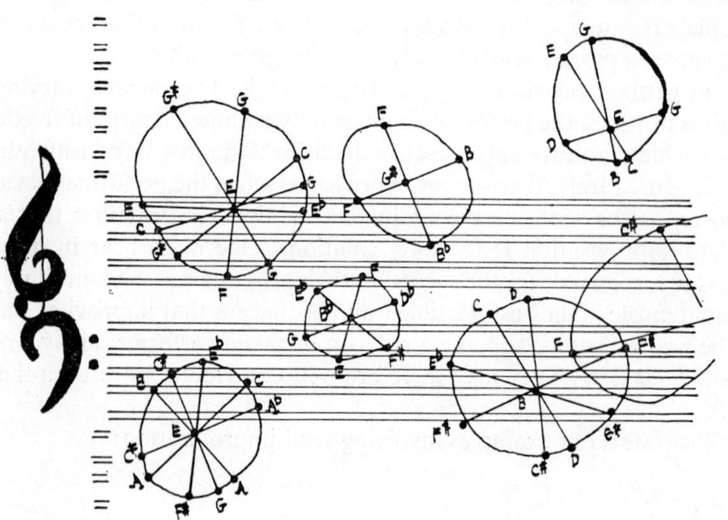

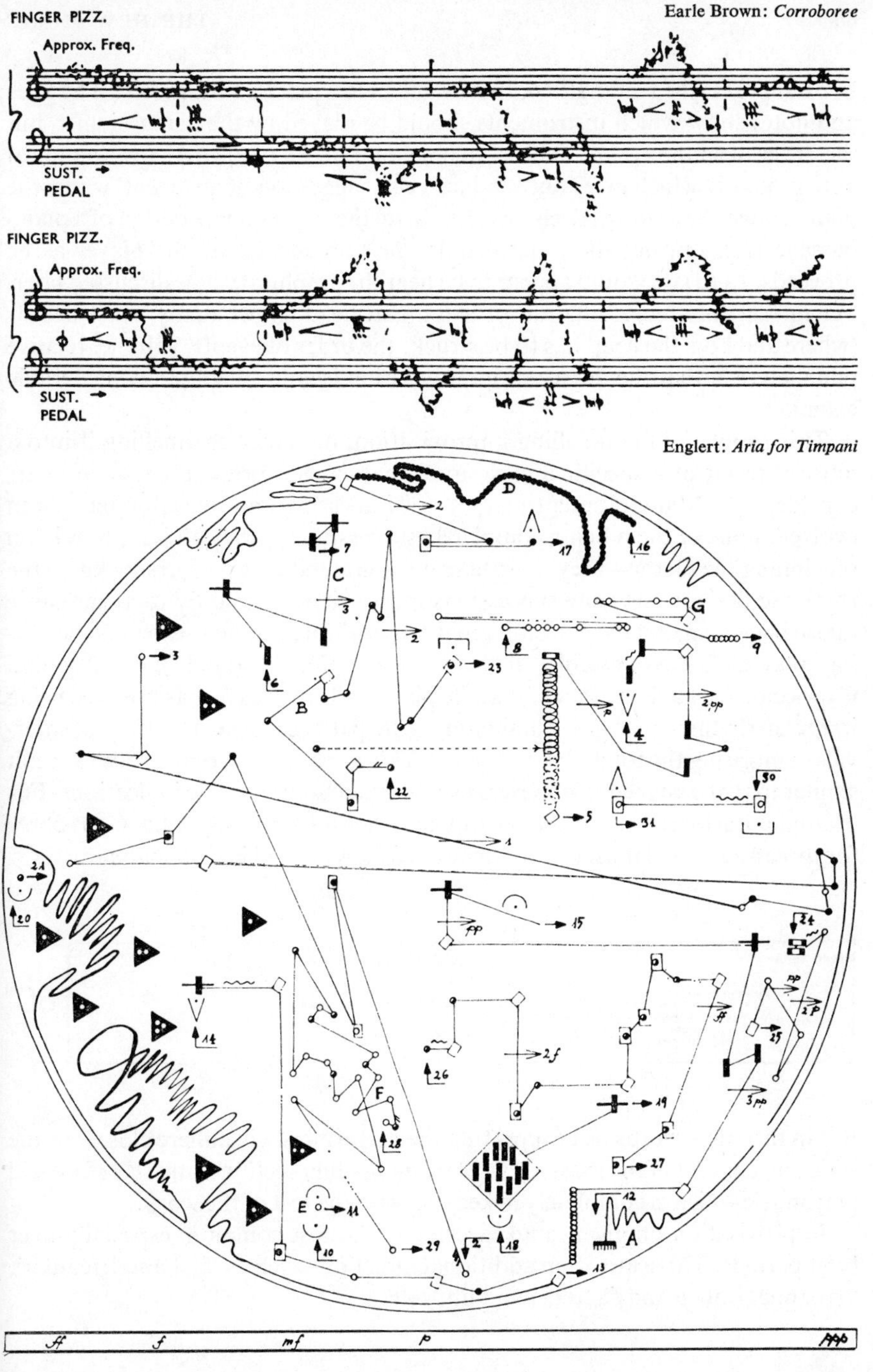

Earle Brown: *Corroboree*

Englert: *Aria for Timpani*

In example (a) the rectangles or 'boxes' indicate a precise time period. The lines and notes show which instruments should be played by the percussionist, but the order of sounds is left to his own imagination. Example (b) shows a typical note grouping which gives only an imprecise suggestion of an 'event' which the pianist must shape into a decisive form. In (c) the approximate design of a piano passage is given, but the exact details must be created by the player as he proceeds. At (d) we would appear to be near the graphic designs discussed later, but in fact this representation of a timpani head shows many exact details (where and how the head has to be struck, the order of events, volume, relative pitch, etc.) so that the degree of improvisation is controlled to a considerable extent.

This problem of controlling improvisation, or rather channelling it into a musical result of a specific and desirable nature, has preoccupied composers considerably. Many different methods of indicating improvisation have been evolved, none of them being completely successful, for they all have to rely on one intangible factor—they must take it for granted that performers know the rhythmic designs and note successions most suitable not only to avant-garde music in general, but to each individual composition. It is no use merely indicating 'play as fast as possible', if the result is going to sound like a Paganini Capriccio. We have to assume that the player will play as fast as possible using irregular rhythmic designs, eliminating scale patterns, using a variety of intervals comprising the total-chromatic, etc. This is why, in order to ensure a result similar to that designed, composers usually make some specific indications. For example, Earle Brown, in the second and eleventh sections of his *Corroboree* for three and two pianos, merely writes as follows for all instruments:

FREE AREA

Performers Initiative:—
Any of the *written* material in any sequence and tempi. Loudness, timbre and register relative to ensemble correlations.

60"

But in these few words he ensures that the performers will adhere closely to the style and content of the music as written out in other sections, and therefore will play music which is completely in keeping with the rest of the work.

Improvisation on given note successions is most common, especially over brief periods. There are often additional directions such as 'fast and irregular', 'dynamics only *p* and *f*', 'repeat ad lib.', etc. :

Smith Brindle: *Three Dimensions*

Sometimes composers resort to fairly evolved systems as a basis for improvisation:

(a) Donatoni: *Black and White*

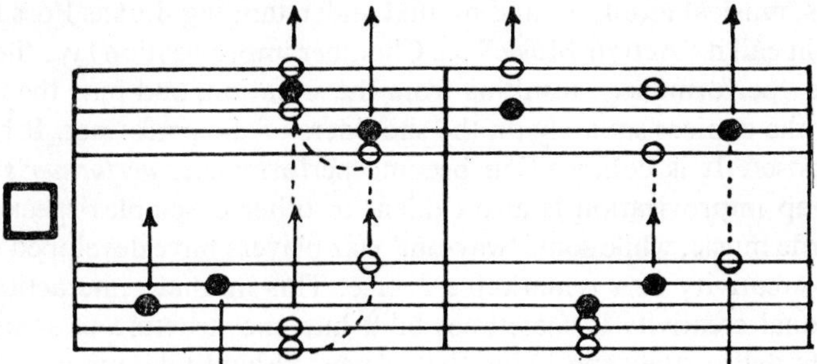

(b) Cardew: *Solo with Accompaniment*

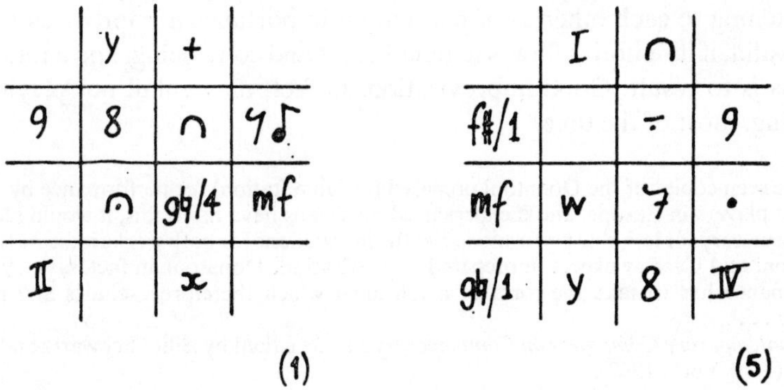

	y	+	
9	8	∩	𝄾♪
	∩	g♮/4	mf
II		x	

(1)

	I	∩	
f♯/1		÷	9
mf	w	7	•
g♮/1	y	8	IV

(5)

It is not necessary to go into the considerable descriptive details which preface the above works. Briefly, the score of Donatoni's *Black and White* for two pianos indicates only which fingers are to be used (each line of the two staves indicates a specific finger), and whether to play naturals (○) or sharps (●). Otherwise, precise notes, durations, and dynamics are omitted. The Cardew example involves the use of symbols (indicating fairly precise musical events) which must be well studied and digested before the players can attempt any kind of performance. In fact, both these examples inhibit improvisation so much by their complexity that players have to write out their own music. So what improvisation is this?[1]

The essence of improvisation is spontaneity, so that 'controlled' improvisation or 'semi'-improvisation can never fully release the performer's true fantasy and ingenuity. Several means have therefore been devised which exploit players' extempore qualities more fully. One method has been that devised by the American Lukas Foss—'group improvisation'—in which chosen players, with gifts of spontaneous creativity, are welded together by common stylistic objectives, musical intuition, and mutual understanding. Lukas Foss has said: 'One might call it "Action-Music" . . . Chamber improvisation lays the emphasis on the "performance" resulting from the situation, and puts the responsibility for the choices squarely on the shoulders of the performer. It by-passes the composer. It is composition become performance, *performer's music*.'[2] Such group improvisation is also evident in other ensembles specializing in avant-garde music, while some 'way-out' jazz players have developed this kind of group creativity to a remarkable degree. This intimate interaction of improvisational creativity is sometimes built into the structure of some works, composers deliberately specifying that players should take up cues they may hear someone else play, and then produce similar material themselves (as in Stockhausen's *Prozession* and Christian Wolff's *Duo II for Pianists*). This action of 'listening to each other' is of paramount importance if improvised music is to be valid, if its emotive flow is to be coherent and convincing, and a total formfulness is to result. Good improvisation, in fact, may entail not playing, but listening, most of the time.

[1] I have seen copies of the Donatoni prepared (in full notation) for performance by some of the best players in Europe, and if experienced musicians have to do this, it would seem even more necessary for less able performers. Yet the instructions for both works indicate that both Donatoni and Cardew expect unprepared improvisation. Donatoni, in fact, says 'A concert performance has to take the form of a rehearsal which therefore excludes any previous reading . . .'.

[2] cf. *Contemporary Composers on Contemporary Music*, edited by Elliot Schwartz and Barney Childs (New York, 1967).

Good improvisation can produce some of the most convincing music of our time. As a member of a jury in a composition competition I recently had to listen to tapes of a number of new works, many of them based on improvisation to some degree. As far as performances went, the difference in performance quality between improvised and non-improvised works was striking, so much so that one was tempted to dismiss 'through-composed' works and listen only to those which entailed improvisation—which was absolutely wrong.

More radical means of stimulating improvisation without the stumbling block of notation have been used—graphic scores, and what one might term 'text scores'. Either of these may form a whole composition, or only part of it. Some graphic scores may indicate distinct musical parameters, as in the Feldman, Stockhausen, Ligeti, Haubenstock-Ramati, and Renosto examples quoted on pp. 67–76 and 79. Other graphic scores may deliberately omit any notational sign or indication of a musical shape. The composer's one aim is to stimulate the performer's musical creativity through a graphic design. Some composers are extremely able draughtsmen, and obviously find it irresistible to turn a musical score into a work of art. Sylvano Bussotti, for example, is quite outstanding both as an artist and as a musician, so that in some cases one wonders whether the final page of a score is the consequence of a primarily visual conception, or whether the music came first. The following example was derived from a drawing made in 1949 and reset as a music score in 1959:

Bussotti: *Five Pieces for David Tudor*

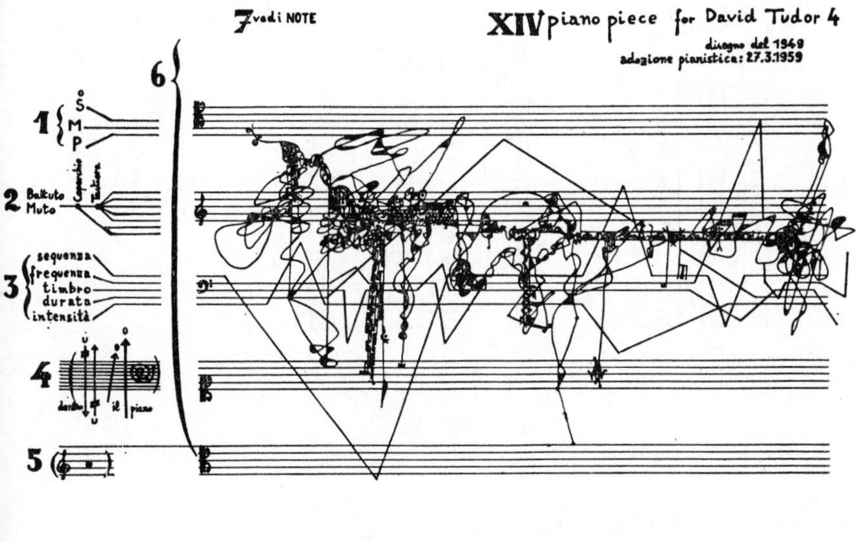

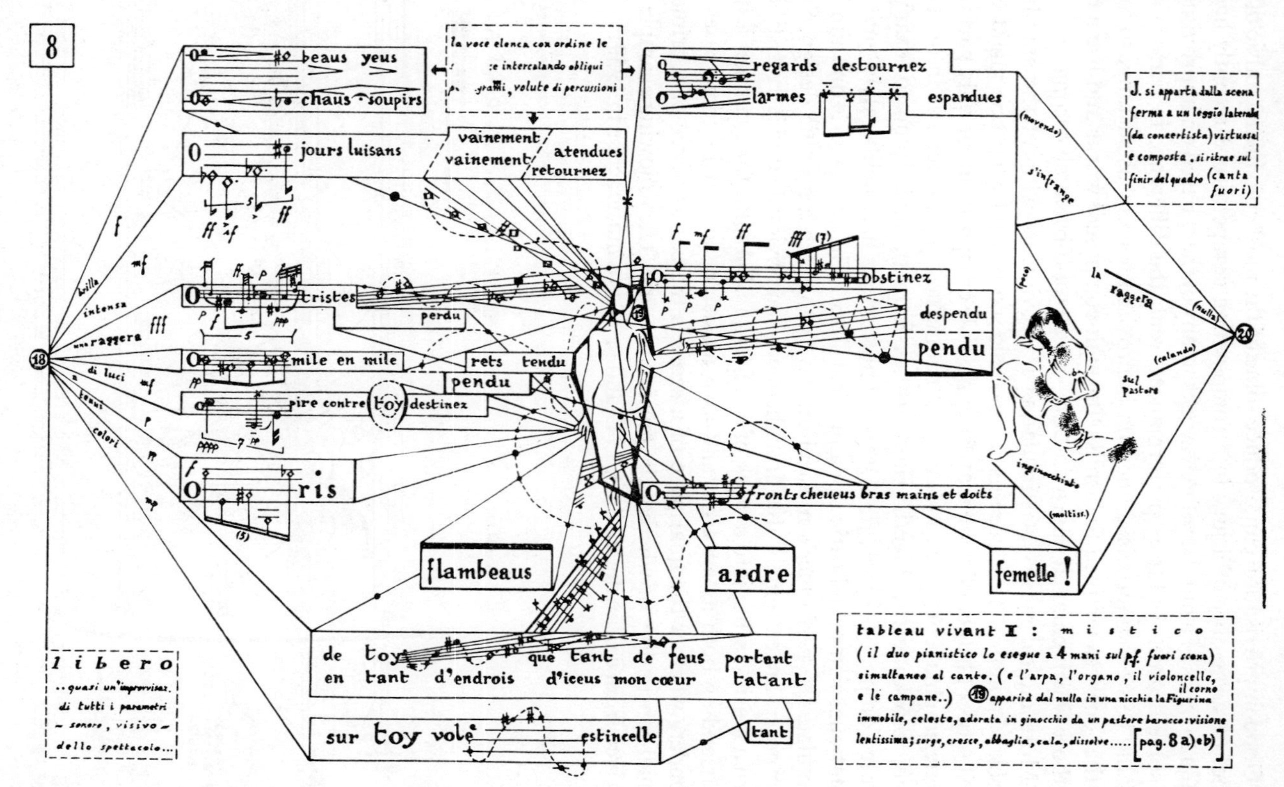

Bussotti: *La Passion selon Sade*

Some of Bussotti's scores, through their pictorial presentation, became very enigmatic as music, and the only way to interpret some of his notation would seem to be through well prepared improvisation. The example opposite from *La Passion selon Sade* (1966) shows all kinds of elements—stage directions, lighting indications, fragments of music, words to be sung (or spoken?), instrumentation, gestures, etc., but the exact performance of this page (which represents up to two minutes of music) will need considerable preparation if a consistently good presentation is to be guaranteed. More enigmatic still is the fact that, in spite of all the detail given, Bussotti writes in the bottom left-hand corner: 'Free . . . almost an improvisation of all visual and sound aspects of the spectacle'.

Earle Brown produced graphic scores in the early Fifties in America, one of his main influences being the work of artists in New York in the post-war years. The origin of Brown's artistic influences really goes further back to the 'art of determined relations' or 'constructivism' of an earlier European period, and there is a distinct resemblance between some of his scores and certain pictures of Piet Mondrian, Bart van der Leck, Gerrit Rietveld, and (later) Victor Pasmore and Fritz Glarner. The following page from Brown's *Folio* has strong affinities with van der Leck's *Geometrical Composition* of 1917. It can be performed in any of four positions, the black rectangles indicating various musical properties such as durations, intensities, intervals. The same score can be used by several players, who may use different positions of the page, and whose interpretation of the blank space as silence may vary considerably as to duration, so that any performance of the work will be an improvisation with quite unpredictable results:

In this case there can be very little possibility of co-ordination between the performers, or of that 'intimate interaction' which makes for good improvisation. It is therefore possible to deduce that if this score, when played by a group, represents 'chance', that chance occurs in the form of a tyranny which precludes what, by mutual improvisation, could be the 'best' result. But of course one of the main principles in accepting chance operations is that of accepting without reserve (and hence without any desire to 'improve') whatever happens. Chance—in theory—can have neither good nor bad results, but only events.

On the principle that graphic art should need neither comment nor explanation (and that any good picture speaks volumes) a number of examples of graphic scores follow, without any verbal comment. All these are intended as guides and stimulants for improvisation or as 'plans for performance', though not all are 'abstract' as far as musical details are concerned:

Levine: *Parentheses*

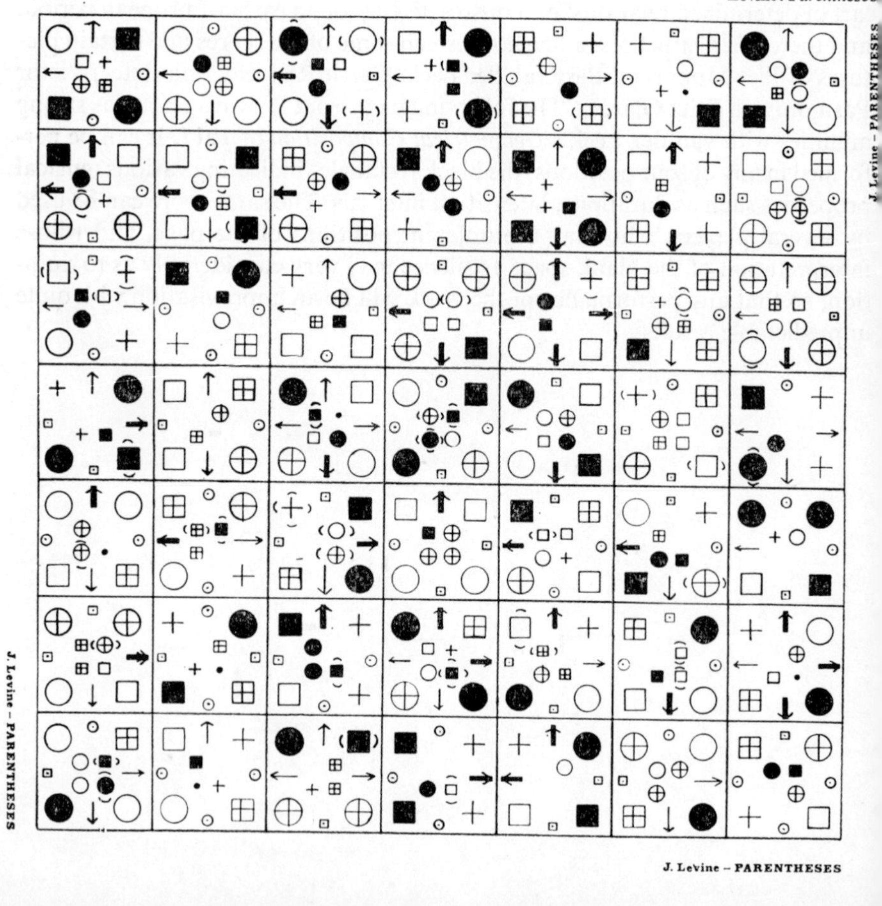

J. Levine – PARENTHESES

J. Levine – PARENTHESES

J. Levine – PARENTHESES

J. Levine – PARENTHESES

Logothetis: *Agglomeration*

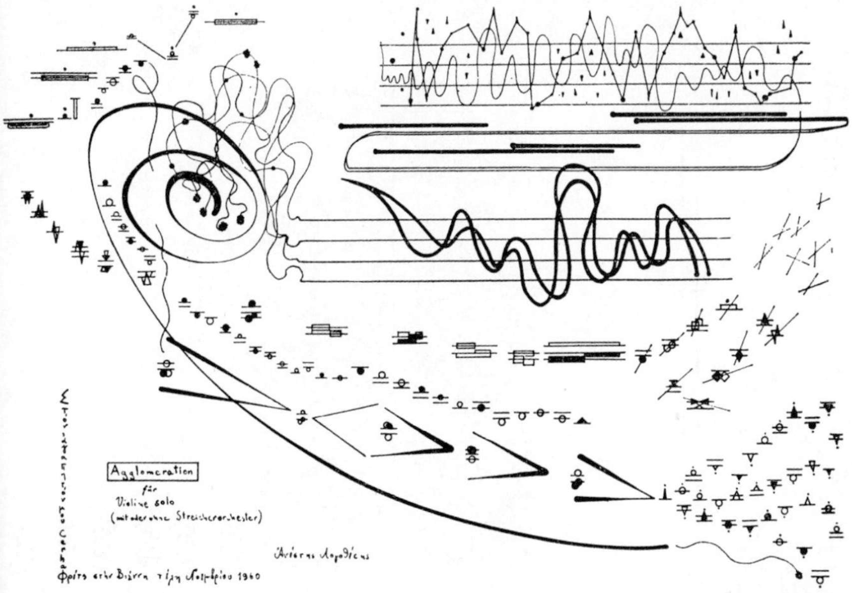

Agglomeration
für
Violine solo
(mit oder ohne Streichorchester)

Buonomo: *Percussion Tiem*

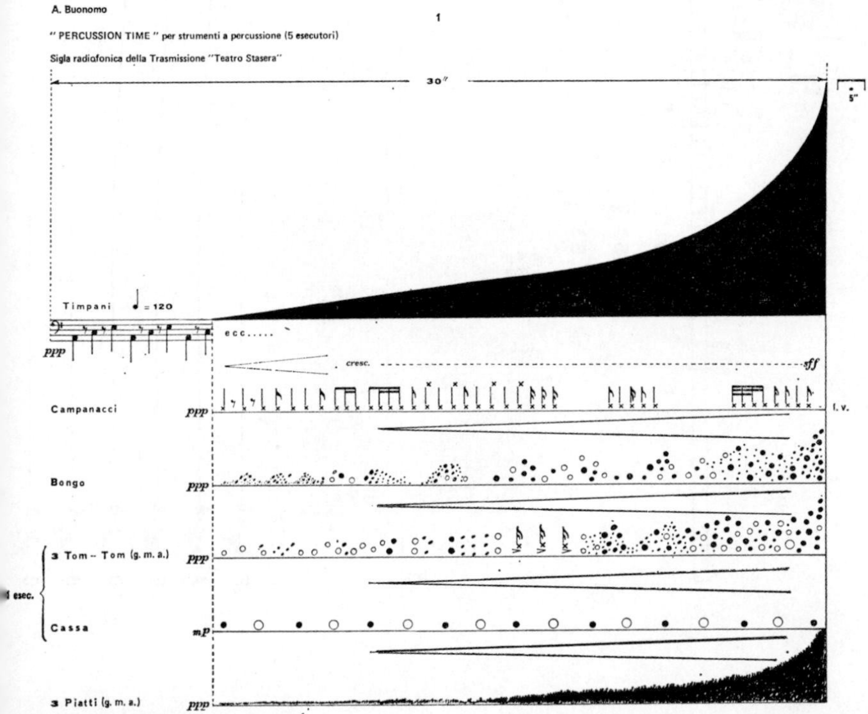

A. Buonomo
1
" PERCUSSION TIME " per strumenti a percussione (5 esecutori)
Sigla radiofonica della Trasmissione "Teatro Stasera"
30"
5"
Timpani
= 120
ppp
ecc.....
cresc.
fff
Campanacci
ppp
l. v.
Bongo
ppp
3 Tom - Tom (g. m. a.)
ppp
1 esec.
Cassa
mp
3 Piatti (g. m. a.)
ppp
Proprietà per tutti i Paesi delle Edizioni SUVINI ZERBONI S.p.A. - Milano, Corso Europa, 5
© Copyright 1972 by Edizioni SUVINI ZERBONI S.p.A. - Milano.
Tutti i diritti riservati a termini di legge. - All rights reserved. International copyright secured.
S. 7243 Z.

Kayn: *Signals*

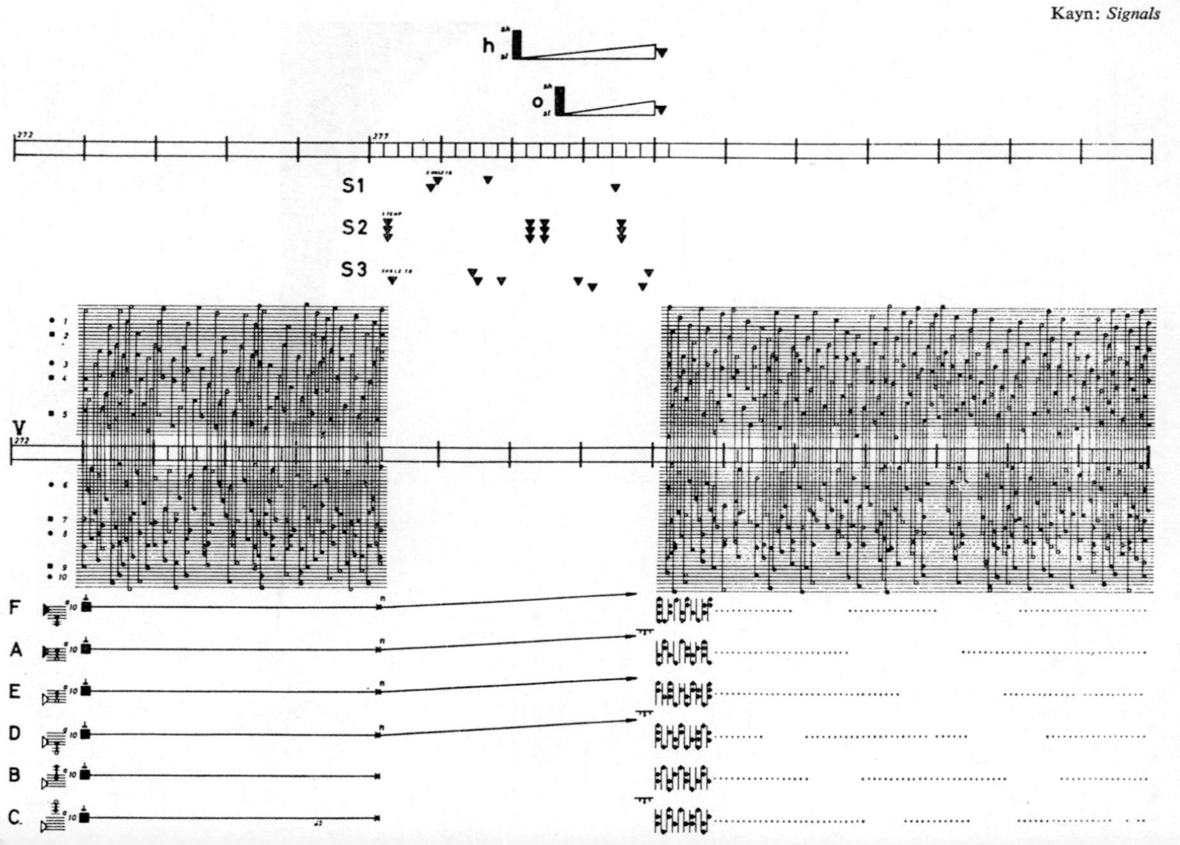

Cage: *Water Music*

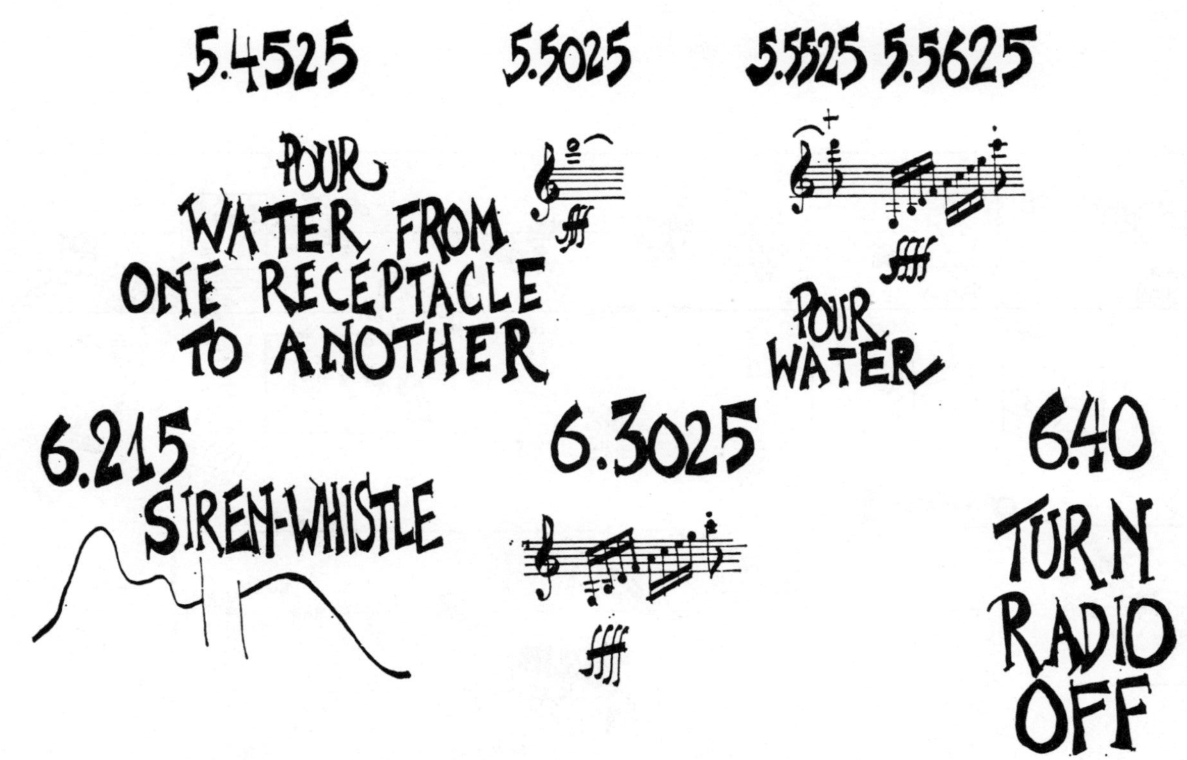

Berberian:
Stripsody

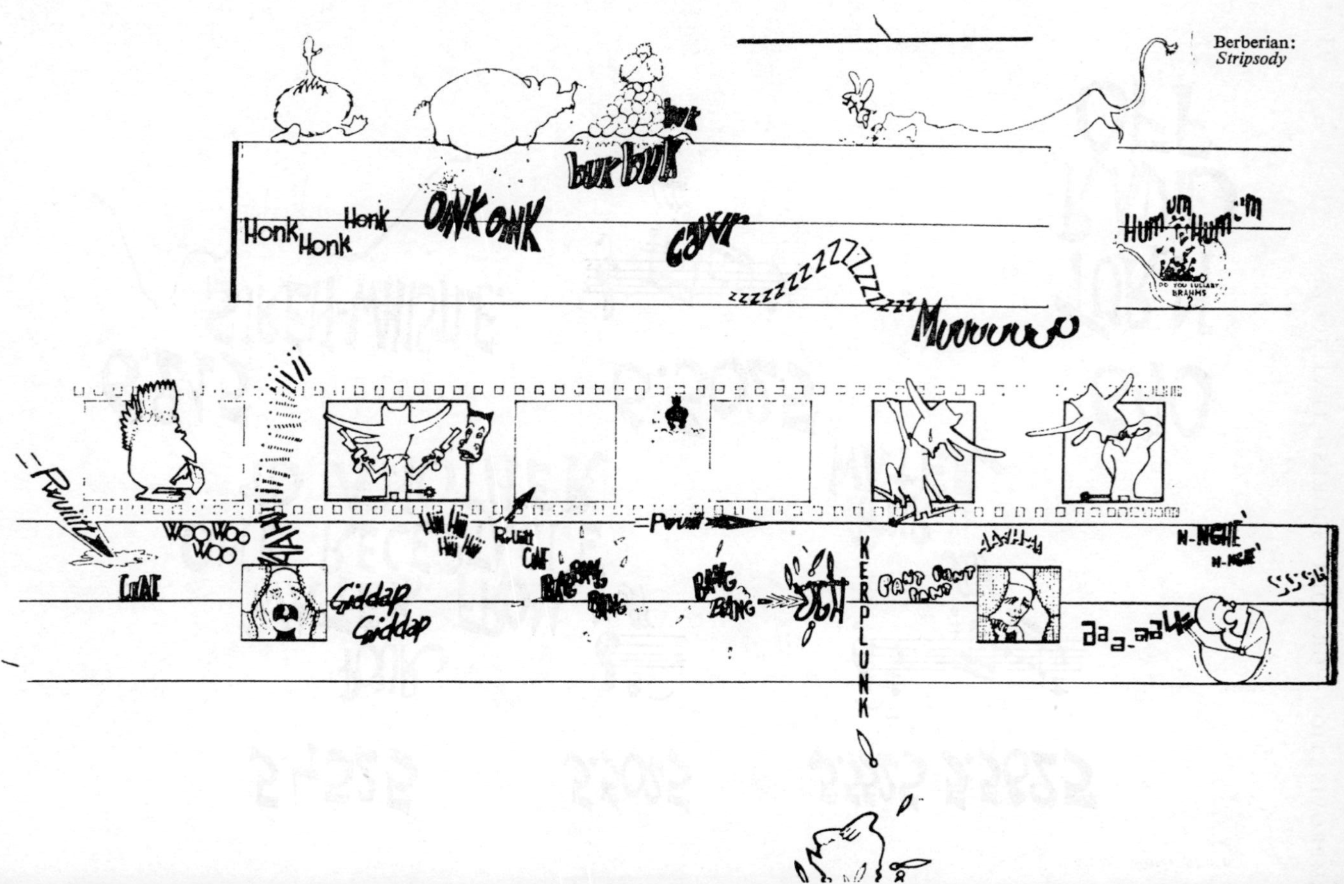

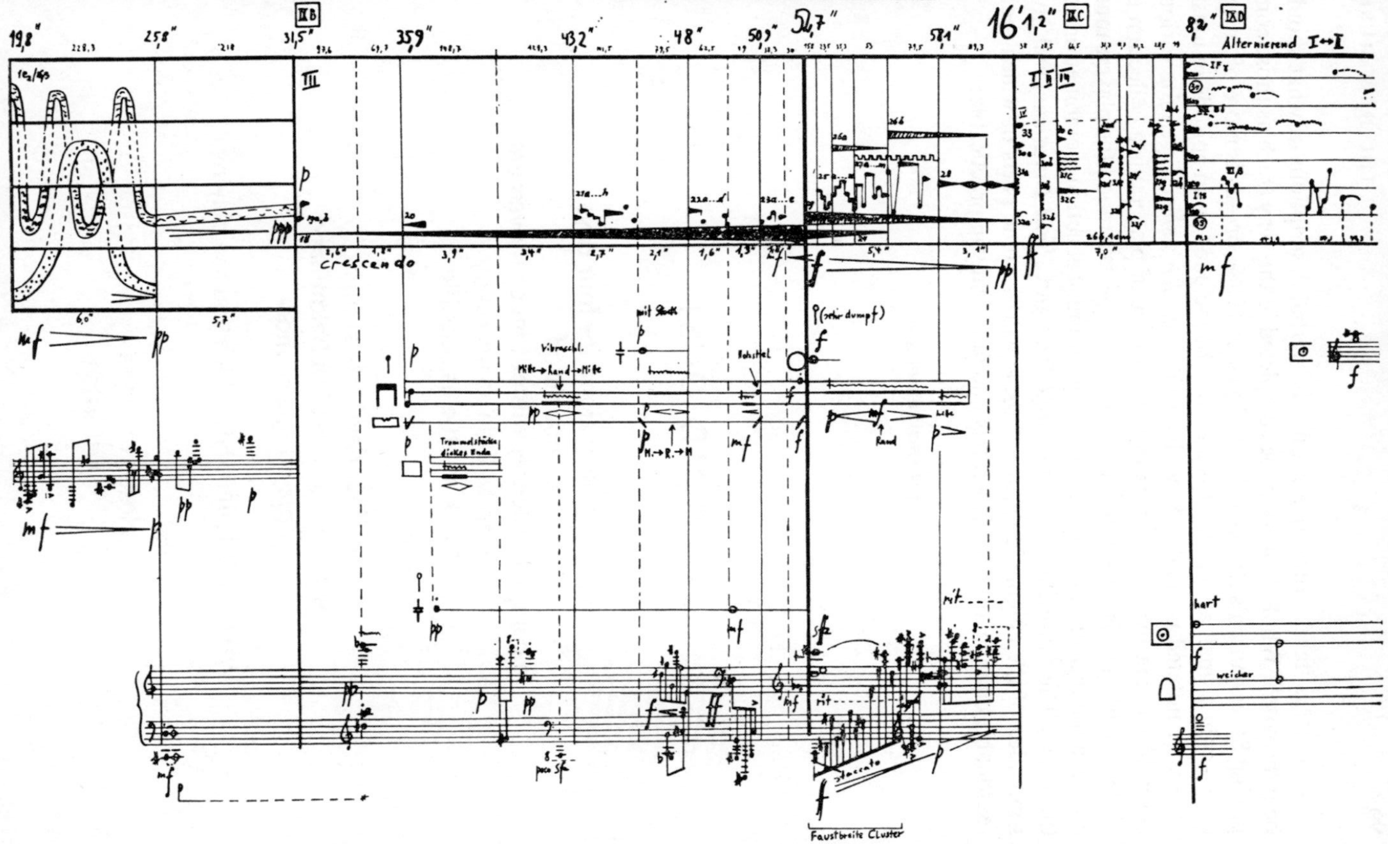

N.B. Only the upper part of this example is a graphic score. It represents the four-channel recording of electronic music and serves as a guide for the two performers (piano and percussion).

As regards 'text' scores, these comprise verbal descriptions of what should be improvised. Whole scores can be completed in this way (such as those comprising Stockhausen's *Aus den sieben Tagen* of 1968), or—as is more often the case—only a small area of 'text score' may be included as an episode in music otherwise notated normally. Stockhausen's *Aus den sieben Tagen* for various ensembles (from three musicians to any number of players) is a collection of pieces, each comprising a verse or text which suggests a mood the players must create, a manner of playing, a certain kind of musical action, combinations of these, etc. The following two texts (*Gold Dust* and *Right Durations*) will give some idea of the enigmatic nature of these works, some parts of which seem reasonable enough, others deliberately and fanatically impracticable:

for small ensemble

GOLD DUST

live completely alone for four days
without food
in complete silence, without much movement
sleep as little as necessary
think as little as possible

after four days, late at night,
without conversation beforehand
play single sounds

WITHOUT THINKING which you are playing

close your eyes
just listen

for circa 4 players

RIGHT DURATIONS

play a sound
play it for so long
until you feel
that you should stop

again play a sound
play it for so long
until you feel
that you should stop

·and·so on

stop
when you feel
that you should stop

but whether you play or stop
keep listening to the others

At best play
when people are listening

do not rehearse

In his *(Sonant 1960/ . . . .)* Mauricio Kagel has one entire movement *(Fin II/ Invitation au jeu, voix)* presented as a text score, each instrument having different instructions. Some parts are to be spoken aloud, others must be read and then interpreted by performance. In the following excerpt of the first fifty-four seconds of the electric guitar part, words in capital letters must be spoken aloud, those in small letters determine musical events and manual actions. In the left-hand margin, total and partial durations are indicated. The pitch of the reading voice must fluctuate 'between normal and quasi falsetto', the intensity 'modulated between very soft (whisper) and very loud (almost shouting)', etc.:

SONANT (1960/....)

for guitar, harp, double bass and membranophones

FIN II / Invitation au jeu, voix

Electric guitar

Mauricio Kagel

T / P

00" / 11" *mf* rall. FIRST, WOULD YOU GIVE A SIGN TO THE OTHER PLAYERS TO MAKE SURE THAT THEY'RE WITH YOU ? AND THEN PLAY chords composed of tones sounding close together, in the middle register, separated by relatively large leaps.

11" / 11" *f* ↓ *pp* (I WOULD LIKE TO CONVINCE MYSELF – WHATEVER ONE'S INTERPRETATION OF THE EXISTENCE IN THE WORLD OF PROBABILITY LAWS – THAT THE SAME PROBLEMS PLAY A PART NOT ONLY IN COMPOSITION, BUT ALSO IN LISTENING.)

22" / 32" Might I be so bold as to ask you to play the chords strictly periodically, but in such a way that the vertical density *mf* – continually varied – suggests to the listener an aperiodicity of the intervals of attack. WHY NOT BRING THE TONE-*p* CONTROL INTO IT ? Have a try. THAT'S RIGHT. A BIT MORE TO THE LEFT . . . and then suddenly way over to the right. Meanwhile keep playing the chords more narrowly and irregularly, till you reach a monodic articulation in low register. Play *f* each note "on the fret". HOW ABOUT A FAST SEQUENCE OF HARMONICS ? If that doesn't appeal to you, slide with fingernail or plectrum slowly along the 6th string. You know that the glissando is brightest when approaching the bridge, and you can emphasize this with the tone-switch, turned to maximum treble.

54" / 20" *pp* rall. ↓ *f* acc. ↓ *p* (THERE ARE SEVERAL MECHANISMS WHICH IT IS IMAGINABLE TO CREDIT WITH THE ABILITY TO TRANSFORM A FLEETING TEMPORAL ORDER INTO A LASTING SPATIAL ONE, AND VICE VERSA. OF COURSE IT'S ALL PURE SPECULATION, FOR WE KNOW VIRTUALLY NOTHING OF PROCESSES AT THE DEEPER BRAIN-LEVELS. IF IT EVER BECOMES POSSIBLE TO SURVEY THE EFFECTS OF THE EMERGENCY-EPOCH IN THEIR TOTALITY, IT WILL BE EVIDENT THAT . . .)

1'14" / 09" Silent barré. Violent movements of the left hand between the VIth and XVIIIth positions. Use the volume pedal to maximum effect. At the same time strike the fingerboard with the fingertips of the right hand from XIXth to the bridge, and then gradually cut down to plucking with the nails.

1'23" / 20" *p* ↓ *mf* *f* rall. (THE AUDIBILITY-THRESHOLD OF THE ROOM WILL DETERMINE THE MINIMUM LOUDNESS-LEVEL OF THE PERFORMANCE. WE HAVE SPOKEN A LOT ABOUT MOTORIC AUTOMATISMS, OR SPONTANEITY OF MOVEMENT.) Play, using the low E-string, a chord consisting of three major sevenths. HOLD TO EXTINCTION !

1'43" / 20" rall. (HOW ARE PARTS CONNECTED WITH A WHOLE ? IN SEARCH OF SWITCH-PRINCIPLES.)

LITOLFF/PETERS 30224

Sonant is in fact a semi-theatrical work where music, speech, and action fuse together into one art—see the chapter on 'theatre'.

We can refer, however, to one characteristic of text scores which should already be apparent from the Stockhausen and Kagel examples: the musical substance of these scores tends to be somewhat meagre, because many words are needed to describe even simple musical events. Many of the fifteen pieces of *Aus den sieben Tagen* create in fact very static musical situations. We must bear in mind, however, that static, slender, intuitive, ritual music was what the composer desired, so that perhaps the suggestive, inspirational verses were the best guide for the players to compose their own inspired sounds. Perhaps, indeed, the text serves better than any notated score, for it so strongly evokes mood rather than action.

10

Concrete Music

There are said to be over 6000 serious works of electronic music today, most of them produced only in the last decade. The amount of concrete music must be equally vast. This creative activity has developed mainly through the invention of two comparatively cheap pieces of equipment—the tape recorder, and the electronic music synthesizer—which together need cost no more than a moderately priced grand piano. Yet though these inventions are comparatively new, the idea of electronic music (or some similar kind of sound) has been in some men's minds for decades. One can imagine that forty, fifty, even sixty years ago, men like Russolo, Varèse, Schillinger, and Busoni[1] would almost have given their eyes to have the electronic devices we have today. They had the vision, but not the means, or at least not quite the means. Electric valve oscillators did exist in their time, and even the Hammond electronic organ was a product of the Thirties. But the actual recording facilities were the problem. (One of the first electronic music compositions—John Cage's *Imaginary Landscape No. 1* (1939)—had oscillator frequencies recorded on two 78 r.p.m. gramophone records, but normally such a system was too expensive and inflexible to be practicable.) It took a world war to produce what was almost the right instrument—the wire recorder—which was later replaced by the tape recorder, so flexible, versatile, and economical that sound could at last be recorded, altered, manipulated, made permanent, or discarded, with incredible ease and at negligible cost. Once the tape recorder was perfected (about 1950), and its potentialities fully realized, other electronic sound equipment (either already existing or suitably modified) could be assembled to form the first electronic music studio. But before discussing early electronic music, we must first turn aside for a moment to observe another artistic development which flourished through the medium of recording alone—the *musique concrète* of Pierre Schaeffer.

Musique concrète—'concrete music'—was originally so called to indicate

[1] cf. Busoni's *Entwurf einer neuen Aesthetik der Tonkunst* (Leipzig, 1910).

that the music was made up of really existing sounds and not of electronic tones. The sound material comes from real life (it is, in fact, usually carefully studio-recorded) and is not artificially or synthetically created by electronic means. Schaeffer's work is therefore somewhat in opposition to electronic music proper. Indeed his work in Paris and the Groupe de Recherches Musicales which he established at the French Radio has always firmly stood its ground in regarding living sound and no other as its basic musical material. Schaeffer has always collaborated actively with other composers since his first success in *Symphonie pour un homme seul* (1949), and musicians such as Messiaen, Varèse, Boulez, Stockhausen, Berio, Luc Ferrari, and Xenakis have been invited to work in the Paris studio since its early years. Indeed the artistic influence of the Groupe de Recherches Musicales has been very wide indeed.

Concrete music is a 'montage' or assemblage of live sounds which are subjected to two main kinds of treatment: (1) tape manipulation and (2) electronic modification. Through these two means, relatively familiar sounds can be made unrecognizable and then reassembled to give the most unexpected results. The original sounds recorded can be very few indeed; the important thing is that they should be rich, complex sounds, capable of substantial modification. Tape manipulation comprises the following main techniques:

1. *Changing speeds*. A tape can be recorded at one speed and replayed at another, thus raising or lowering the pitch of sounds. In a single operation sounds can be raised or lowered several octaves. This also brings about considerable modifications in timbre. Tape speeds can also be changed *during* a recording, to produce glissandos up or down.

2. *Reversing tape direction*. A sound played backwards can sound quite strange. For instance, a reversed percussive sound starts softly, increases to a climax, and breaks off. Even the tone quality is almost unrecognizable. For instance, a long piano chord sounds almost like an organ.

3. *Tape cutting and editing*. Any part of a sound can be cut out and rejected, or retained for separate use. Our ears recognize many sounds only by the character of the 'transient' or initial attack, and if this is removed the remainder of the sound can seem unfamiliar. Cut off the transients of metallic noises and they sound quite smooth. Use these transients alone and they sound like breaking glass. Short lengths of such transients assembled together can give astonishingly rapid and complex effects. More generally, sections of tape can be cut and reassembled in any new order.

4. *Tape loops*. Short lengths of tape can be made into loops so that when played back they repeat sounds in ostinato fashion, or perhaps sustain long sounds almost like organ tones. These are often used for background effects.

5. *Superposition of sounds.* Sounds from one recording can be added to another, dynamic levels being controlled and varied in the process. This used to mean running two different tapes on separate recorders and passing the sounds for recording on to a third instrument. Today using 'sound on sound' facilities this process can be done with two machines only, one recorder simply adding new signals to its own tape. Sound on sound controls, in fact, allow one to add layer on to layer of sound and build up very complex effects even with a single tape machine. In the process, however, progressive deterioration of the first signals is inevitable.

6. *Multi-track recording.* Tape recorders were first available only in single-track versions, but two, four, eight, or sixteen tracks may be used today. Recordings can be made on multi-tracks, and then a master tape made giving a final 'balance' to all the material, in which the volume relationships of the original tracks may be altered considerably.

7. *Stereophony and Quadraphony.*[1] Sound from different tracks can be fed into two, four, or even more widely spaced speakers for what are called stereophonic or quadraphonic effects. There are several different reasons for this usage, though they may or may not all apply in any one composition. Stereophony (sound produced from two speakers fairly widely spaced, but facing the listener) originated with two main objectives. Using two-channel recordings, different sounds can issue from each speaker, so that the listener experiences directional effects. Instrumental groups can be made to seem in different positions, antiphonal effects can be introduced, or one kind of sound can be made to 'talk' to another. But an almost greater function of stereophony is the illusion of space it can suggest. Whereas with a single speaker sound merely enters a room through a small porthole, with effective stereophony it seems to exist over a broad area. With still more speakers (quadraphony, etc.) sound can seem to come from all directions, giving an illusion of great space. In addition, sounds on each track can be 'panned' to different speakers in turn so that the music seems to gyrate in space. Quadraphony can also be made to simulate special acoustic conditions. Through transmitting delayed, attenuated, and 'coloured' sounds, secondary speakers can be made to give the reflected sounds characteristic of a great cathedral, or a cavern, or empty city streets. All this adds a wonderful new dimension to sound. I have heard multi-directional transmissions of concrete music by the Paris Groupe de Recherches Musicales in the great hall of the Grand Palais of the Champs Elysées, and the effect was far beyond all expectations.

[1] Though stereophony and quadraphony are not, strictly speaking, aspects of 'tape manipulation', they are included here as they derive from the exploitation of multi-track techniques.

Electronic modification of the real sounds used in concrete music usually takes three forms:

1. *Filtering*. Electronic filters in their simplest form are like the tone controls of a radio, which allow one to add more bass or more treble. In a more developed form, filters are designed to attenuate frequencies within several frequency bands: for example, an eight-octave filter permits frequencies to be subdued or eliminated in any one or more one-octave bands over a range of eight octaves (most of the audible range). In this way, any complex sound can be made to seem smooth, hollow, brittle, bright, metallic, or mellow. This is why the sounds used in concrete music should have a rich sound spectrum. A simple sound (like a flute) cannot be modified very much, because there is so little to filter out.
2. *Reverberation*. This simulates the rapid sound reflections which occur in most enclosed spaces. Slower, perceptible repetitions of sound produce echo. Reverberation can be varied so that sounds are either dry and 'near', or prolonged and distant as if in a bottomless pit. It gives life to sounds and can simulate varied acoustic conditions. Reverberations can be achieved by several means—echo chambers, reverberation plates, tape-delay recordings, electronic reverberators, or spring devices. Most of these colour the sound slightly, which may itself in many compositions be a desirable feature.
3. *Ring Modulation*. Sounds can be distorted out of all recognition and rendered extremely complex through ring modulation. Though this treatment can be applied to the sounds of concrete music, it belongs more legitimately to the field of electronic music and will be discussed later.

Concrete music has been made with very varied sound sources, though the basic material on which many pieces are built is often very slender. 'Piano-tape' music was very popular in the Fifties, as piano sounds are most adaptable and a few basic sounds can go a long way. In their *Notte in Città* Berio and Maderna included a long section of piano-tape music which was made entirely of only four chords. Pieces have been written using only the sounds of scissors or drops of water falling into a bucket. The manipulation of vocal sounds can produce a very rich effect. Stockhausen's *Gesang der Jünglinge* (1955–6) is a very extensive piece made up substantially of the spoken and sung voice of one boy, so manipulated and multiplied that at times there seems to be a vast multitude. Electronic sounds are added but these are always given a simple tone colour, so as to blend easily. In fact the main compositional technique used has been one of serializing an array of vocal sounds and setting them in a precise structure.

Inevitably, concrete music has become more and more complex and accomplished. Multi-track recordings encourage the use of contrasting sound types, but in general, to be coherent and logical, a babel of jumbled sounds has to be avoided. So composers still prefer to select a limited amount of sound material and build large areas of their compositions with nothing else. The composer's bravura may in fact be demonstrated by just how far he can go with very little.

Though the Groupe de Recherches has preferred to remain isolated from electronic music, others have taken the very logical step of combining both concrete and electronic sounds. After all, the aural results of the two methods are very similar, and while a composer may find it easy to synthesize certain sounds electronically, others are easier to produce by live recordings. So inevitably concrete and electronic music are become blood brothers to a considerable degree, especially, as we shall see, in the latest developments.

11

Electronic Music

Electronic music, particularly in the early years, was composed in a different way from concrete music, and this was perhaps a main reason for the initial separation of the two schools. Concrete music begins with prepared sound material, which is moulded into its final form by a process of experiment, trial and error, perhaps following unexpected paths to goals which were never foreseen initially. Electronic music, however, was composed like traditional music, being first conceived in the mind of the composer, then written down, and finally realized in sound.

The first electronic music studio was established at the Westdeutscher Rundfunk, Cologne, in 1951 under the directorship of Herbert Eimert. Initially the medium was developed at a slower pace than Schaeffer's Concrete Music. It was not until 1953 that the first demonstration took place, and the first concert of compositions was not broadcast until late in 1954 (pieces by Eimert, Pousseur, Stockhausen, Goeyvaerts, and Gredinger). By 1956 the first plateau of artistic achievement had been reached with works of undisputed aesthetic value such as Eimert's *Fünf Stücke*, Stockhausen's *Gesang der Jünglinge*, and Křenek's *Spiritus Intelligentiae Sanctus*. In the meantime, an electronic music studio had been established at Radio Italiana in Milan, where Berio's *Mutazioni* and *Perspectives* and Maderna's *Notturno* followed closely on their jointly composed *Notte in Città* (a montage of concrete music, voice, and electronic sounds). Subsequent studios followed in locations as far apart as Princeton and Tokyo.

This slower development of electronic music, as compared with concrete music, according to Eimert 'seems to lack completely that surfeit of abundant vitality which so often characterizes new movements'. But the slow development was inevitable: (1) very few composers could gain access to studio facilities, (2) whereas concrete music could be composed quickly (complex sounds being recorded, modified, and reassembled) the electronic music composer had to labour slowly from the simple towards the complex, each individual sound having to be built up of various elements, (3) the early studios lacked those electronic aids which make for rapid sound synthesis, (4) composers were entering a new unexplored territory, which seemed so forbiddingly vast that method had to be established before even a small area of possibilities could be used. Unfortunately, the method chosen was itself a slow and laborious process, that of total pre-determination.

The beginnings of electronic music coincided with the development of integral serialism in conventional instrumental/vocal composition. In all probability this was no coincidence, but rather the consequence of a close similarity of ideas in a small group of composers whose sound ideals (whether in the electronic or conventional media) were very similar. Eimert's words on electronic music composition[1] read very much like the integral serialists':

> In electronic-serial music . . . everything, to the last element of the single note, is subjected to serial permutation, resulting in a completely new way of composing sound—the poetics of sound, as the medieval theorist would have called it.

Early electronic music was therefore predetermined—or rather precalculated, for it was much more practical to use pitch frequencies (expressed in c.p.s. or Hz) than the conventional names of notes in the chromatic scale. (In fact any association of electronic sounds with notes of conventional pitch was avoided from the beginning.) For instance, a sound could be made up of four tones of unconventional pitch such as 240, 380, 524, and 632 Hz. These could be set up on calibrated dials, and then recorded together. As well as the frequencies of sounds, several other parameters had to be indicated—duration (in tape length), volume, attack, decay, reverberation time, etc. These data were best indicated on graph paper, or in some diagrammatic form, so that each sound structure could be built up in turn, recorded, and spliced on to the master tape. The recording process was therefore very laborious. A composition could comprise hundreds of separately recorded sound events, which might need superposition one on another, so that the composition of a few minutes of music could entail weeks of work.

Very few scores of electronic music composition have been published, as with this medium it is much easier and certainly more profitable to hear the music than to look at it. Also, a score of electronic music cannot possibly show all the details involved with sufficient clarity and completeness. For example, the simplest modification in timbre of a sound would need very complex indications in a graphic score. Sometimes, however, a score can be used to show the general overall workplan, giving the durations, volume, and decay of sounds, but omitting other more precise details. The score on page 106 of *Music for Magnetic Tape No. 1* (1963) by Andrzei Dobrowolski is such a simplified working

[1] Herbert Eimert: 'What is electronic music?' in *Die Reihe* 1 (Vienna, 1955).

Dobrowolski: *Music for Magnetic Tape No. 1*

MUZYKA NA TAŚMĘ MAGNETOFONOWĄ Nr 1

ANDRZEJ DOBROWOLSKI (1963)

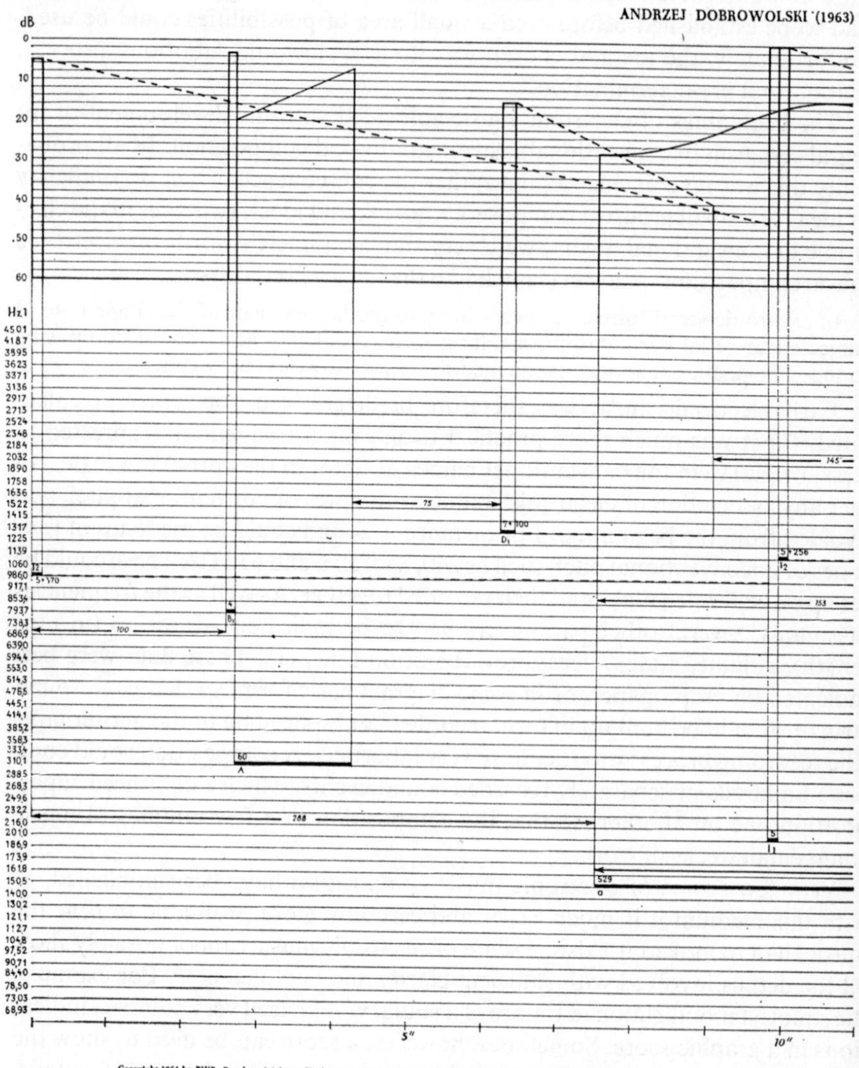

record of music which comprises electronic 'tone-mixtures' and a number of 'concrete' sounds (principally sounds recorded in a piano through sympathetic vibration of the strings with shouted vowels). The score shows a succession of tone-mixtures indicated by capital letters (I_2, B_1, A, D_1, etc.) each comprising up to twelve sine tones at various pitches and volumes. The duration scale is 19 mm. to 1 second (horizontally) in the lower part of the diagram, the exact duration of each sound also being shown in figures. For example, the first sound (tone-mixture I_2) is shown as 5 mm. plus 370 mm. decay. The top part of the diagram shows the intensity, covering a range from −60 dB ('silence') to 0 dB (*fff*). The first sound begins at −5 dB for 5 mm and then declines to −44 dB over 370 mm. The fifth sound (after 288 mm.) indicated by a small 'a' is a recording of the vowel 'a' shouted into piano strings. As will be seen, it lasts for 529 mm. and increases in volume as shown in the upper part of the diagram. This score therefore represents a much more complex situation than is at first apparent, though in actual fact (in that it uses only sine tones) this is fairly simple electronic music.

The early 'classical' electronic studio of the Fifties would comprise the following sound sources:

1. *Sine-Tone Generators*. Sine tones are the purest musical sounds, having no harmonics and comprising a single frequency of even dynamic level. They are called 'sine' tones because in the graphical representation used to show the air displacement of various types of vibrations, a pure tone is shown by sine curves. (Other wave forms similarly applied to electronic sounds are square waves, saw-tooth waves, ramp forms, triangular outputs, etc.) The possibilities of a classical studio depended on the number of sine-tone generators available. In order to build up a complex tone of individual timbre, at least eight sine-tone generators are necessary, so the tendency was to exceed this. Naturally, the timbre produced depends not only on the disposition of the frequencies (and their phase-relationship to each other) but on their relative dynamic levels. In any single superposition of sine tones, even a small rearrangement of the relative volumes of the component frequencies can make a significant change of tone colour. Sine-tone generators usually cover the whole audible range, to produce frequencies from about 40 Hz up to approximately 20,000 Hz.

2. *White Sound Generator*. White sound or 'noise' comprises all audible frequencies sounding together. The distribution of frequencies is apparently even, though to the human ear lower frequencies decrease in intensity while sounds in the upper region tail off at the threshold of an individual's perception. No frequency remains at a steady dynamic level, so that white sound seems to have a rapid internal motion within an overall total sound.

3. *Square Wave Generator*. Square waves have a rich harmonic content and therefore produce sounds which contrast with sine tones and are highly desirable in the classical studio. Square-wave generators were not always used in

early studios, but later became standard equipment on account of their richer sound resources.

The above sound sources, essentially simple in themselves, can be modified and transformed by various means. We have already discussed tape manipulation methods for concrete music, and all these are equally valid for electronic music. We have also mentioned means of electronic modifications. These are again valid, but need to be enlarged on:

1. *Filters.* Filters could modify considerably the white sound of early studios or the complex wave forms which were still to come. In early studios it was particularly important to be able to modify the only complex sound source—white sound—so a large bank of filters was used, filters which could attenuate or cut off sounds within narrow bands over the whole sound spectrum. It was thus possible either to cut out a narrow band from the white sound spectrum, or to cut off all sounds except very few. Filters were developed to such an extent that a single sine tone (or very near it) could be extracted from the whole of white sound. As we have noted, the frequencies in white sound are 'mobile', they vary continuously in dynamic level in a random manner, so that filtered bands of white sound seem to be in movement—an attractive characteristic and in useful contrast to the static quality of sine tones. This random pulsing of filtered white sounds will be again noted in discussing the dynamic suppressor.

2. *Ring Modulation.* When two frequencies are fed into each input of a ring modulator, only the combination tones (summation and difference tones) are heard. For instance, if a sine tone of 300 Hz is fed into input A and another of 220 Hz into input B, we will hear the summation tone 300+220 = 520 Hz and the difference tone 300−220 = 80 Hz. These are combination tones of the 'first order'. Other tones of the 'second order' would also result, being the sum and difference of one of the generators and one of the first-order tones, and so on. In theory, second-order tones would be as follows:

2nd Summation tones (*Hz*)	*2nd Difference tones* (*Hz*)
300+520 = 820	
220+520 = 740	300−80 = 220
300+ 80 = 380	220−80 = 140
220+ 80 = 300	

In practice, second-order tones are much fainter than first-order combination tones, but are sufficiently strong to influence the tone colour. The important point to bring out, however, is that from only two sine tones, the ring modulator has effectively produced eight of varying intensity. Considerable modification has therefore been effected.

But the above example is of only a simple situation. In usual practice, several tones are fed into each input of the ring modulator, so that its output consists of a multiplicity of combination tones of rich effect. In addition, if the relative volumes of the input tones are altered only slightly, the output timbre can be significantly altered. In later usages, more complex signals such as square or sawtooth waves are fed into the ring modulator, so that very dense sounds are produced. The danger here is that distortion sets in, and one effect becomes indistinguishable from another.

3. *Reverberation.* Electronic studio reverberation facilities are as described previously under concrete music. One might add, however, that electronic sound (unlike the sounds of concrete music) is particularly dry and lifeless. Reverberation is essential to give it vitality. Electronic composers often went to great lengths in the use of the echo chamber, tapes being run in both directions and re-recorded to give pre-echo as well as reverberation. The resulting tape would then be played through the echo chamber again, even several times, until the whole character of the original sounds was transformed.

4. *Variable Speed Tape Recorders.* Varying speeds are used to speed up or slow down specific effects. This normally involves pitch changes and glissandos. The *Telefonbau Normalzeit*, however, is designed to change the speed of a rhythmic passage without altering the pitch on the final tape. That is, tape can be fed into the machine at one speed and across the recording head at another, without any pitch change taking place on a subsequent replay at the 'new' speed.

5. *Dynamic Suppressor.* This device allows signals to be cut out below a chosen dynamic level, and in early studios was one of the few possible means of introducing random or 'chance' elements. For example, any fluctuating signal, such as the random pulsing of narrow bands of filtered white sound (mentioned previously), can be passed through the dynamic suppressor so that only peaks above a certain volume are recorded. Several recordings can be made at other pitches and with varied suppression, and then the results superposed in various ways on two recording channels. Finally, signals from the two tracks can be passed into the inputs of a ring modulator. The resulting output is a completely new sound with random movement, varied timbre, etc., which can be used or discarded, passed through the suppressor and modulator again for new effects, and so on. Such random qualities were hardly looked for by the early composers, as they preferred predetermined events, but they were eventually welcomed as the self-generating musical possibilities of electronic equipment became evident.

Unfortunately, if an electronic studio has no semi-automotive processes (such as are found in the later voltage-controlled studios) composition is a slow, laborious process. With relatively static sounds the composer has himself to prepare every single element of change, and where change is frequent it may take several hours to assemble a few centimetres of tape. If all events are predetermined, and every sound has to be built up, processed, and spliced bit by bit into a master tape, the work becomes a drudgery which no mercurial personality can tolerate. Thus after an initial honeymoon period with electronic music most composers abandoned the medium, so that it is quite usual, before Moog invented the synthesizer, to find many composers producing a single electronic work and then no more. This also possibly explains why the works of the dedicated pioneers seemed to make most impact on the musical world, while those that followed have seemed less significant and often of limited aesthetic value.

Perhaps indeed if Robert Moog had not invented voltage-controlled oscillators and amplifiers, and then assembled voltage-controlled and selected non-voltage-controlled components into the so-called 'synthesizer' (about 1965), electronic music would have ceased to be of significant interest to composers. But the synthesizer changed the situation dramatically. Here was an instrument which was not only highly labour-saving, and a fascinating and seemingly endless source of new sounds, but could be made virtually to play itself in highly mobile sound patterns which might be either recurrent or completely non-repetitive. By using a sequencer, the synthesizer can in fact memorize long complex musical structures and play them live without recording and tape editing. The old predetermined drudgery has therefore gone by the board, most of the tape splicing and cutting can be forgotten, and at last the composer is free as never before. For he is free not only to discover the sounds he wants and control their every nuance, but to work with sounds *in movement*, to move with them through space by any devious path he may choose, and finally, having discovered and charted a new sound world, to hear it again at the touch of a finger. This is truly contact with living sound as never before.

The word 'synthesizer' is perhaps unfortunate. It implies that the synthesizer's objective is to imitate, to create something artificial and therefore by implication inferior. But in reality it is a highly refined musical instrument in its own right, with far greater resources than any other, and capable of producing sophisticated music of no mean aesthetic value which represents our age as no other. This is the kind of music which interests serious composers—not the synthesized Bach and pop music which has hit the headlines, and incidentally synthesized a fair fortune. To reproduce instrumental music on the synthesizer is highly entertaining in the short term, but to the serious musician the real potentialities of this miracle box only begin where imitation of any kind leaves off.

As this is not a treatise on electronic music, it is not possible to dedicate a large amount of space to the intricacies of synthesizer functions. But it is necessary to outline their principles in a brief and general survey, showing how they differ from the 'classical' studio. The sound sources in synthesizers are usually few (as compared with the number of sine-tone generators in classical studios). This is because the sound sources are usually rich sounds which can be modified or filtered to give very varied tonal spectrums. For instance, a square-wave oscillator can be 'shaped' to any form between , through its standard form to . Triangular outputs ( ) can be shaped into or , and so on. These shapings not only produce different tone colours but, as will be seen, can influence significantly the outlines of musical structures.

The main working principle of the voltage-controlled synthesizer to be understood is that though oscillators are used as sound sources, they may also be used to 'control' each other. As a simple example, supposing oscillator 1 is set to sound a pitch of say 440 Hz, it will emit this tone continuously. If, however, it is 'controlled' by oscillator 2, a square wave, set to a sub-audio pitch of 6 Hz (six pulses a second) its pitch will fluctuate according to the signal strength of oscillator 2. If the level of the latter is weak, oscillator 1 will have a gentle vibrato. Increasing the level of oscillator 2 will make the six steps a second in oscillator 1 gradually larger, passing through interval leaps approximating roughly to quarter- and half-tones, to tones, thirds, etc., right up to leaps of very high to very low pitch. This may be graphically illustrated as follows:

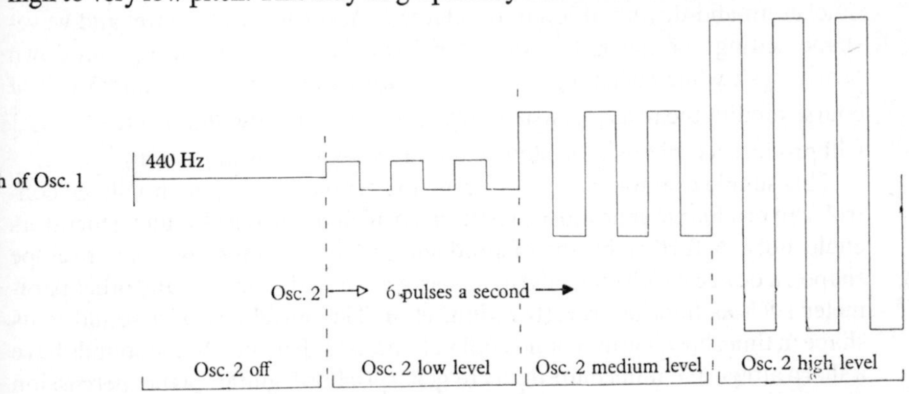

If the shape of oscillator 2 is changed to ⌈⌊ the high sound will be short and the lower one long, and so on. If instead it is changed to a triangular wave (/\/) oscillator 1 will not leap up and down to notes of precise pitch, but will execute glissandos, the size of 'sweep' being governed by the strength of control signal of oscillator 2. Changing the shape of /\/ to /|/ or |\| will make the upward glissandos shorter or longer with respect to the downward ones.

If a third oscillator is introduced, still more complex results can be obtained. For example, when oscillator 1 is controlled by both oscillators 2 and 3, using waveforms of differing periodicity, it will produce sound patterns characteristic of both waveforms combined. Suppose oscillator 3 is set to a very slow pulse (say 0·1 Hz, or a complete cycle every ten seconds) with a triangular waveform, while oscillator 2 is set as before at 6 Hz with a square-wave signal adjusted to make oscillator 1 fluctuate up and down over a small interval, both controls combine to produce a stepped or 'staircase' formation:

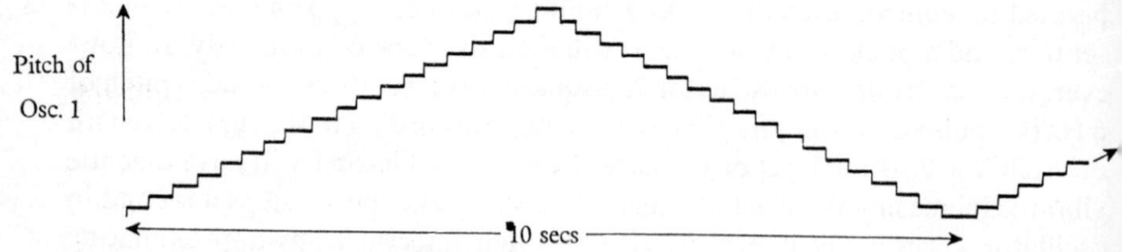

On the slow rise and fall of oscillator 3 (every ten seconds) is superposed the quicker up-and-down motion of oscillator 2. According to the level and wave-shape settings of the latter, the 'steps' can be scalewise, or up-and-down 'warblings'; while reshapings of the wave forms of oscillators 2 and 3 will of course modify the results considerably (e.g. modifying oscillator 3 to |\| will produce a rapid rise and slow fall in the general musical pattern).

This simple example has shown how the synthesizer, through voltage control, can produce mobile musical patterns (which the classical sound generators could not). A further means of producing mobility is through the envelope shaper, a device which controls the shape of a musical sound (or any other parameter such as filtering, reverberation, etc.). The 'envelope' of a sound is its shape in time, how it grows, holds full volume, and then dies. Some sounds have a sharp attack and immediate decay (e.g. harpsichord, guitar, piano, percussion in general) while others grow over a discernible period, are held at constant volume, and then die quickly (e.g. piano accordion, organ pipe, flute, clarinet). The envelope shaper has controls to establish the time of attack, sustain, decay, and 'off', so that a repeating sound envelope could be formed as follows:

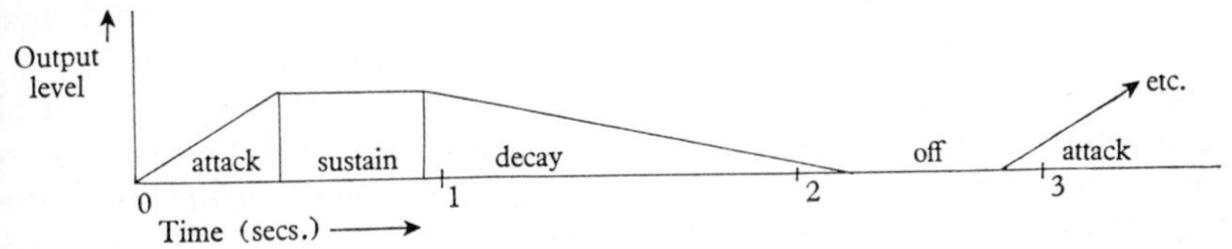

The duration of an envelope can be set up so that the cycle is complete in a fraction of a second, or may cover a long period, such as twenty seconds. (If the repetition is sufficiently rapid, the envelope shaper will become a sound source, having its own audible frequency.) Usually the 'off' position can be set for manual control (normally through a keyboard) so that the envelope shaper can be set in motion exactly when required (e.g. for playing melodies, or initiating a cycle of mobile patterns).

The two ways of achieving mobile events so far described can now be combined to produce a degree of unpredictability in musical results. If we set up the staircase pattern as above (oscillator 1 controlled by oscillators 2 and 3) and put oscillator 1 through the envelope shaper set out of synchronization with the slowest oscillator, we will have random samples of the staircase pattern which fade in and out according to the attack and decay settings. If oscillator 2 or 3 is also controlled by the envelope shaper, considerable modification of the musical designs can now be produced. And so on.

Synthesizers usually have artificial reverberation facilities and filter controls. These too can usually be voltage-controlled or shaped by the envelope shaper. In this way, the degree of reverberation may be made to fluctuate during a certain musical period, or the sound timbre change from mellow to shrill, etc. Ring modulation and white sound are also available.

Devices for altering any parameter (oscillator frequency, filter or decay settings, etc.) are usually built in, and may comprise a two-way joystick, or a keyboard. The keyboard may have its own tuned oscillator, or it may be set to act as a voltage control on any other parameter, so that it must not be regarded only in its conventional sense as something used to play tunes, but as a mechanism which can accurately control all aspects of the synthesizer's performance.

Further means of voltage control are available through peripheral devices such as the random-voltage generator and pitch-to-voltage converter. The random-voltage generator has voltage control functions similar to oscillators, except that the voltages produced are irregular and unpredictable. Voltage changes can however be controlled as to their rapidity of change and the relative span of voltages produced, so that the effect of the random-voltage generator can be modified to suit specific needs. The pitch-to-voltage converter can change musical sounds to voltages, which can then be used for voltage control.

Sequencers are commonly included in synthesizers so that sets of musical events can be memorized. They are small special-purpose digital computers, to provide sequences of control voltages to be used on any of the devices in the studio. Sequencers allow what is played to be recalled and altered in any way, though the small scale of the device makes for a memory of only a few hundred events. Some sequencers are able to deal with several musical parameters at once, so that fairly complex patterns can be built up and stored, to be later replayed and combined with yet other material if necessary.

Normally, a small synthesizer would have two output channels, each with filters and level controls, and 'panning' devices so that sounds can be gradually transferred from one output channel to the other. Whereas in early studios connecting leads had to be fed from one unit of equipment to another, creating a baffling tangle of patch cords hanging like festoons, the modern synthesizer has a neat, small matrix board with several hundred holes, and it is sufficient to push a pin into a hole to connect one device to another. This makes the most complex patching simple, as long as the functions of the matrix board are clearly understood. In order to show the use of a matrix board, the figure below shows a simple nine-pin patch on the London-made VCS3, indicating the path followed from sound source to speakers. The sound source is white sound, fed into the filter at H7. The filtered sound is fed into the envelope shaper at D10, and the result is directed into two output channels at B12 and C12. Various controls have however been introduced: the filter is controlled by a slow pulse from oscillator 3 (triangular form) at N6, while the decay is controlled by both oscillator 1 (ramp shape at L2) and oscillator 2 (triangular shape at L4) again set to slow pulses. At O16 and P15 the joystick controls the output amplifiers to swing the sound from one speaker to another and alter its volume. This patch will produce filtered white sound in repeating irregular waves which can be made to sound like seawaves beating on the shore, or rolling bursts of thunder, gusts of wind, etc., according to the various oscillator, filter, and envelope settings:

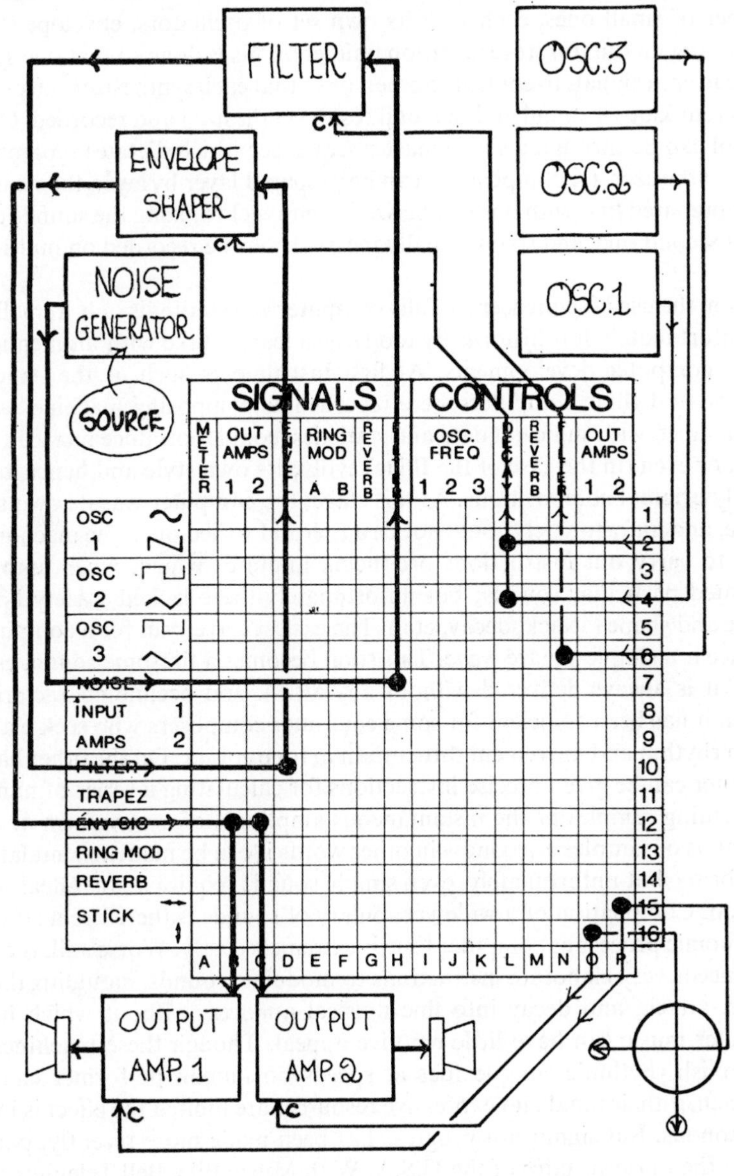
FILTER
C
ENVELOPE SHAPER
C
NOISE GENERATOR
SOURCE
OSC.3
OSC.2
OSC.1
SIGNALS
CONTROLS
METER
OUT AMPS
1 2
RING MOD
A B
REVERB
OSC. FREQ
1 2 3
REVERB
OUT AMPS
1 2
OSC 1
OSC 2
OSC 3
NOISE
INPUT AMPS 1 2
FILTER
TRAPEZ
ENV SIG
RING MOD
REVERB
STICK
1 2 3 4 5 6 7 8 9 10 11 12 13 14 15 16
A B C D E F G H I J K L M N O P
OUTPUT AMP. 1
C
OUTPUT AMP. 2
C

Larger synthesizers are usually based on the concept of building together a number of small ones, each with its own set of oscillators, envelope shapers filters, ring modulator, reverberation unit, etc. This is done so that one synthesizer can emit signals to control another, or so that each synthesizer can produce a different kind of sound and the total result synthesized and recorded. Overall control can be through a single master sequencer which dictates separately to each synthesizer. (A composition can be prepared layer by layer, the sequence being prepared first with one synthesizer, then synchronizing the sounds of this with a second one, and so on. Finally the work may be recorded on multi-track tape.)

From the use of sequencers to fully computerized studios is only a small step but unfortunately it is historically too large a leap to take without mentioning earlier computer developments. At first instruments such as the American Dataron and Illiac computers were regarded as composing machines which programmed with sufficient data and statistics, could reproduce music in given styles, or even (in the case of the Illiac) evolve its own style and hence its own entirely original compositions. At this stage, the computer was its own sound source, and unfortunately could not be a rich and varied one. The machine was made to carry out instructions producing impulses which, when amplified generated particular sounds; but unfortunately these lacked variety both in timbre and shape (attack, decay, etc.). The easiest waveform for a computer to produce is a simple square wave. This soon becomes a tiresome sound, especially if it is always delivered without any attack and decline characteristics, though it has been sufficient for some computer composers who seek elaboration in rhythm and movement rather than in tone colour. On the other hand, a computer can be given precise instructions for calculating a series of numbers representing samples of the instantaneous amplitude of a waveform at many thousands of samples a second—in other words it can be made to simulate any waveform—but unfortunately, even simple sounds require a great deal of calculation. Compilation of a wide vocabulary of sounds is therefore a slow and uneconomic process as computer time is extremely costly. Worse still, the computer needs very elaborate instructions to modulate sounds, moulding them in timbre, attack, and decay into fine musical nuances, without which finesse computer music can have little emotive appeal. Though these machines can accomplish rhythmic complexities at speeds no human performer can ever approach, if their tonal and expressive resources are limited the effect is indeed monotonous. But significant progress has been made more recently, particularly in the Eastern states of the U.S.A. With Music File, Bell Telephone, etc. the resources of impressive polyphonic structuring are being realized, while with the use of the digital analogue converter rich waveforms are being created which can simulate instrumental sounds to perfection. Not only that, but the physical and temperamental characteristics of performers can be reproduced to an astonishing degree. For instance, one feels the gathering of a (simulated) trumpeter's energies as the music climbs and intensifies, there is a significant pause for breath before the climax, and then a relaxation of physical concentration as the music declines into repose. Such performance finesse is indeed admirable (though its validity may be questionable), and one must recognize that without it computer music would remain on an inferior aesthetic plane.

The use of computers with synthesizers, however, is quite another matter. As we have seen, sequencers can memorize a certain number of musical events and give precise instructions to a number of synthesizers for performance. But their memories are limited. On the other hand, even a small desk computer is a source of immense memory, and coupled with the highly versatile performance possibilities of synthesizers makes for a very flexible and widely expressive musical instrument.

The new generation of computerized studios has in fact a different objective from the old. Whereas previously the computer was regarded as a superhuman composing machine, producing compositions of its own from given data, in the new studios the computer is used largely as a memory bank, capable of producing any sound the composer desires (through synthesizers), memorizing the sequence of events he establishes, and finally playing the complete work whenever required. Information is usually fed to the computer by teletype keyboard or a special manual controller, though the composer can also override the computer and add musical details through conventional keyboards by switching the synthesizers by hand. Unfortunately the method of storing up the computer's memory ('programming') and releasing it in musicianly fashion is still a complex affair, particularly as so many items of 'hardware' are involved. The figure on page 118 shows the layout of a computerized studio set up by Peter Zinovieff, David Cockerell, and Peter Grogono, and for which the most sophisticated communication language so far evolved ('MUSYS') has been invented.

Computer music therefore need no longer be regarded as a mechanized musical language, but rather one in which the composer's free inspiration can be brought into play. He can think in sound and have it reproduced at will, so that, to a large extent, he can work as subjectively as did Mozart or Rossini. As yet, however, no computer music of the new generation has made a significant mark in the musical world; which brings us to a strange paradox. This music is so greatly superior to early electronic music, both in artistic stature and technical brilliance, that it merits wide recognition, and yet it has not

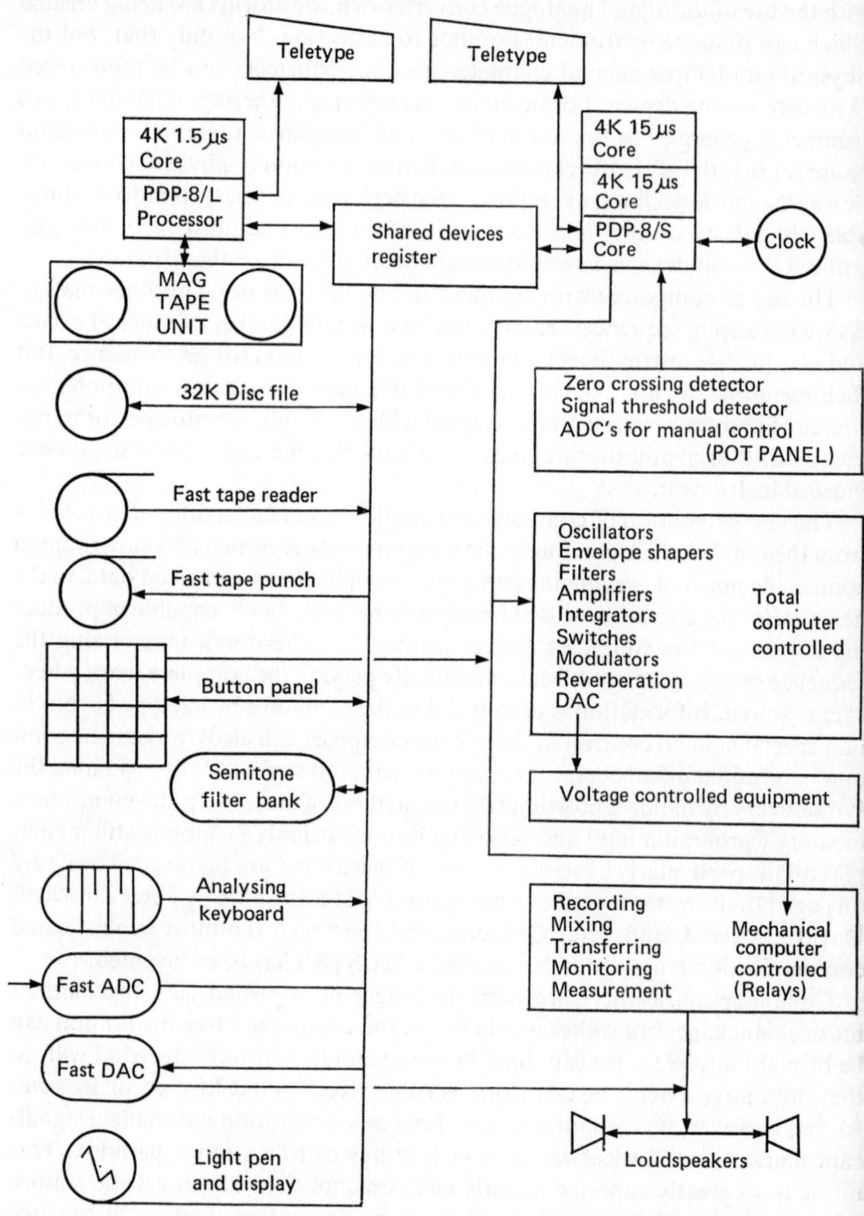
Teletype
Teletype
4K 1.5 µs Core
PDP-8/L Processor
4K 15 µs Core
4K 15 µs Core
PDP-8/S Core
Shared devices register
Clock
MAG TAPE UNIT
32K Disc file
Zero crossing detector
Signal threshold detector
ADC's for manual control
(POT PANEL)
Fast tape reader
Fast tape punch
Oscillators
Envelope shapers
Filters
Amplifiers
Integrators
Switches
Modulators
Reverberation
DAC
Total computer controlled
Button panel
Semitone filter bank
Voltage controlled equipment
Analysing keyboard
Recording
Mixing
Transferring
Monitoring
Measurement
Mechanical computer controlled (Relays)
Fast ADC
Fast DAC
Loudspeakers
Light pen and display

achieved a fraction of that éclat which greeted the first rudimentary pieces of Eimert and Stockhausen. In fact this lack of recognition for any particular piece of electronic music has been a characteristic phenomenon of musical life during the last decade—even though interest in electronic music is such that synthesizers are spreading into every university, college, school, and even home. Perhaps it is the *kind* of music which has not caught on. It is certainly not the *medium*—the momentous success of Walter Carlos's *Switched-on Bach* proves that!

Lastly, we must note the vast change in compositional techniques since the early Fifties. The first steps in the electronic world were calculated and carefully measured; the new-found territory was so immense that, fearing its extent, composers worked only with slide rule and graph paper. But now, if one excepts certain areas such as the computer studios of the Eastern States, and occasional European installations such as the IBM at Pisa university, all can be free, composers need no longer fear the immensity of sound-space, and total organization can at last give way to spontaneity, ingenuity, and free invention—that is, if composers so wish.

To sum up, electronic music seemed to promise so much in the early Fifties, but that promise has not so far been fulfilled. Today, technology offers us even more tantalizing resources. But will great art be achieved? Those of us who were impressed by the first electronic miracle may prefer to hold a watching brief, but there is no doubt that for many of a younger generation the future of music lies in electronics; its artistic validity is beyond dispute and great works are bound to ensue.

Viewed dispassionately, however, it must be admitted that electronic music, *as concert music*, is no great success. It seldom evokes a warm audience response, in fact it sometimes generates no response at all. It is not easy to identify the reason. Perhaps it is simply that an audience does not care to applaud loudspeakers; and without applause, a concert is dead. Composers tend therefore to avoid the 'captive' audience, and have their music played as an environmental atmosphere at (for example) art exhibitions, where the viewers need not behave as an audience at all. The truth is that an audience needs to respond to a living presence, to personal artistry. This is why one of the most successful applications of electronic or concrete music is as an accompaniment to performers whose musical role is dominant. In such pieces as Babbitt's *Philomel* and Nono's *La Fabbrica Illuminata*, the solo singers hold the stage, while tapes provide a full-bodied accompaniment. In Stockhausen's *Kontakte*, the four-track tape gives out a substantial mass of electronics, but our attention is focused on the pianist and percussionist, for they are the 'presence' of the music. In such 'live' situations, electronics can be a resounding success, and it is perhaps in such scores (and in film and television sound tracks where again there is the visual dimension) that the most certain future lies.

12

Cage and Other Americans

It is impossible not to write at some length about that engaging and polemical figure who has taken Europe by the ears and shaken out the dross—John Cage.

Perhaps the clue to Cage's music is in his writings—*Silence* and *A Year from Monday*.[1] These are mostly derived from his lectures, which are occasionally very revealing as to his music and philosophy. More often they reveal him as a master of anecdote (the story of Cage poisoning himself through eating skunk cabbage is told with a simplicity and skill worthy of Saroyan), while other lectures seem purposelessly absurd, provocative or meaningfully meaningless, e.g. *Lecture on Nothing*, *45′ for a Speaker*, *Where are we going? and what are we doing?* This last (1961) is a set of four independent lectures of forty-five minutes each, one read by a speaker, the others recorded on tape and played simultaneously, or in other combinations. Cage says, 'I have therefore made a lecture in which . . . meaning is not easy to come by even though lucidity has been my constant will-of-the-wisp.' A lecture on *Indeterminacy* (1958) consists of ninety stories which he has recited with piano accompaniment and radios, or with a tape recording of his *Fontana Mix*. Each story must last one minute, whether it is short or long, and may therefore be unintelligible even if it is audible.

Strangely enough, even in his enigmatic pieces one is left with the impression of extreme lucidity; something has been greatly clarified. But what? Perhaps a psychological clarity has been achieved through the growing need to pay no attention to words, to dissociate oneself from any meaning or emotion. Perhaps sheer boredom brings liberation, and suddenly things are seen to be so simple, all the complexities fall away like meaningless sounds. . .

These writings have analogies with Cage's music. This may be listened to, or

[1] *Silence* was originally published in the U.S.A. in 1961. Both books were subsequently published in London in 1968. From a musical point of view *Silence* is much more interesting. *A Year from Monday* is more socially and politically orientated, as its dedication confirms: 'To us and all those who hate us, that the U.S.A. may become just another part of the world, no more, no less.'

half-listened to, or not at all. It needs a new listening attitude. As Cage says: 'New music: new listening. Not an attempt to understand . . . Just an attention to the activity of sounds.'

This new attitude has not come easily to Europeans, who listen at an intense level and strive to 'understand', even when there is nothing to be understood. We are so accustomed to delving into a hurly-burly of sounds to grasp the real core that with the sparseness of Cage we are apt to miss what is nakedly clear. Sound, for Cage, need have no associations: 'A sound does not view itself as thought, as ought, as needing another sound for its elucidation, as etc.; it has no time for any consideration—it is occupied with the performance of its characteristics. . . .' A sound exists in isolation: 'Urgent, unique, uninformed about history and theory.' And paradoxically: 'A sound accomplishes nothing; without it life would not last out the instant.'[2]

To be concise, Cage's music, like his writings (and lectures), does not necessarily go anywhere; it can exist without meaning, it can be sound, or it can be silence. Furthermore, all sounds are legitimate and admissible, whether conventionally 'musical' or otherwise.

As Cage rightly points out, silence is only relative. His recurrent theme is that in an anechoic chamber[3] we do not hear silence, but a pumping of the heart and intoning of nerves, while in a concert hall, on these are imposed inhalations, exhalations, ambient sounds, traffic noises, etc. 'Silence' is therefore a substratum of sound at about 25–30 dB, while on this, other ('musical') sounds can be overlaid, not in continuity, but casually, now and then. This is why he can write pieces such as *Solo for Sliding Trombone* with 20% or less of instrumental sound in the total time-duration. This is why—to emphasize the real nature of silence—Cage wrote *4′ 33″* (1952), for any instrument or ensemble, with one instruction—*tacet*. Music, for Cage, is therefore silence (which is sound at one level), plus other sounds (at a higher acoustic level). The nature of these sounds is often largely immaterial—they can be radios, speech, instruments, scratched gramophone pick-ups, and so on.

For Cage, too, music is action. A player's body, gestures, speech, and actions are an extension of his instrument, an enlargement of its personality. Cage's music can therefore involve players in speech, movement, and gesture, in theatricalisms which are quite alien to the almost impersonal 'white tie and tails' tradition of European instrumentalism.

Cage was early attracted to Oriental music and philosophy, and he seems to have been so impervious to Western traditions that the main characteristics

[1] 'Experimental Music' in *Silence*. [2] ibid.

[3] A completely silent room without reverberations.

›f European music are quite absent from his work. From his first works in 1933 o the String Quartet of 1949, his music emanates much more of the East than he West. There are melodic lines reminiscent of the rhythmic repetitive cycles ›f Indian ragas and talas, placid ostinatos, gentle sonorities which recall the ;amelans of Bali and Java, and the bare percussive clarity of Chinese theatre nusic. His music is largely devoid of directional harmony (except for the simple ree pentatonic semi-consonance of the String Quartet), and is basically either ntirely melodic or percussive, or combines both elements. The example below ›f the prepared piano in *Amores* (1943) shows the weaving, repetitive melodic lesigns with a floating, non-directional harmony which rests as a static back-:loth to the entire musical section. The strings of all the notes shown are pre-›ared with either bolts, nuts and bolts, or pieces of rubber. The objective is to ›roduce sounds which are rich in harmonics (those with bolts), resonant in a netallic way (those with nuts and bolts), or dull but prominent in harmonics where rubber is used). Cage says: 'The total desired result has been achieved if, ›n completion of the preparation, one may play the pertinent keys without ensing that one is playing a piano or even a "prepared piano". An instrument aving convincingly its own special characteristics, not even suggesting those of piano, must be the result.' The following example does not therefore sound as ›ianistic as it looks. The tone is subdued and evanescent, prominent in har-nonics and percussive sounds of different colour:

In 1947, Cage was notably influenced by Zen Buddhism, which leads to a nistrust of the rational mind and a searching out of ways to nullify its powers ›f decision. From this point we find him using various systems with which to :ircumvent the memory and constructive will. I have already mentioned his use n 1951 of *I-Ching* in *Imaginary Landscape No. 4* for twelve radios and *Music of*

Changes for piano, in which coins (or marked sticks) are thrown for chan numbers. Hexagrams of thirty-two or sixty-four numbers are formed, and fro these the various musical elements are determined. Strangely enough, this for of constructivism was closely allied to European integral serialism which w emerging almost contemporaneously. The principles are similar, but it is to b noted that the results, in Cage's hands, are much more gentle. *Music of Chang* is slender and reflective—as if his oriental thought cannot be purged:

This points in no uncertain fashion to the fact that neither Cage's *I-Ching* n the integral serialist's systems can really override the composer's own instinc and inventive desires; they can only clothe them in a different language.

After using *I-Ching* in *Music of Changes*, various other means were devise to cultivate the element of chance. Template stencils were made and laid ov manuscript paper in various positions, so as to give fortuitous dispositions notes. Imperfections in manuscript paper were pinpointed and became th sources of sound structures. In *Atlas Eclipticalis* (1961) an immense mass material in eighty-six instrumental parts was evolved by laying transpare paper over star constellations and then transferring them to music manuscrip

It would seem that complex methods of cultivating chance such as *I-Chi* were gradually abandoned, Cage coming to rely on what we may call 'huma indeterminacy'. Players are given a certain amount of material (as in the Co cert for Piano and Orchestra of 1957–8 quoted on p. 82), but may choos any note-group at random and play as they wish, or not at all.

Eventually, any involvement with notation is abandoned. The *Aria* for sol voice (1958) is merely sets of words arranged in bizarre patterns, adjoinin linear pitch indications drawn in colours which suggest mood or manner performance. It may be sung with *Fontana Mix* (tape) or with parts of the Concert for Piano and Orchestra. In other pieces schemes are provided from which performers may prepare parts (*Variations I and II*), or which indicate certain activities (*Cartridge Music*, 1960 and *Water Music*, on p. 93). Cage thus gradually disengaged himself from musical definition in any aspect, his main concern becoming the theatrical exploitation of human indeterminacy in the three parallel paths of sound, text, and vision.

Some of his theatre seems farcical and provocative, though it is perhaps not deliberately so, as Cage takes his art most seriously. For him the action is an integral part of the music—which Europeans failed to understand. Cage outraged the critics from his first debut in Europe, and this 'shocking' reputation has remained with him. (H. H. Stuckenschmidt describes the 1954 debut of Cage and Tudor at Donaueschingen in a typically hostile fashion: 'One of the pieces . . . *12′ 55·677 for two Pianists* . . . lasted for about thirteen minutes of chirping, drumming sounds, mostly ejected as explosive staccatos. Occasionally Tudor got hold of a whistle or a toy trumpet and blew cat-calls. Then he began to bang on some metal with a hammer. Eventually he crawled under his piano to make running repairs, leaving Cage to play on undisturbed.')[1]

As early as 1937 Cage drew attention to the possibilities of the electronic synthetic production of music' and inevitably taped music of the 'concrète' variety has featured in his output over a long period. His most grandiose theatre has been the result of a year's work with the Illinois University computer Illiac) in 1967 composing *HPSCHD*. This work, based on harpsichord-type sounds, comprises fifty-one tapes each of twenty minutes duration which can be played in any combination, or all at once, together with seven live harpsichords. The first performance in the assembly hall of Illinois Urbana Campus included numerous films and slides projected kaleidoscopically on a 340 foot screen and several transparent plastic curtains. In this way the eyes and ears were subjected to such a massive corpus of sight and sound as the senses have rarely experienced. The result, however, must not be regarded as anything but an environment', a background which is alive, but in which nothing can be heard or seen except in a fleeting manner. Such a work needs not only passive listening, but passive looking! (Not an easy accomplishment for music critics, if one reads their comments on the 1972 London Round House production.)

To sum up, Cage has let an enormous draught of fresh air into the stuffy fug of concert halls. His actual musical influence is hard to pinpoint, for in many ways his is largely a negative musicality. In America his influence is of one kind—his cult of 'silence' and isolation from musical tradition—whereas the

[1] H. H. Stuckenschmidt: *Twentieth-Century Music*, London, 1969.

'shocking' Cage has been more noticed in Europe. His has above all been a liberating force, a new philosophical vista, a psychological disinternment from the nightmare *Moses und Aron* heritage. He has let us see again the old simplicity of things, how a single curve can say more than a labyrinthine delineation, how music can be rid of the over-sophistication and return to a primeval state of innocence.

Cage associated closely with Morton Feldman, Earle Brown, and Christian Wolff in the post-war years. Though all were composers, their main source of common interest was the visual arts, especially the work of the then thriving New York school and particularly Jackson Pollock, Willem de Kooning, Philip Guston, Franz Kline, and Mark Rothko. Later associations with Jasper Johns and Robert Rauschenberg were particularly close. As composers, they were all non-European in the sense that they felt no close ties with conventional musical history and tradition, so that they were particularly inspired by a school of painting and sculpture which began from the raw soil of America and forged its own future. Regarding art in New York in the early Fifties, Feldman writes admiringly that: 'Anyone who was around in the early 50's with the painters saw that these men had started to explore their own sensibilities, their own plastic language . . . with that complete independence from other art, that complete inner security to work with that which was unknown to them . . . That was a fantastic aesthetic accomplishment. I feel that John Cage, Earle Brown, Christian Wolff and I were very much in that particular spirit.' Each of these four, in his own way, pioneered accomplishments in music. Each worked with 'that which was unknown' in such a manner as to influence the future of both American and European music.

Their common ideal was to discover means of composing which, like Cage's use of *I-Ching*, destroyed conventional musical continuity and liberated sounds from the governance of memory, desire, and the rational mind. Cage says: 'Where people had felt the necessity to stick sounds together to make a continuity, we four felt the opposite necessity to get rid of the glue so that sounds would be themselves. Christian Wolff was the first to do this. He wrote some pieces vertically on the page but recommended their being played horizontally from left to right as is conventional. Later he discovered other geometrical means of freeing his music of intentional continuity.'[1]

Geometrical means, or 'graph scores', were to be a common working method for Wolff, Brown, and particularly Feldman for some considerable time. His numerous *Projections* and *Intersections*, as well as a large corpus of other works, are all written according to the graphic system already shown on

[1] Cage: *History of Experimental Music in the United States* in *Silence*.

pp. 61 and 67. The simplicity of this system is extreme; it makes composing look easy, almost too easy. Perhaps Cage's remarks on this are apt:

> There are people who say, 'If music's that easy to write, I could do it.' Of course they could, but they don't. I find Feldman's own statement more affirmative. We were driving back from some place in New England where a concert had been given. He is a large man and falls asleep easily. Out of a sound sleep he awoke to say, 'Now that things are so simple, there's so much to do.' And then he went back to sleep.[1]

In case this seems to throw doubt on the validity of Feldman's graph scores or to the degree of his personal involvement in his compositions I myself must resort to anecdote. When I first heard Feldman's solo percussion piece *The King of Denmark* I was so struck by the extraordinary beauty of the music that I wrote to the publisher for a copy. When I saw the score I was much disappointed—for it showed me nothing of the sounds I had heard, but only squares, rectangles, and numbers. It looked barren, and I assumed the music I heard had really been improvised. But of course I was looking for what was not there (conventional notation) and ignored the fact that Feldman's squares and numbers were indeed an accurate representation of his music.

With Feldman's graph scores we must therefore not jump to conclusions. If they look so devoid of significant sounds, and yet produce music of a specific quality (allowing for some degree of indeterminacy), we must at least give him credit for inventing one of the simplest and most effective notations ever used.

I have already illustrated the early graph scores *Projection I* and *Intersection I*. This notation served Feldman as a basic method over almost ten years. Various extensions of this essentially simple graphic principle were devised, usually aimed at indicating more movement of sounds than the early scores permitted. For example, in his *Atlantis* of 1958 the graph indicates the number of sounds to be played within each time unit (each 'box' of the graph is equal to 92 MM). Some instruments may combine these sounds into chords (harp, piano, xylophone, and vibraphone), but usually they are played as soft, flowing phrases:

[1] ibid.

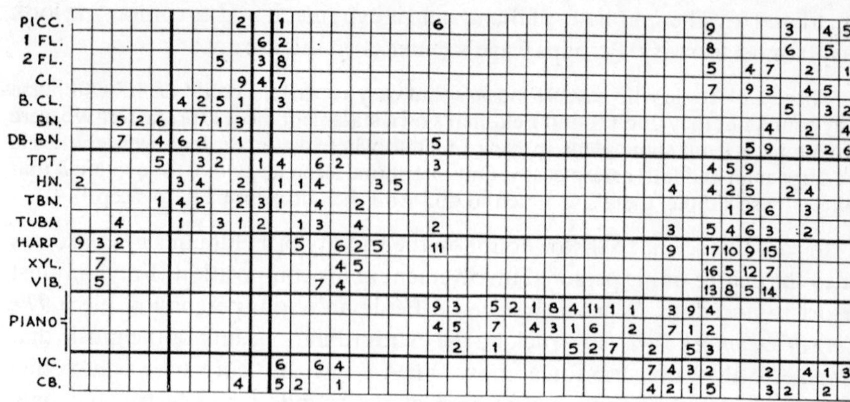

However, beginning with the *Durations* of 1960, Feldman moved gradually into the realm of precise notation. A large number of works are based merely on successions of sounds of imprecise duration, where instruments begin together and then play on in their own time:

Sometimes instruments in an ensemble play from 'one identical part but at their own speed, in their own time, slowly over-lapping their defined pitches like a series of reverberations from a single sound source'. (It will be noted that this situation, where only sound durations are indeterminate, is the exact opposite of the procedure in his early graph scores, where the duration of sounds was the only determined factor.) Eventually, even this factor of indeterminacy was abandoned in works such as *Christian Wolff at Cambridge* (1963), for unaccompanied choir:

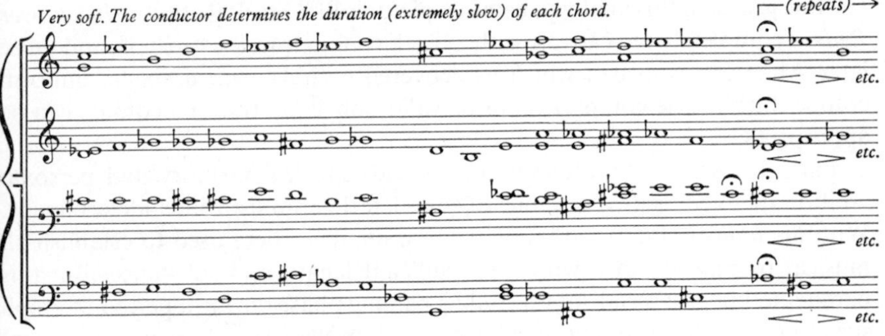

This piece, without any text, amounts to no more than sixteen chords, sung very softly and slowly, and then repeated. Could anything be more simple? Or is it too simple?[1] On the surface, Feldman is arriving at normality, his quality as a revolutionary has disintegrated, and his work can be compared, perhaps not too favourably, with that of the 'ordinary' composer. Later Feldman works such as *False Relationships and the Extended Ending*, *On Time and the Instrumental Factor*, and *The Viola in My Life*, are even written in metre, with conventional note values, and so on, so that all aspects of indeterminacy are completely eradicated. Perhaps this complete definition is what Feldman had always searched for, and this comparatively 'European' solution would have served him all along. Curiously enough he says of his early graph pieces: 'After several years of writing graph music, I began to discover its most important flaw. I was not only allowing the sounds to be free—I was also liberating the performer. I had never thought of the graph as an art of improvisation, but more as a totally abstract sonic adventure'.

This 'sonic adventure' of his is just what has appealed to us, for it emanates a very quiet, cool, and clear vision, a pale, tranquil, almost colourless landscape which breathes peace and rest as does little other modern music. It is deliberately eventless, hypnotic, and without emotion. Admittedly this is only art of a limited scale, but as Feldman says: 'a modest statement can be totally original, where the "grand scale" is, more often than not, merely eclectic . . . My compositions are really not "compositions" at all. One might call them time canvases in which I more or less prime the canvas with an overall hue of music.'

[1] One of Feldman's latest works, *Madame Press died last week at the age of ninety*, for instrumental ensemble, features two notes a minor third apart played on the flute throughout, supported by slow, vague chords. This 'cuckoo' theme (played perhaps ninety times) is certainly the ne plus ultra of musical simplicity, but is it too much so?

His music lies, in this analogy, between pictures like Mark Rothko's *Black over Reds* (a completely red canvas, with a black rectangle in the top half) and those later American canvases which are covered entirely with a single, uniform colour. But for the comparison to be valid only cool, tranquil colours can be appropriate.

Earle Brown's early attempts to override musical memory and personal volition spanned the two extremes of complete determinism and indeterminacy. With his *Indices* (1954), tables of random numbers were used to establish all musical parameters in a work of significant length and substance. But this parallel to integral serialism was only a passing phase during a period of graph structures which are more radical in conception than any other composer conceived at that time. Inspired by Alexander Calder's 'mobiles', Brown designed graphic scores which could be used in various ways, to give different sound interpretations of structures which were almost completely indeterminate in musical terms.

Brown's *Four Systems* and various pieces in *Folio* (1952) are based on music which can be played forwards or backwards, or upside down, or on designs which can be played in any position, by any number of players. The designs often comprise black rectangles of various sizes which are arranged vertically and horizontally on the page (see Ex. 54), but they have no specific musical significance. They can be regarded as indicating pitch, volume, duration, and so on, but these details are best arranged between the players themselves, as long as unpredictability is preserved. Brown's objective is to provide a 'programme' which can be given identity of a different kind at each performance. In other words, we have here that mobile, open form which European composers were to reach out for in the early Sixties, and of which Brown was the real originator.

After such completely indeterminate graphic forms, Brown (like Feldman) moved towards more precise notation, though preserving the open-form principle. Such works as *Available Forms 1* and *2* (1961–2) are written out in score, but with the final form left open. For instance, in *Available Forms 2* the orchestra is divided into two groups, with separate independent conductors. Musical sections are numbered in such a way that each conductor can signal his group to play a certain section when he thinks its material suits the situation of the moment. The form of any particular performance therefore depends on the reactions of the interpreters and on their mutual understanding. The musical material also has a certain improvisatory character. The material Brown calls 'explicit' is fairly fully notated, but that which is 'implicit' comprises linear patternings which merely indicate a certain kind of activity:

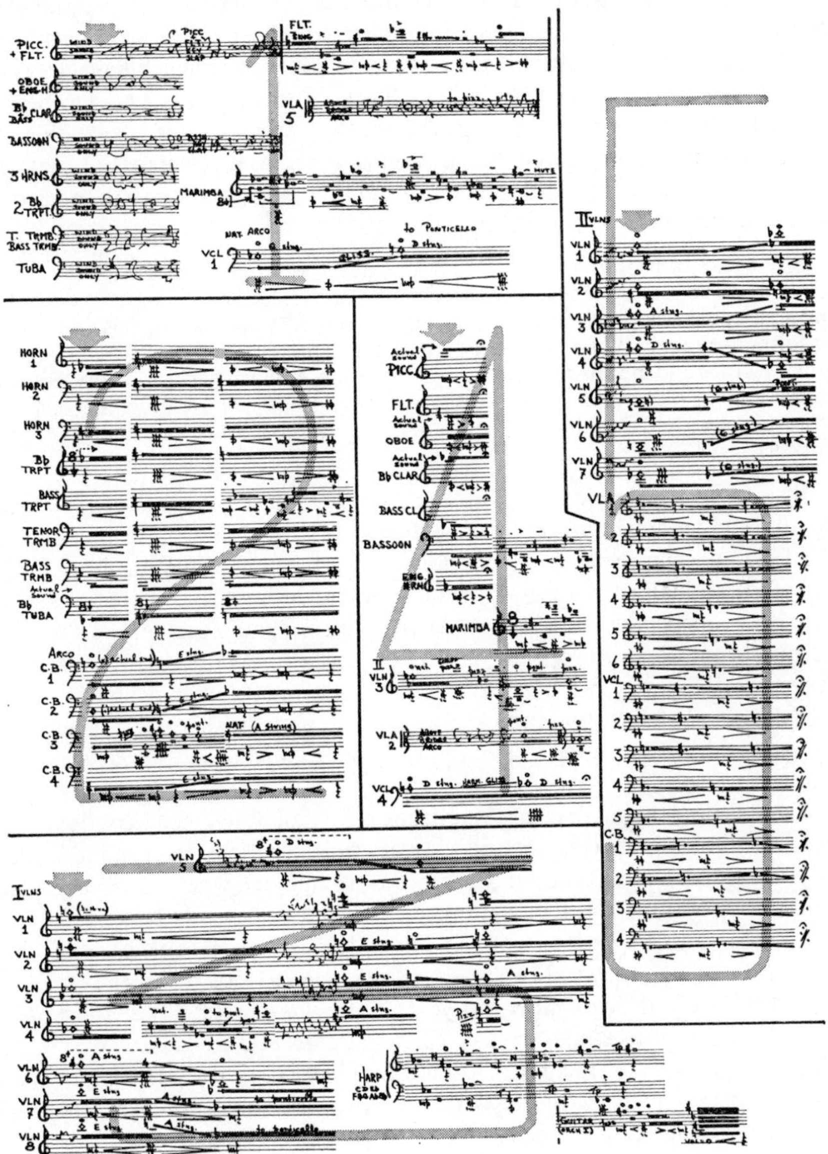
PICC. + FLT.
OBOE + ENG. H.
Bb BASS CLAR
BASSOON
3 HRNS
2 Bb TRPT.
T. TRMB. BASS TRMB.
TUBA
FLT.
VLA 5
MARIMBA
NAT. ARCO
to PONTICELLO
VCL 1
GLISS.
D stng.
II VLNS
VLN 1
VLN 2
VLN 3
A stng.
VLN 4
D stng.
VLN 5
VLN 6
VLN 7
HORN 1
HORN 2
HORN 3
Bb TRPT
BASS TRPT
TENOR TRMB
BASS TRMB
Actual sound
Bb TUBA
ARCO
C.B. 1
E stng.
C.B. 2
C.B. 3
NAT (A STRING)
C.B. 4
Actual sound
PICC.
FLT.
OBOE
Bb CLAR
BASS CL
BASSOON
ENG. HRN
MARIMBA
II VLN 3
VLA 2
VCL 4
D stng.
HARM. GLISS.
VLA 1
VCL 1
C.B. 1
VLN 5
I VLNS
VLN 1
VLN 2
E stng.
VLN 3
A stng.
VLN 4
Pizz.
VLN 6
VLN 7
to ponticello
VLN 8
HARP
GUITAR

In the course of time Brown, like Feldman, has become more conventional in that his music has become increasingly defined. The open-form concept has latterly been abandoned in favour of fixed overall forms which have areas of flexibility within the inner structures. That is, while works like the String Quartet (1965) and *Corroboree* for three (or two) pianos, are written with both explicit and implicit notation and are sectionalized so as to be played 'straight through', the players should interact, moulding one section into another in a flexible and spontaneous manner. He says:

> What I am trying to imply is not only a great responsibility on the part of the performers to perform the work 'as written', but also an intense awareness of ensemble and individual flexibility *within* the material as written and within this concept of performance relativity. I would like to think that an intensified sense of human and sonic *presence* and intuitive performance contact can be extended beyond the 'normal' precision-goal of most chamber music performing, into an area of immediacy of action-reaction and flexibility, while maintaining the *basic* shape and character of the work.[1]

By altering a couple of words or so, this statement could be taken as an ideal for all chamber music, however conventional. It serves to illustrate how Brown, like Feldman, has perhaps unconsciously grown *towards* the European tradition after originally denying its influence. Though intimate friends of Cage, they have been independent of him and beaten their own paths, arriving as it were in Europe, while some Europeans have been journeying with Cage to America. This underlines what we brought out at the beginning of the chapter on indeterminacy. In aspects of musical creation, the paths of many Europeans and Americans have converged, arriving at a common ground about the mid-Sixties.

There is no denying that the Americans have had much to contribute to the more adventurous aspects of contemporary music; in fact, their influence can only be regarded as a healthy one. It is hard to imagine what European music would have become if it had continued in isolation, possibly heading further and further into the complexities of integral serialism, or at least still overburdened with its own weighty tradition. We tended to look down on American art and culture in the early post-war years, but in the end it has been the Americans who have let us see how music can legitimately be considerably different from anything we ever imagined. Their music has led us along fascinating new paths, and taught us many important lessons, the most important perhaps being that Europe can no longer afford to live in artistic isolation.

[1] Notes to String Quartet.

13

The Search Outwards—The Orient, Jazz, Archaisms

There have been clear signs that, for some composers, what one might call the 'classic'[1] avant-garde idiom is not enough. Perhaps it is too narrow in its field of expression, perhaps it is too stereotyped. Certainly it is a kind of communal language on which it is not easy to impress the stamp of one's own identity. Perhaps on the other hand there is nothing wrong with the idion, but some composers are restless for change. (Boulez has shown little desire for change over twenty years, whereas Stockhausen has knocked down his own house and built it in a different way for every new work.) Whatever the reasons, composers have begun to search outwards to enlarge the idiom, gathering inspiration from the orient, from jazz, from the classics and medieval and renaissance music. In short, the avant-garde has not only looked 'forwards' but 'sideways and backwards'. In this chapter I shall examine the main directions of search.

Musically, the East and West have been rubbing shoulders for only a few decades, yet already the integration between the two has gone some distance. Air travel has bridged the chasm which separated the occident and orient, migrations of peoples (Pakistanis to England, Jews to Israel, Chinese and Japanese to the U.S.A.), and armies of occupation (in Japan, Korea, and Vietnam) have all made for a rapid intermingling of peoples and cultures.

Earlier, the influence of Eastern on Western music was often a matter of atmosphere rather than real musical fact. Debussy's brief experience of Eastern music at the 1889 Paris exhibition led him to the gentle pentatonicisms of *Voiles* (middle section), *La Fille aux cheveux de lin*, and *Pagodes*, but not to a deep acquaintance with oriental music. Yet Debussy's orientalisms, so perfectly wedded to his seductive, impressionist idiom, became an integral part of French music—the hesitant, pliant melody and semi-immobile harmony, the subdued tone and lush colouring. Puccini's *Turandot*, on the other hand,

[1] Of course in a constantly evolving art such as that of the avant-garde, there is no such thing as a 'classic' idiom. By classic, I mean well-established, central, mainstream, something like the largely undeviating art of Boulez.

though oriental to a similar degree, had no such influence on Italian music.

Messiaen's studies of oriental music, particularly Indian, were much more thorough (see his *Technique de mon langage musical*). Scales and modes were

Messiaen: *Chronochromie*

analysed, the rhythmic structures of melodies codified, and the results set in rigorous order. Curiously enough, Messiaen's music is often very unoriental in effect, far less so than, for example, Varèse's *Density 21·5* for flute solo (which one could trace back to Debussy's *Syrinx*). Though Messiaen's melody may be based on Indian raga principles, it sounds aloof and Northern, and is in any case often pushed into the background by a surging flood of complex chromatic harmony usually presented in dense patterns. The oriental quality of Messiaen's music is much more evident in those passages where all the harmony moves in parallel with a melodic pattern, especially when he evokes the gamelan sound with keyed percussion groups such as glockenspiel, marimba, vibraphone, xylophone, bells, etc. as in the example opposite.

This gamelan sound, also propagated by Messiaen's pupil Boulez, has been quick to spread through Western music. But we must recognize that though the origins may be Balinese or Javanese, only the Eastern colour remains, for the real essence of the music may be quite European.

In the U.S.A. composers were much more open to Eastern influences. Their lack of a national tradition led them to throw the net wide in their search for idioms which could be adapted and personalized. Henry Cowell, Alan Hovhaness, Lou Harrison, Harry Partch, and John Cage experimented with percussion instruments which evoked oriental effects—gongs, glass bowls, pyrex dishes, tom-toms, indian drums—while, following Cowell's experiments, Cage evolved the prepared piano, with its gentle, naïve tone and percussive colourings. As we have seen in Cage's *Amores* (p. 123), the harmonic 'problem' could be sidestepped altogether, while with composers such as Hovhaness harmony can be trance-like, almost immobile, with a bare shifting of emphases within an organum-like amalgam of pentatonic notes. Varèse, too, developed a melodic idiom which with its peregrinations around, above, and below a central note seems directly descended from the Indian thematic principles of embellishments of a single tone:

Varèse: *Intégrales*

Quite apart from direct musical influences, some composers have been drawn towards oriental religious thought, with its stress on contemplation, and the seeking of psychological states beyond the level of consciousness. Music's purpose is 'to sober and quiet the mind', to induce a state of trance in which one is completely passive, yet acutely perceptive of divine influences. Such trance-inducing music has, as we have seen, been Feldman's purpose, with his long-held, almost inaudible sounds, shifting almost imperceptibly in timbre and tone. Stockhausen's first product after his visit to the East (*Telemusik*) may have been purely documentary. But *Stimmung*—his real admission of oriental influences—is the extreme of contemplative, static passivity. Six singers sit cross-legged around a bowl of light, six electronic tones emerge from concealed speakers, the singers take up these same sounds, which remain unchanged and immobile for an hour and a quarter:

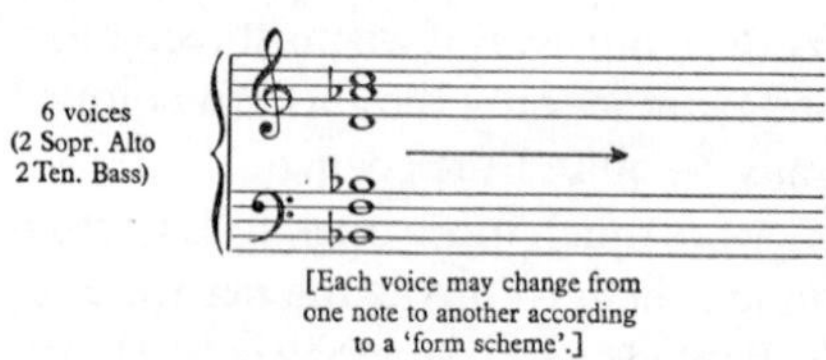

[Each voice may change from one note to another according to a 'form scheme'.]

There are 'magic names' and poems which singers take up in turn, according to a complex system of chance; after a lead from one voice, the others gradually follow and merge together until a new lead is given. Words are sometimes repeated insistently, faster and faster; vowels are taken up and reiterated, their harmonic contents exaggerated so as to create colour contrasts; consonants are formed into semi-percussive utterings; almost imperceptibly, the balance of the chord is changed, so that first one note is dominant and then another. This is very slender material for seventy-five minutes if the audience is listening in a Western way, expecting change, forward movement, and development, but if one listens passively, allowing the trance-like experience to flow warmly through to the nerve-ends, inducing a yoga-state of peaceful non-perception, one has for a while won that liberation from earthly ties which Eastern philosophies cherish.

In some ways, oriental influences have spread over a much wider area than is at first apparent. For example, the extreme harmonic simplicity of Terry Riley's *In C*, the perpetual ostinatos and tonal immobility of his *A Rainbow in Curved Air*, the raga-type melodies, all these surely have Eastern origins? The String Quartet by Tomas Marco, in which there is only one note—middle C—played in a thousand ways: is this European or Oriental? The dispassionate immobility of Feldman's music—is this not a child of Eastern thought?

This Eastern immobility is one of the most peaceful things that has happened in Western music. The restless inquietude of European avant-garde music has never been able to give the world those moments of peace which are its greatest current need (hence, perhaps, the listener's flight back towards the renaissance and baroque), so it is to be augured that the more pacific aspects of oriental religion and philosophy will continue to penetrate our music. Unfortunately, as imitators of Feldman have discovered, static music has not an infinite market. And now that Stockhausen has written *Stimmung*, such a tour de force has eliminated any possibility of imitation.

So far, we have only looked at Western composers' appropriations of Eastern music and philosophy. But there is another side to the coin. European music has long penetrated Japan (once a big importer of Western musicians) and other Eastern countries, so that oriental musicians have eventually begun to compose in the European manner. As we can well see with Japanese and Chinese copies of our own instruments, the orientals are extremely quick at assimilating techniques and reproducing our own originals, often with vast improvements (whether in music and art, or the material junk of our lives, such as transistors or motor cars). So it is not surprising that some Eastern figures have become prominent in post-war music: the two Matsudairas, the 'Cageian' Toshi Ichiyanagi, Toshiro Mayuzumi, Fukushima, Toru Takemitsu—all Japanese; the Korean Isang Yun, and the Chinese Chou Wen Chung, whose objective is a fusion of oriental and occidental idioms. All these write in what one may call a contemporary style, and show how the cross-fertilization of East and West is creating a truly international musical language.

Perhaps Cage was right in looking East. If we can ignore the more superficial and precious *chinoiserie* which has been thrown up, we must welcome that clarification which contact with the Orient has wrought in Western music. After all, the complexity of Stockhausen's *Gruppen* for three orchestras was in danger of leading towards works as hysterically verbose as Schoenberg's *Moses und Aaron*. To compare it to the slender grace of Balinese music is like comparing the evocative simplicity of a Chinese poem with the weighty obscurity of *Finnegans Wake*.

A final comment: it is all very well to talk about fusion of the East and West, the creation of an international musical language, and so on, but if this implies a subsequent disintegration of native music cultures, the prospect is bleak. The levelling out of all cultures to a common mean would surely be an artistic impoverishment. A sameness the world over would be even more stultifying than a classless society which levels out all social differences. Fortunately, however, ethnic music cultures have a vitality which may not easily be suppressed.

Jazz[1] and pop have one characteristic which makes them almost incompatible with avant-garde music—they are based on a powerful 'beat', which is just

[1] Today, the word jazz seems to be acquiring a limited meaning, almost as an antonym to pop, signifying a complex, improvised beat music. I use the term in its wider sense as rhythmic music of U.S. Negro origin, developing through ragtime, dixie, and New Orleans styles to swing, hot jazz, progressive, cool, etc.

what avant-garde composers want to avoid. At the same time they both have simple melodic lines and conventional harmonies, which again are anathema to the radicals. So the influence of jazz and pop has been minimal. Nevertheless, there have been repeated efforts to bridge the gap between jazz and 'classical', sometimes in what may be called parody, sometimes in earnest. Indeed, before the Second World War composers of considerable stature had lively, if brief, flirtations with jazz (notably Stravinsky's *Ragtime* and *Histoire du Soldat*, Milhaud's *La Création du Monde*, Křenek's *Jonny spielt auf*, Gershwin's *Rhapsody*, Copland's *Billy the Kid*, Hindemith's *Kammermusik No. 1*, Lambert's *Rio Grande*, and Weill's *Mahagonny* and *Dreigroschenoper*—all pieces which have stood the test of time). In the Fifties, 'progressive' jazz was introduced as an art-form associated with the concert hall. The 'big band' of Stan Kenton became 'classical' or the Dave Brubeck Quartet joined up with the New York Philharmonic Symphony. Conversely 'serious' composers such as Seiber associated with Johnny Dankworth to join jazz band and symphony orchestra together; Rolf Liebermann, Berio, and Maderna wrote jazz works for symphony orchestra. Richard Rodney Bennett has written highly competent jazz scores (including the ballet *Jazz Calendar*), while Berio's *Allez Hop* is a kind of semi-opera based on popular song, blues, etc., with scoring of the 'big band' type. Perhaps some of these works were written to appeal to popular taste, but their success has not been spectacular. The real truth is that the sounds of the jazz band and symphony orchestra don't mix well, nor do jazz idioms and symphonic styles. While the one is Dionysian, of the earth, the other is Apollonian, of the spirit, and our individual sensibilities are attracted to one or the other, but never to both, at any particular time.

Much happier results came from a different kind of jazz in the Fifties, which, in contrast with the nervous, forceful be-bop of the Forties, aimed at restraint, clarity, and intellectual appeal. Different brands were called 'cool', 'west coast', or 'third stream', but in essence they all shared the characteristics of almost baroque repose, tight contrapuntal constructions or thin textures supporting meagre, aloof melodic lines. Gunther Schuller, an American avant-garde composer of some distinction, wrote a fair corpus of 'third stream' music which reveals how jazz can reach a high art form in the hands of a trained musician, and can even be compatible with a twelve-note idiom.

At the same time, one must recognize that jazz improvisers with no real musical training such as Charlie Parker[1] and even the distant Django Rheinhardt and Coleman Hawkins laid the foundations for that nervous, concen-

[1] Parker begged Varèse to give him lessons in 'structure', but died before this could be arranged.

trated, almost erratic kind of improvisation which is the basis of much avant-garde performance. For decades, the only tradition of improvisation had been in jazz (indeed, in the previous century it had become almost a lost art except in the organ loft), and without that tradition it is hard to conceive how performers could have faced the challenge of the virtually blank page. More recently, this improvisatory situation has had a new kind of feedback. Modern jazz has become completely divorced from its origins, the style of some specialist groups becoming more and more rarefied. The basic elements—melody, harmony, beat—have been thinned off until they exist no more. There is no sign of basic harmony, there is no rhythmic pulse. The only constructive element is an 'idea', which is briefly mentioned here and there. In truth this is group improvisation of a kind which is almost indistinguishable from 'classical' avant-garde improvisation, except that the former features the jazz structure of solo instrumental 'choruses' and is probably consistently louder and more frenetic, and lasts longer. Indeed sometimes the same players play both kinds of music. This shows how the improvisatory muse has gone full circle.

To complete the picture of how jazz and classical are drawn together (though here it is jazz that does all the borrowing) we can briefly mention the parasitic filching of Mozart, Tchaikovsky, etc. by pop groups, the re-rediscovery of Bach through the Swingle Singers, and the switched-on Bach, Scarlatti, and Monteverdi by the Carlos & Co. synthesizers. Electronic music is of course commonly used to make pop—even the village record shop makes a good turnover of records of synthesized jazz. Thus that 'diabolus in musica'—electronics—has become a highly successful tool for commercial exploitation, and why not?

The search outwards for an expansion of the avant-garde idiom has occasionally been turned towards the past. But as one of the cardinal principles of the post-Webern school has been to wipe out what has gone before, and begin a completely new language, any association with the past has usually been carefully avoided. And quite rightly. For the quotation, amid sounds in an advanced idiom, of anything classical or romantic (such as a Beethoven theme or an excerpt from Verdi) would be like a sock in the eye. Certain things just are not compatible!

However, looking further back, medieval and even pre-medieval music seems to offer possibilities. It is so pure, untainted with the more obviously emotive elements of later music, that it can fit alongside or within an advanced modern idiom without being incongruous. We must not forget that it was the use of early renaissance proportionalisms and structures which Webern passed on as a heritage to the post-war generation, and it was these proportionalisms which some used in their particular brand of integral serialism. Some of the post-Webernites, too, must have researched into early renaissance music, but in those years there seems to have been only one attempt to unify old music with the new language—Bruno Maderna's *Musica per Orchestra No. 2.* (Maderna had a great enthusiasm for medieval and early renaissance music and he used to exchange puzzle canons with Nono as a pastime, rather like an interchange of chess problems.) Maderna's *Musica* is based on a logical growth process which is very successful: a plaintive gregorian-type monody is introduced, which expands into harmony through organum; counterpoints based on proportionalisms begin to break up the texture, and these move into the serial sphere until a pointillist idiom is arrived at. The composition then goes into reverse, the musical texture gradually returns to the clarity of the beginning, and the piece moves back to the original canto fermo.

This excursion into archaism does not seem to have been followed up on the Continent (where the accent has been so much on 'looking forward'), but in a more retrogressive musical nation such as England, where in any case there is a great reverence for early music, the recuperation of elements from the distant past has come quite naturally. Peter Maxwell Davies showed an early interest in the use of medieval and renaissance structural techniques in his *Prolation for Orchestra* (1958), though the music reveals no really obvious audible relations with the past. (He gives as his main source of information Morley's *Plaine and Easie Introduction to Practicall Musick.*) Similarly, in works such as *Alma Redemptoris Mater* (1957) and *Ricercar and Doubles* on the medieval carol 'To Many a Well' (1959) it is hard to pick out the elements derived from old music. The general musical texture is in fact rather Webernian, either in a pointillist manner, or (as one would expect) based on rhythmic proportionalisms, with the usual diminutions, augmentations, retrogrades, etc. In later works, however, there is a much bolder confrontation of the old music with the new. For instance, in *Seven In Nomine* (1964), pieces by Taverner, Bull, and Blytheman are quoted in relatively undisguised fashion, interspersed by variants in modern idiom. The problem, of course, is that simply to oppose the old and the new would be crude and painful. But to integrate them into an expressive unity is by no means an easy operation. Perhaps one of Maxwell Davies's most successful blends of the old and new is in *Antechrist* (1967), where the archaic theme *Deo Confitemine* (see 'a' below) runs right through the music, sometimes in old-fashioned clothes (doubled at the fourth below in quasi-organum, or written in double canon by contrary motion, etc.), sometimes integrated into a complex rhythmic structure which ignores tonal centres (as at 'b'):

It would seem that in such a score, and his later *Hymn to St. Magnus* (1972), Maxwell Davies has worked the more obvious Webernisms out of his system, and harked back to a more flowing contrapuntal idiom which, apart from its non-tonalism and metrical conflicts, is a direct descendant of early renaissance times.

While Maxwell Davies has worked consistently at a music whose idiom spans many centuries, others have made more sporadic attempts to gather the distant past within a modern idiom, notably Roger Smalley (using Blytheman's *Gloria Tibi Trinitas* in a large group of works including *Missa Brevis*, *Missa Parodia I* and *II*, and *Gloria Tibi Trinitas I* and *II*), John Tavener, and the American Charles Wuorinen. There is no doubt that this is a fairly fertile field, the first fruits of which have barely been seen, but it is also a dangerous one, for the successful fusion of such contrasting idioms calls for great artistic discrimination.

Later music (classical, baroque, romantic, etc.) has not yet been successfully integrated within a contemporary idiom, but more recently there has been a strong movement towards pastiche and the use of parody. Berio's *Sinfonia* for orchestra, singers, speakers, etc., can be likened to a newspaper, with its serious pages, the sports section, foreign news, fashions, the arts, etc.; or to standing on a street corner and hearing radios that play symphony and jazz, Swingle Singers and opera, which is blotted out now and then by people who pass by, speaking in different languages. Berio uses sizeable sections of Mahler's Second Symphony, and makes references to Bach, Schoenberg, Debussy, Ravel, Strauss, Boulez, Pousseur, and others. Readings include passages from Beckett's *The Unnamable* and James Joyce, as well as odds and ends in different languages. Altogether, this mélange is extremely attractive and of course superbly conceived. If it is meant to divert, it certainly succeeds. Yet one has the uneasy feeling that in the *Sinfonia* Berio's musical idiom, usually so constant and incorruptible, has for once failed him, and he has fallen back on pastiche as a commercial surrogate. However, he says 'I consider this *Sinfonia* also an exercise on "relativity" of perception of music history', which statement, if it can be clarified, perhaps explains the issue.

Peter Maxwell Davies's use of parody in '*Missa super L'Homme Armé*' has a much more censorious intent. The interruption of the Mass with foreign elements (the foxtrot, a speeded up gramophone record, honky-tonk ostinatos, etc.) is intended as critical comment, depicting the mass as having become degenerate through what he calls 'the corruption of the Mass from the inside'. Though such a concept may be questionable, there is no denying the force with which Maxwell Davies makes his point. As one can imagine, the juxtaposition of old music with garish trivia of more recent contrivance is harsh, even brutal, but of course this is what the parody is intended to be.

Some younger composers, like their contemporaries who wear Victorian clothes (or accept what we once regarded as overblown, degenerate art as quite normal), show an unexpected liking for nineteenth-century trivia. John Tavener, a truly masterly composer who delights in smarmy Victorian hymns, has featured the luscious 'Lead kindly light' in his cantata *The Whale*, with admittedly powerful effect. In other cases those who integrate popular music and 'our beloved classics' into an avant-garde texture may be merely indulging in parody. Perhaps there is an ironic twist to Stockhausen's use of national anthems in *Hymnen*. In some cases one wonders whether the use of large blocks of old music is either just laziness or the inability to create original material. We know that in the past composers borrowed freely from each other. But surely today, if a composer writes a piece of theatre which contains no other music than Brahms, he is not a creative musician at all.[1] The only musicianship required is in the choice of musical material.

One sometimes wonders whether the 'search outwards', in the case of composers with lesser gifts, is not some form of exhibitionism. On a Saturday afternoon in Chelsea, one can see people dressed in every manner, in military uniforms, Victorian gowns, Indian robes, completely naked except for a newspaper, in cowboy outfits, and so on. What is it all for? Is it merely the need of individuals to assert themselves, to be different, to escape the sameness of a monotonous people and a monotonous existence? Perhaps indeed some composers are not composers at all, except in an effort to be different (though being

[1] I have in fact heard pieces based on Brahms and Wagner.

different and being highly individual are not the same thing). Hence perhaps some of the need for pastiche and parody—easy ways of filling the creative void, easy ways of turning an ironic, critical glance at our society.

To end this chapter on the search outwards, mention must be made of a curious phenomenon which may have portents for the future—what could be called a 'search inwards' by composing back towards basic material. Through a form of 'retro-composition' or 'de-composition', a piece of music is made to disintegrate gradually into its basic elements—the exact reverse of normal compositional processes. Were it not for the stature of the composer who is leading this school—Franco Donatoni—one could ignore such extraordinary concepts, but as his 'de-composed' works (those written since 1965) have been played internationally, his ideals must be considered. Donatoni's principles are complex and cannot be compressed into a few words. His own extensive theories (cf. his book *Questo*),[1] written in a singularly competent but impenetrable language, make tough reading. To put things in a rather simple way, it would seem that Donatoni regards basic sound material as having an identity of its own, an identity which for centuries has been smothered by the ego of the 'composer-creator'. For him, only a truly impartial artisan can take this sound material and work with it without imposing his own self, allowing it to crystallize of its own accord into pure music, uncontaminated, pristine, and ageless. His method of working is usually to take a fragment of music (by any composer) and work with it as 'material', gradually liberating the sounds until they are freed from the original straitjacket, and speak for themselves. For instance, in *Etwas ruhiger im Ausdruck* (1967) for flute, clarinet, violin, cello, and piano, the piece begins with part of the eighth bar of the second of Schoenberg's *Five Piano Pieces*, Op. 23:

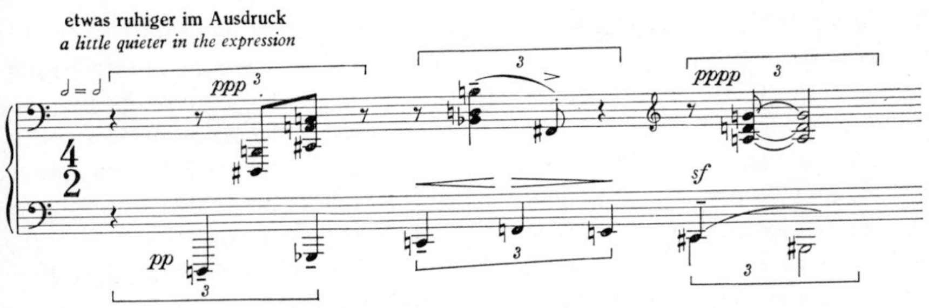

This material is subjected to Donatoni's 'artisanship'—a tour de force of technical contrivances such as the transposition, inversion, and retrograde of note

[1] Adelphi (Milan, 1970).

patterns, the formation of chords from note-successions and note-successions from chords, the diminution and augmentation of note durations, 'accumulations and condensations', 'dispersions and rarefactions', and so on. All this sounds rather like the machinations of serialism, but of course no conventional series are used. In actual practice the music gradually loses its rhythmic physiognomy, and becomes ironed out into evenly flowing note patterns which have no particularly distinctive shape:

The last episode, in the composer's words, is 'an attempt, without success, at reconstructing the original material with the precise scope of re-integrating Schoenberg's text. The end must be regarded as an arbitrary interruption of an experiment which failed.'[1] There is a curious excess of rigour in Donatoni's attitude. Just as one may note that the only dynamics he permits throughout *Etwas ruhiger* are limited to the *pp–pppp* zone of Schoenberg's own example, so also we can see how every technical gambit is worked to its utmost conclusion, while no individual 'touch' is tolerated. No wonder, with such absolutism, that it was impossible to return to Schoenberg's original text!

Though one must concede that Donatoni's 'retro-composed' works have brilliant qualities, particularly in texture and austere, monastic tone, it is diffi-

[1] op. cit.

cult to see how one work can differ widely from another. Differentiation depends precisely on sculpturing sound material into decisive shapes. This means imposing one's will on sound material (which in itself has no will of its own). But this is precisely what Donatoni denies. Perhaps indeed, Donatoni may deny that it is necessary for one work to be recognizably different from another; in fact he would probably agree that the liberation of all sound material, and the elimination of self, can only arrive at a uniform language. Finally we must observe a curious concordance as well as an opposition between Donatoni's work and indeterminacy. While the one is absolutely precise in every detail and the other more or less indeterminate, in both cases the composer is at the mercy of the sound material, for it is the quality of the basic material which determines the ultimate result.

To sum up, the search outwards has both positive and negative aspects. It may have been instigated by a feeling that the classic free twelve-note idiom of avant-gardism is too communal, that real self-expression or individuality can only be achieved through grafting on something more distinctive. This need for bizarrisms may indeed only be a form of shallow exhibitionism without deep artistic purpose. But viewed as a whole, the search outwards has inspired a rich variety of music over an extended period, making an impression of rapid and continuous 'developments'.

In reality, however, the situation has been much more static than at first seems apparent. The basic language—free twelve-note music—has remained the same. The departures from it have been many, but they hardly constitute real progress or development towards a new authentic language. They are really excursions which have given novelty and interest to a period which otherwise could have been rather dull. After all, how infinitely boring would it have been if we all (including Stockhausen) had kept on writing more and more *Gruppen* for more and more orchestras! In actual fact we have lived through years which have been as exciting as any others in musical history, even though many of the changes and developments have been more apparent than real.

14

Theatre

As the exponents of 'theatre' or 'theatrical-performance music' rightly point out, the visual dimension of music is no new phenomenon. Since the early civilizations, music has been a part of ritual; in religious celebrations and pageantry, music, action, and audience reaction have been closely bound together. It is therefore logical to extend modern music through visual interest, and to try to evoke audience response of a more direct nature. The old concept of concerts performed in comparatively stiff immobility, with a completely passive audience, is regarded as obsolete. As we have already observed with John Cage, music can be action—the performer's movements and gestures can be an extension of his instrument, an enlargement of its personality. If at some point performers speak, there need be no surprise if we take this as an integral part of the sound patterns (note the speech sections we have already cited in Kagel's *Sonant 1960/ . . . .*) (p. 98).

'Theatre' has a longer history in the U.S.A. than in Europe, and has become much more widespread. European tradition still clings to conventional 'concert' presentations and continues to aim at music of high aesthetic quality, whereas in the United States a fair proportion of young composers recognize that if they write a symphony, opera, or oratorio it can never be played (there are no radio promotions, and concert societies are generally conservative). They prefer to write (in fact they can only write) for the University campus, and for limited performing means. Their work, having little future, is more ephemeral than that of their European counterparts,[1] and it is only natural that ephemeral musical quality should be given more artistic substance through the quality of theatre. The Universities of Michigan, Illinois, and California are particularly encouraging towards theatre (whereas Columbia and Princeton, with their middle-generation reputation for integral serialism, are much less so),

[1] The European cult of the 'first performance', however, hardly encourages music of lasting quality. Composers know that second performances are so little in demand that they will probably never take place.

in fact the ONCE group festivals in Ann Arbor, Michigan specialize in giving opportunities to any composer's theatre, with no limitations. It is an open forum, where anything can be tried once. The ONCE creed can be summed up as follows:

> ... the dynamics of recent musical evolution have led creative artists to consciously explore those performance elements which extend beyond the realm of 'pure music' and sound. These performance elements can be included in the category of 'theater,' and include *dance* (physical activity, human gesture, and movement of all sorts), *staging* (lighting, the juxtaposition and manipulation of stage properties), *natural sounds* (the artistic integration of stage-activity sounds and speech), and the *spatial disposition* of performance (the means of involvement and confrontation of the audience-spectator with the performance activities).

Theatre scores can comprise conventional notation, coupled with instructions for movement, etc., but more generally they comprise instructions for gestures, speech, movement, and free sounds. There may be no score in notation. Essential aspects of performances are lighting effects and the inclusion of films, slides, sounds on tape, etc. In fact, the objective is to produce a mixed-media influence on the senses in general. If words are used (some theatre is entirely wordless) these may be abstract, meaningless, or occasionally of a protest or semi-political nature. However, theatre does not seek to get too involved with real life, so that if there is any meaning at all, it is commentary rather than propaganda. Certainly it is never militant.

Indeterminacy is often a cardinal factor in Cage's theatre; the elements (music and movement) are given, but their ordering (or omission) is not determined but must be planned by certain rules within a given time-span. For instance, his *Theatre Piece* (1960) may be performed by from one to eight performers ('musicians, dancers, singers, et al. To be used in whole or part, in any combination'). Actions are to be made within certain time periods, the actions being chosen from a range of twenty nouns or verbs by the performer. Their significance changes at certain points so that each part can comprise up to a hundred different actions. The composing means are the materials of *Fontana Mix* (a tape montage). Needless to say, the result is a display of unassociated actions and situations, an assault on the senses of incoherent and inconsequential material which must be observed impartially and dispassionately in the way we have learned to listen to Cage's music as 'just an attention to the activity of sounds'. Intense listening could only lead to exasperation.

The question of audience participation has never been successfully resolved. Concert audiences are particularly passive. They may laugh occasionally at Cage's bird calls,[1] but the direct participation that Cage and the exponents of

[1] As in *Water Music*.

theatre hoped for has never come. Some theatre deliberately seeks to provoke audience participation: the performers move around the audience and into it. Sometimes there is even a 'performing' audience placed within the real one. But the real response has been negligible. Perhaps indeed active audience participation is not wanted. The first performance of Nono's *Intolleranza 1960* was interrupted by a political fracas, with fisticuffs in the stalls and stinkbombs in the orchestra. This is hardly what theatre means by audience participation.

In Europe, though composers have felt the need to accentuate the visual aspects of performance since the late Fifties, theatre in the American style has got off to a poor start. True, there has been a certain amount of Cage-inspired lighthearted play, performers crawling inside and underneath grand pianos at the Palermo Festival, bursting balloons, setting music on fire, etc., but audiences have not been co-operative. The ensuing scandals have discouraged concert promoters from repeating the experiments. (One notes the rapid demise of the Palermo Festival, a regionally financed project which was hardly the right shop-window for avant-garde activity, particularly theatre of the horseplay variety.) Even Stockhausen's adventure in buffoonery—*Originale* (1961)—has remained an unloved essay.

Theatre in Europe tends to be musically more highly developed than its American counterpart; in fact the theatre element may be minimal. In Berio's *Circles* it only involves the singer moving to various positions (to complete the 'circle') and playing on wood chimes. (The surprise that such minimal movement evoked in 1960 shows how differently European and American audiences react.) In Kagel's *Match* the theatre element is only evident in a very roundabout way—indeed the music is so complete in itself that some people may never notice the subtlety of Kagel's joke. His programme note is a serious account of how, like Tartini, he dreamed an identical dream on three consecutive nights. Each dream was a complete performance of the same piece of music for two cellos and percussion. After the third dream Kagel wrote out the music exactly as he had dreamt it. In the performance (which needs virtuosity of a high order) the two cellos seem to be playing a duet with percussion accompaniment, but one gradually becomes aware that in reality they are trying to better each other's efforts, while the percussionist acts as a referee, interrupting now and then with a musical comment. In the end, he breaks up the competition with a flexatone solo, and shakes hands with the cello he declares the winner. Of course this is all a legpull, but done with great musicality and refined wit.

Kagel, whom one can regard as Europe's leader in theatre, attempted one work which is more on the American pattern—*Sur Scène* (1959/60). This fairly extended work, called 'chamber music theatre in one act', is for speaker, mime, recorded tape, singer, and three instrumentalists. The performers appear, and practise spasmodically. The mime enters and performs inconsequent actions. At last a speaker appears and hesitantly begins a lecture about contemporary music. As he rambles on, the singer enters, and gradually interrupts, the instrumentalists' musical comments become louder, taped sounds increase, the babble grows greater, and the lecture becomes incomprehensible. A musical interlude calms the situation, then the lecture begins again, and so on. On page 150 is a sample of a more comprehensible part of the lecture.

Sur Scène has never been a spectacular success, and not many attempts have been made in Europe to surpass it. In 1968, Stockhausen made a further essay in this medium which was relatively unsuccessful for such a successful composer. This 'Theater Piece' called *High and Low*, which is the centre point of *Aus den sieben Tagen*, is perhaps more in the American style, but whether this is so or not its subsequent obscurity is significant. Surely this means that for Europe works on this pattern have little permanent place, even if written by a composer of renown.

In order to appreciate the real nature of this kind of theatre, it is worth quoting the entire piece, which though lasting 'at least forty minutes', only occupies one page of the score:see page 151. The theme is obviously a contrast between degeneracy and nobility, or 'beauty and the beast', but the reader must decide for himself how forty minutes can be made absorbing with the ideas given. The music to be played should presumably resemble Stockhausen's *Kurzwellen*, though this is not specifically stated.

In Europe theatre is usually allied to music of good quality, and has perhaps moved towards two main concepts, one where lighting effects are coupled with music (as in Stockhausen's *Trans* of 1970, again a 'dream' product) or one which is virtually semi-opera with well defined subject matter. For instance, Nono's *Intolleranza 1960* uses film, slides, recorded sounds, and stage action ingeniously representing situations (social, political) by lighting effects and minimum action. Such works as *La Fabbrica Illuminata*, for recorded tape and solo voice, are political propaganda, which can only be successfully put across if lighting effects and film are used. Maxwell Davies's *Eight Songs for a Mad King* has each instrumentalist in a cage, representing both visibly and in music the birds of the mad King (baritone) who has the rest of the stage to himself. Sylvano Bussotti's *Passion selon Sade* (1966) is an excellently conceived amalgam which, in spite of a certain decadent quality of dadaism, turns chamber music into semi-opera. An organist in a blood-red robe plays massive clusters. The stage becomes dark. Occasional spots pick out instrumental soloists, the singer enters in costume, sings, lies on a couch. Darkness. Chains are dragged

Kagel: *Sur Scène*

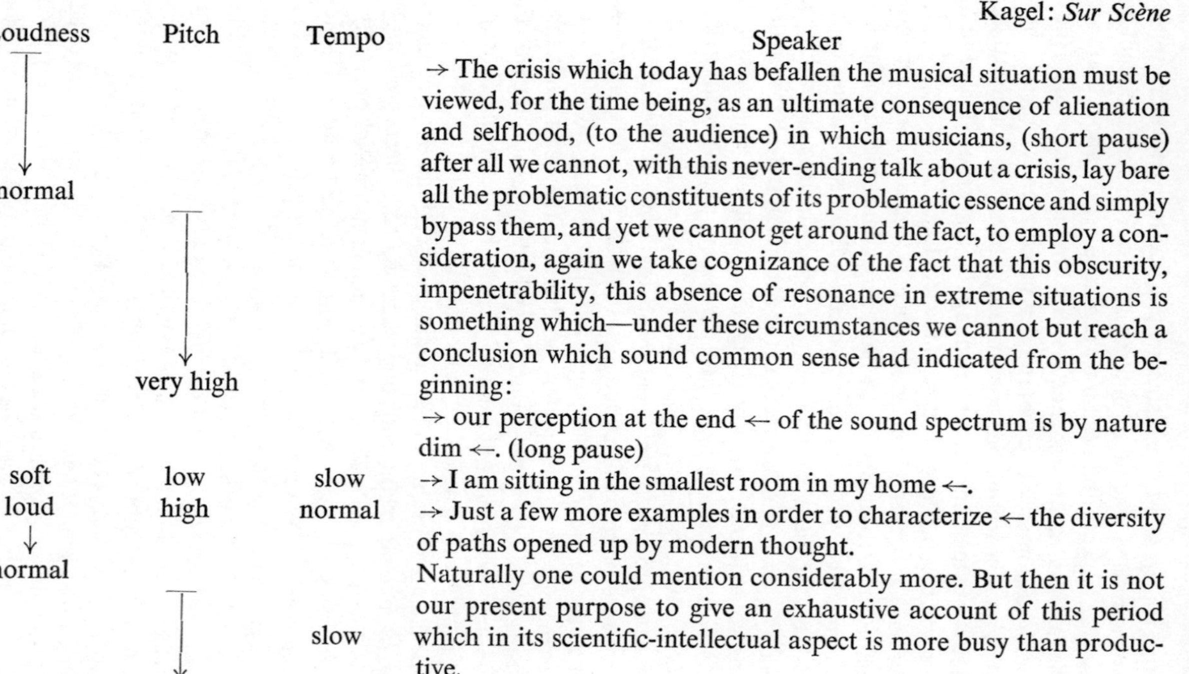

Loudness	Pitch	Tempo	Speaker
↓			→ The crisis which today has befallen the musical situation must be viewed, for the time being, as an ultimate consequence of alienation and selfhood, (to the audience) in which musicians, (short pause)
normal	↓		after all we cannot, with this never-ending talk about a crisis, lay bare all the problematic constituents of its problematic essence and simply bypass them, and yet we cannot get around the fact, to employ a consideration, again we take cognizance of the fact that this obscurity, impenetrability, this absence of resonance in extreme situations is something which—under these circumstances we cannot but reach a conclusion which sound common sense had indicated from the be-
	very high		ginning:
			→ our perception at the end ← of the sound spectrum is by nature dim ←. (long pause)
soft	low	slow	→ I am sitting in the smallest room in my home ←.
loud ↓	high	normal	→ Just a few more examples in order to characterize ← the diversity of paths opened up by modern thought.
normal	↓	slow	Naturally one could mention considerably more. But then it is not our present purpose to give an exhaustive account of this period which in its scientific-intellectual aspect is more busy than productive.

theater piece

HIGH AND LOW

MAN left	CHILD center	WOMAN right
on the floor shabbily dressed degenerate, an animal	sits on a chair	stands at a lectern beautifully dressed noble, angelic
sounds, words, sentences movements, gestures of the most disgusting gruesome, depraved kind	all three look at the audience they speak independently with pauses of varying lengths all at once, alternating	sounds, words, sentences few movements, gestures of the most refined, exalted and devout nature
curses, protests against EVERYTHING!	in each performance a different order —to some extent a renewal— or words and gestures	consolation, devotion in EVERYTHING
the MAN mixes his words with those of the WOMAN "shit—God"		the WOMAN also has words of the MAN in her vocabulary but she may choose whether or not to say them

The CHILD repeats words that it hears.

This lasts very long (at least 40 minutes). Then the MAN goes to the WOMAN and dances with her for a couple of minutes (waltz? in any case, they embrace), meanwhile they continue to call out their words: mixed, alternating, together, in the rhythm of the dance, with long pauses, during which only the shuffling of their shoes is heard.

From the beginning, two noisy, richly-noisy instruments (for example viola with contact microphone and filter and tamtam with microphone and filter) play along with the man; they suggest to him things ugly and disgusting in nature and expression, or comment, support, ape, complement what he says and does (also when he says words or makes gestures belonging to the woman). Two instruments with clear pitches (for example piano and electronium) play along with the WOMAN, correspondingly pure and beautiful.

MAN and WOMAN react to their instrumentalists, freely adding words and gestures (of a similar nature) that occur to them or are suggested to them.

The musicians prepare themselves for each rehearsal and performance by playing KURZWELLEN, while the MAN and WOMAN listen.

A different CHILD should be used for each presentation.

may 9, 1968

across the stage. Spots reveal the singer and conductor embracing, general musical dénouement. This seems slender material, but the music is striking, the general effect superb. This seems to be the best category of European theatre—chamber music expanded through association with a subject or ideal, where lighting effects and movement make for suggestion rather than action, and where musical substance is maintained at a high level.

To sum up, European theatre tends towards a continuation of European tradition (musical substance, relevant meaning). American theatre, on the other hand, is a forum wide open to experimentalism, creating its own traditions and conventions. Musical quality is not necessarily relevant: theatre can be merely a 'happening' blessed with spontaneity and nothing else. The concept of the extra musical dimension (music as vision, as well as sound) is in itself an excellent one. As we have already seen, it has existed through the ages. Yet we must have no illusions. If music is allowed to expand too much in its 'visual dimension', while its substance in sound falls into superficiality, its quality may be highly questionable.

We must not take Cage too literally. His writings regarding theatre are so persuasive that we are induced to agree that almost anything is valid. But is it? Just how valid will 'theatre' be in the future, unless it has substance?

15

Colour—New Instrumental Usages

While previous developments in instrumental usages were comparatively slow, in this century they have surged ahead at an accelerating pace. This increasingly frenetic search for novel instrumental possibilities has been due primarily to a need for colour contrasts, and for the creation of that brittle, almost metallic kind of sound which is so representative of our age and has come to dominate our music. Contrasts in timbre have long contributed to the beauty of music, especially in the Romantic period, but as modern composers have gradually discarded the more conventional elements of music—melody, harmony, metre, etc.—tone colours have become one of the main weapons in the composer's armoury.[1] In 1908 Schoenberg may have introduced *Klangfarbenmelodie* ('melody of tone colours') in his *Five Pieces for Orchestra* as a novelty, but by now for some composers it is the most vital compositional factor. Indeed, today's music is made of such shifting and changing sounds, transmuted in such subtle ways, that the old, more mechanically contrived *Klangfarbenmelodie* can be forgotten except as an historical point of reference.

Colour contrasts in modern music up to the Post-Webern period are generally used in three ways. (1) In the pointillist style, one instrument plays no more than a very few notes (often one only) at a time, the sounds passing successively to instruments of contrasting timbre. (2) Broad areas of a composition may be given over to contrasting tone colours (for example, in *Chronochromie* Messiaen allots entire sections in turn to tuned percussion, strings alone, the woodwind group, etc.). (3) Timbre contrasts may be obtained by exploiting the various

[1] Colour research is by no means a recent phenomenon. The following is from a letter written by Tchaikovsky in 1880: 'It seems to me that our period differs from earlier ones in this one characteristic: that contemporary composers are engaged in the pursuit of charming and piquant effects, unlike Mozart, Beethoven, Schubert, and Schumann. What is the so-called New Russian School but the cult of varied and pungent harmonies, of original orchestral combinations and every kind of purely external effect? *Musical ideas give place to this or that union of sounds. Formerly there was composition, creation; now . . . only research and contrivance.*'

tonal possibilities of single instruments (for instance, in his string music Webern calls for rapid successions of contrasting sounds—bowing, pizzicato, tremolo, harmonics, flautato, etc.—giving a kaleidoscopic effect of fluctuating timbres). This last usage—the exploitation of individual instrumental effects—has brought about an increased use of solo instruments and mixed ensembles, while conversely the preference for 'solo' sounds has created a demand for an ever wider gamut of solo instrumental effects.

In more recent years, however, the rather contrived pointillist and Webernian-type colour contrasts have fallen out of use in favour of more refined timbre mutations. This is a direct result of electronic music influences. Any composer who has worked in an electronic music studio knows that immensely varied sounds are at his fingertips, but the secret of success lies in limiting the sound-colour palette to a few associated colours only. One must work within these limits, avoiding the temptation to introduce other sound-types. (There is an analogy here with painting. Too much colour contrast makes for blatancy. Good art is often made by the blending in infinite shades of very few colours.) Music for orchestra or ensembles too now involves the 'blending' process, where few colours are chosen, but given extensive variation, even distortion (including electronic filtering and ring-modulation). For instance, the strings in Penderecki's *Threnody to the Victims of Hiroshima*, the brass in Roger Smalley's *Pulses*, the single tam-tam of Stockhausen's extensive *Mikrophonie I*, and the six singers of his very lengthy *Stimmung*—all these are single colours only. But through changing and blending of the shades, the composers have discovered enough colour-mutation to sustain interest over considerable time periods (especially in the last three works). At the same time—and this is important—music based on uniform colour has a monolithic strength often absent from pointillist-*klangfarben* compositions. The accent now, therefore, is on discovering and exploiting the timbre-contrast potentials of each instrumental group, and thus inevitably of each single instrument.

In the last two decades, while the structure of instruments has generally remained unchanged, some have revealed rich, formerly latent possibilities, others have not to any great extent. But before dealing with each instrumental group, it would be best (to avoid repetition) to mention certain effects which are common to most instrumental groups. For instance, most instruments now produce rapidly reiterated sounds: woodwind and brass fluttertongue, string tremolos, percussion tremolos and rolls. As composers become ever more conscious of the need to 'mould' and transform sounds, strings, woodwind, and brass are expected to produce various kinds of vibratos and undulations, as well as 'straight' tone, and to merge one into the other. Most sustained-tone instruments are expected to play in quarter-tones or to use similar micro-intervals, while the use of glissandos, muting, harmonics, and various mechanical noises and tone distortions is common to all groups.

The strings have been a somewhat disappointing source of instrumental novelty since 1945. This is because composers such as Bartók and Webern had already explored their resources so thoroughly that there has seemed little else to discover. All the main techniques had been exploited: various bowing positions (normal, near the bridge, on the fingerboard), normal pizzicato and pizzicato with the string rebounding against the fingerboard, natural and artificial harmonics, tremolo (with the left hand or with the bow), bowing with the wood of the bow ('col legno'), beating the strings with the bow, 'flautato' (a soft, pale sound obtained by light left-hand pressure) and so on. However, in their striving for contrasts composers now use certain effects such as harmonics, tremolo, glissando (both bowed and pizzicato), and 'col legno' considerably more than in any pre-war music.

Two new usages have come into prominence. One is bowing between the bridge and the tailpiece. The sounds are naturally out of tune and rather toneless, so that on a single instrument the effect is poor. But used with a mass of strings a pale, ethereal sound results, which resembles soft electronic white sound (cf. Penderecki's *Threnody*). The other new usage is the creation of mechanical noises—tapping the instruments with the bow or fingers, slapping the strings with a wire brush, and so on.

It is possible that we are on the threshold of further developments in string techniques. Garry Carr, Barry Guy, and other jazz bassists playing amplified bowed and pizzicato double bass reveal enormous advances in playing agility: rapid passages in double stoppings, polyphonic playing, the extraction from such a ponderous instrument of an infinity of light and airy harmonics contrasted with harsh, barking timbres and bitter scrapings—all these, coupled with wide varieties of pedal-controlled amplification, reveal an unexpectedly overwhelming gamut of sounds from an obviously neglected instrument. In the more 'classic' field, Bruno Bartolozzi (whose *New Sounds for Woodwind* has created revolutions in the use of woodwind) is now working on developing string sounds further, though the results have still to become common usage. These comprise fingerings (similar to artificial harmonic fingerings) which produce what he calls 'sonoric amalgams'—combinations of various sounds—and which produce novel timbres, at least thirteen types of pizzicato, a wide range of modifications to bowing techniques, etc. Again, the main accent is on timbre modifications and the discovery of new sound effects.

Woodwind instruments once seemed to have little new to offer, but they have now revealed rich new fields which are still not fully explored. Whereas previously the ideal woodwind tone was one of a uniform colour throughout the instrumental compass, it is now common for composers to exploit and seek to exaggerate the inherent contrast in tone between the various registers of each instrument. Furthermore, not only has it become obvious that each instrumental register has its own special colour, it is being discovered that there are big colour contrasts *within* each register (for instance, the lower notes of the flute and clarinet can be smoothly mellow or quite harsh—or anywhere between these limits—according to the way they are blown). Also, deliberately unorthodox timbres and attack characteristics ('transient' sounds) are being cultivated which would once have been quite unacceptable (e.g. 'breathy' tone, untongued attack, fluttertongued and sung attacks, squeaky sounds, etc.). Many of these unusual timbres and transients are produced by lip control, but recent discoveries reveal that sounds of the same pitch can be given quite different colours by the use of a multiplicity of unorthodox fingerings. Woodwind players can now therefore 'sculpture' sounds in an extraordinary way, varying the timbre, attack, and speed or depth of vibrato from moment to moment, so that their instruments have a rich variety of expression hitherto undreamt of.

Recent research has yielded yet other possibilities. It has been found that each woodwind instrument can play a considerable number of chords, comprising from two to six prominent sounds. Sometimes the component sounds have the same tone colour, sometimes they are in contrast. These chords are produced by special fingerings and lip usages, which serve also to produce unusual tones (e.g. 'broken sounds', the 'smorzato', etc.) and for playing in quarter-tones. At the moment, professional players show some difficulty in absorbing these new techniques, but there is no doubt that we are on the threshold of a new era in woodwind music. For instance the passage on page 157 from Bartolozzi's *Concertazione a Quattro*, so full of chords, quarter-tones, and unorthodox fingerings, has already been played and recorded not by wind virtuosos, but orchestral players. His recent opera *Tutto ciò che accade ti riguarda* contains many similar passages for a larger wind section.

Some performers have developed the use of microphones placed inside the sound tube of woodwind, not for amplification, but to obtain tone modifications. The sound waves within woodwind tubes have many nodes (corresponding to harmonics, formants, etc.) and a microphone placed at such a node will enhance particular sounds, while others remain subdued. This produces sound colourations which have a certain, though limited use. A further source of new colours is for the player to sing while playing. This can produce quite varied and unexpected results, according to whether the performer sings in unison with his

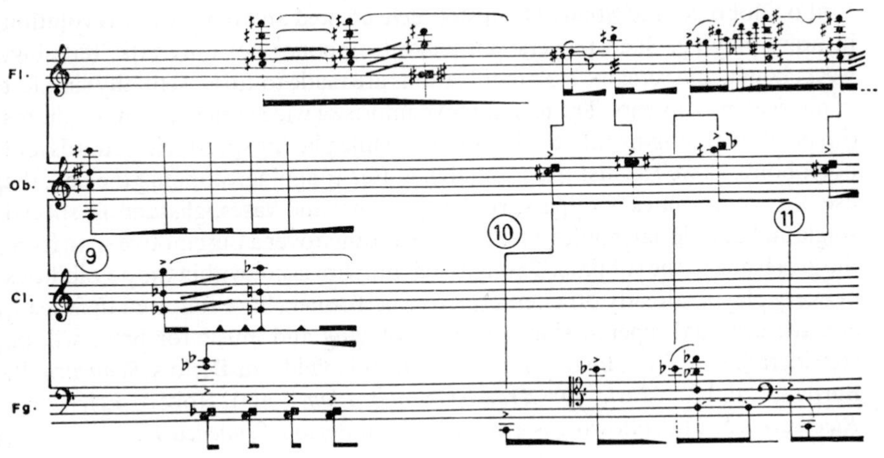

instrument, at the octave, or at some other interval. Singing can make for varied tones, ranging from a slight coarseness in the instrumental sound to very distorted timbres. Singing at the octave below, especially with the flute, produces an attractive sound which appears to be flute sound in low and high zones, with a 'hole' between, and with rough vibrations momentarily interrupting the normal tone. These effects are particularly suited to flute, clarinet, and saxophone. They are less easily accomplished on the oboe and bassoon, which can, however, produce a rough initial sound (sung), followed by normal tone (unsung).

Both woodwind and brass (including horns) have a whole range of mechanical and 'blowing' sounds (sounds made without producing normal instrumental tone) which can be used effectively, especially with electronic amplification and manipulation. Heinz Holliger's *Pneuma* for wind ensemble is a very effective example. A very substantial part of the work consists of mechanical noises (keys rattling, etc.), blowing into various holes of the instruments without producing real tone, singing into the tubes, and so on. Even when the instruments are at last played 'normally', the sounds are so modified electronically that real woodwind tone is never heard in the whole of the work. This again shows the influence of concrete music and electronic music.

The brass and horns are also entering a new period which will see enormous technical developments. While symphonic players have long been stolidly unenterprising, jazz musicians such as Armstrong, Dorsey, and James have shown not only the great agility and compass of brass, but their wide tonal and expressive characteristics. More recently, such avant-garde performers as

Vinko Globokar and Stuart Dempster have created an even greater revolution in brass playing. Such players can make trombones not only talk, but sing, weep, laugh, and scream. No modifications are made to this essentially simplest of musical instruments. The techniques comprise a wide variety of embouchures (lip positions), singing into the instrument while playing (producing chords and polyphony, as well as distorted sounds), flutter-tonguing, stopping the bell, the use of various mutes, stoppers, rubber plungers and vases, glissandos, special single and double harmonics, etc. The effects range over a big emotive span from the grotesque to the sublime. Though such bravura is not within the possibilities of every player, already other enterprising performers have followed their lead, and the eventual repercussions on brass playing and music for brass will be considerable. A few outstanding works in this field are Berio's *Sequenza V*, Barney Childs's *Music for Trombone and Piano*, and Robert Erickson's *Ricercare a 5*. The following is an extract from Berio's *Sequenza V*:

N.B. The performer uses a metal plunger mute for open (◯) and closed (+) sounds, according to the indicated pattern. Fast and continuous movement of the slide is shown by a visual pattern at the point marked 'slide', the performer producing instrumental sounds as shown above the stave without concern for the movement of the slide. There are 7 dynamic steps from 1 (as *p* as possible), as 7 (as *f* as possible). Notes with a line through them: as short as possible; others: held to the next sound.

So far, we have only considered the more conventional instruments. We now turn to that instrumental group where by far the greatest developments have taken place—the percussion. Whereas previously percussion instruments were regarded as the 'noise-makers' of the orchestra, or were introduced occasionally for some special exotic or colouristic effect, by now percussion has not only become an essential instrumental group equal in status to strings, woodwind, and brass, but frequently plays the major role in orchestral and ensemble music. Strangely, the revolutionary Viennese School hardly used percussion at all. But since the Second World War leading composers such as Messiaen, Boulez, and Stockhausen have brought this group to the fore (though we must recognize that the percussion ensemble was pioneered in the Thirties by Varèse and Cage in their more obscure days).

Percussion's leap into the limelight has been partly due to the contemporary composer's desire for novelty of effect, but there is a more cogent reason. As outlined at the beginning of this chapter, modern music relies more and more on timbre contrasts. A rich colour spectrum is one of the composer's most vital means of making music, and to him the vast variety of percussion sounds has been like manna from heaven. Whereas conventional instruments have had little new to offer, and, worse still, tend to sound 'classic' and dated, percussion instruments are a rich source of fresh, unused sounds of tremendous variety and emotive potential. So inevitably the last two decades have witnessed a revolution. The percussion group has moved from 'almost off-stage' to the footlights, and performers have done a lightning change from being the dull boys of the orchestra to playing the role of virtuosos.

Since 1945, the number of percussion instruments in use has been considerably augmented through three sources. Firstly, Messiaen's interest in Oriental music initiated the use of a variety of eastern instruments such as sets of gongs, tamtams, crotales, temple blocks, wood blocks, wood and glass chimes, Chinese cymbals, etc., while he grouped tuned percussion instruments on the Bali or Java 'gamelan orchestra' principle to form an orchestral ensemble comprising xylophone, marimba, vibraphone, and glockenspiel. (These latter instruments had been used to some extent previously, particularly by such enterprising orchestrators as the American Henry Cowell, but had never been brought together as a homogeneous sound mass on a par with strings, woodwind, etc.) Secondly, a large number of Latin-American instruments have found their way into serious music, partly through their increasing use in jazz; these comprise, besides the marimba, several types of drum (bongos, congas, and timbales) and a variety of struck and shaken instruments of indefinite pitch (claves, cabaca, chocolo, cuica, guiro, jawbone, maracas, mexican bean, reco reco, etc.). Africa has been the third source of instruments, mostly different types of drum, many of which, particularly the wooden slit drum or 'talking drum', are capable of emitting various tones.

Apart from these instruments of ethnic origin, Western musicians are inventing new instruments of their own, some with fine sound characteristics—for instance, the lujon (large metal tongues fitted in a resonating box) and boobams (two octaves of small drums fitted with long tuned resonators). The American Harry Partch writes music for an octave divided into forty-three tones, and has built special instruments with very novel tonal characteristics, including sets of enormous glass bells, large marimbas formed of planks and cubes of wood, etc. Finally, some musicians have experimented with contact microphones which give entirely new types of percussion sounds. As contact microphones do not transmit the natural, fully-resonated sounds of an instrument, but only th vibrations of a small part of its surface, the resulting amplified sounds ar limited in pitch and usually have unvarying tone colour quite unlike the rea instrumental timbre.

In sum, there has been a great expansion of six types of percussion sound— produced by metal, wood, and membrane instruments, all in tuned and untune forms. Experiments have been made with various types of glass sounds, bu these have not been generally adopted as yet. There have also been many inno vations in methods of playing instruments. Novel effects can be obtained b playing the most commonplace instrument in unusual ways. For example, whe a cymbal edge is stroked with a cello bow, strange ethereal sounds sing out, bu when it is rasped with a serrated edge such as a file or saw, there is a harsh, brittl jangle of sound. Drums may be played with the fingers, with beaters having wood, plastic, rubber, felt, or lambswool heads, with brushes, with coins, etc. These give a wide variety of tones and dynamics. In fact composers and players are experimenting so intensively that, as far as percussion is concerned, it would be quite impossible to give even a brief summary of today's current developments.

The piano has proved a rich source of new timbres, well suited to the colour palette of post-war composers. Henry Cowell noted its cluster possibilities as long ago as 1930;[1] while John Cage's early experiments with the 'prepared piano' paved the way for a wide range of unconventional usages. In Cage's prepared piano a selection of bolts, screws, and pieces of rubber are so placed that a variety of sounds can be produced. Rubber threaded through the strings at harmonic nodes will give sounds of quiet, pale harmonic quality. Bolts or screws left free to move will produce buzzing tones, while those fixed firmly will make for dull, thudding, percussive sounds with little or no 'piano' tone. The prepared piano is therefore suitable for pieces which are partly melodic and partly percussive in a colouristic way. In Cage's pieces which exploit this medium, ranging from *Amores* (1943) to *Sonatas and Interludes* (1947), the 'tuned' sounds usually form pentatonic scales, and the music has a charming, withdrawn sound somewhat oriental in character. At least in the hands of Cage, therefore, the prepared piano is no strident monstrosity. By other means, however, the piano can be made extremely potent. From early works such as Kagel's *Transicion*, beaters of all kinds have been used inside the piano to strike the strings, producing a remarkable range of colours varying from soft, dull tones to harsh, metallic clangings. Wire-wrapped bass strings can be scraped with knife blades, strings can be plucked with the fingers, fingernails, or a variety of

[1] Henry Cowell, *New Musical Resources* (New York, 1930).

plectra, and so on. The tone can be modified by pressing strips of plasticine over the strings and then playing on the keyboard. Quiet, pale tones will result. If metal rulers are laid over the strings a percussive, clanging effect is obtained. With the sustaining pedal depressed, one can obtain magnificent cluster sounds by rapid glissandos over the strings or by striking several strings at once (with the palms of the hands, knuckles, rulers, blocks of wood, etc.). In short, almost any physical action will produce novel, interesting sounds from the piano, though some damage may result. This is also true of the harp and harpsichord, to a lesser extent (the sounds, not the damage, which will be proportionally greater). Finally, the use of a microphone inside the piano will greatly enhance these sound potentialities.

Electronic amplification, which has been used for some time for instruments of limited volume such as guitar and harpsichord, is now being used for the voice and other instruments, not so much to give added volume as to produce effects of echo and distortion. These effects may be quite unlike the original sounds (as for instance in Stockhausen's *Mikrophonie I* for tamtam), or may simply add some degree of reverberation or echo to give sounds extra warmth and fullness, together with an impression of space. Live sounds are combined with their simultaneous electronic modification in a number of Stockhausen's works (*Mixtur* and *Prozession* for instruments and ring modulators, *Mikrophonie II* for choir, etc.), and inevitably other composers have followed.[1] But unless this medium is carefully exploited, the results can be unsatisfactory. Ring modulation in itself tends to produce a complex tonal spectrum which can be monotonous and uninteresting without further treatment. At its worst it can easily produce considerable distortion.

Lastly, in his search for effect the contemporary composer has taken up the stereophonic usages of the late-renaissance Venetian composers. Stockhausen revived this fashion with his *Gruppen* for three orchestras, each in a different part of the concert hall and each playing different music. Since then, many works have featured two or more instrumental groups or choirs, so positioned that the audience hears music from various directions. Though the results are not always satisfactory (only one small part of the audience can hear a truly balanced multiphonic effect), this use of various sound-sources gives an attractive depth to the music and an added spatial dimension. At the same time an 'action' element enters into the performance, so that instead of looking and

[1] One of the most striking works of this genre is Holliger's *Cardiophonie* for oboe and three tapes, in which the player's own amplified heartbeats and breathing sounds (both live and pre-recorded) produce a sensation of intense disquiet and turmoil. The oboe itself plays only a secondary role.

listening in one direction only, the audience participates more actively by moving its perceptions from one sound-source to another. 'Directional music' has come to be a permanent factor in the act of both sound creation and listening.

It would hardly be fitting to conclude this chapter without paying tribute to those performers who have not only tolerated the endless demands of composers, but have risen to every occasion, taking each new development in their stride. Today we can assume a fairly competent performance, but this was not always so. Not so long ago one went to rehearsals fully prepared for catastrophic results. Nobody played new music willingly. But today the situation is transformed. A new generation of instrumentalists has emerged which is keen to meet every challenge, and offers composers a wonderful collaboration.

Vocal Music—The New Choralism

If instrumentalists have made rapid strides in the last twenty-five years, even their rate of progress has been surpassed by the feats of a new generation of singers, who have not only had to cope with a new kind of music, but have had to acquire the ability to sing perfect pitch in all circumstances, even in quarter-tones, and even when they can hardly hear themselves.[1] Pre-war singers were a rather backward race. Their musicianship was by no means equal to even the mildest 'experimental music', and their sense of pitch could be wildly inadequate (as can be verified by listening to some of the older recordings of works such as *Wozzeck*). But all this has changed. The new singers have a musicality equal to that of any instrumentalist. They have developed a vocal range,[2] expressiveness, flexibility in timbre, and mastery of effect which is far beyond the capabilities of their predecessors.

Apart from more particular trends, there is a general style of expressive melody in the free twelve-note idiom which runs through much modern music—a style which often exhibits a vivid lyricism and capacity for word-painting. The following excerpt from Jean Barraqué's *Sequence* is typical:

[1] Liliana Poli, the Italian soprano specializing in contemporary music, tells me that, singing with an orchestra at high volume, the only way to gauge pitch is by feeling alone, not by sound.

[2] A range of over two octaves is frequently in demand. This is perhaps why the 'medium' voices (mezzo-soprano and baritone) are most in fashion, for they can more easily be extended in compass both upwards and downwards.

The irregular rhythmic patternings, strong dynamic contrasts, and large interval leaps are characteristic of this melodic style. They can often build up to a somewhat over-wrought emotionalism. In fact, if there is a criticism of the way composers have developed vocal writing, it is that there is too much frenetic expressionism and too little introspective, calm contemplation. But this is a characteristic of our times in many things.

Most new vocal usages are primarily directed towards achieving variety of effect and contrast of timbre. Whereas previously the ideal solo voice was one with a relatively homogeneous timbre and vibrato throughout its range, today such uniformity is undesirable. The voice must now be able to produce almost any degree of vibrato between a straight unmodulated tone and a tremolo between notes widely spaced apart. The timbre must be variable at will—dark, light, rich, mellow, thin, vibrant, toneless, and so on. Composers often indicate the more obvious timbre transformations (e.g. humming, singing with the mouth closed or the hand over the mouth, consonant noises, vowel sounds only, 'breathed' tones, 'rolled' sounds, unvoiced sounds, inhaled and exhaled noises, etc.), but the singer is expected to add appropriate personal tonal effects to these. Speaking, whispering, and 'Sprechstimme' (spoken song) may be introduced into sung passages, while words are sometimes broken up into their component vowels and consonants in such a way as to make the text not easily intelligible. Decorations such as rapid grace notes and melismas are often profuse, and form the modern equivalent of the old 'coloratura' style.

The products of integral serialism naturally seldom have the suppleness of the above Barraqué example, and at their worst they tend to be rather rigid and inflexible. The following example from Luigi Nono's *Il Canto Sospeso* is typical of this constructivist style. All durations in this tenor solo are derived from quintuplet semiquavers set in various combinations of the numbers 1, 2, and 7. (Orchestral parts are constructed with the same material.) The result has a somewhat angular frigidity, which produces a tensely controlled agony perfectly in keeping with the hopeless despair of the text (a letter from a young Polish prisoner in a Nazi concentration camp . . . 'If all the sky were paper and all the seas of the world were ink, I could not describe my sufferings, and all I see around me'):

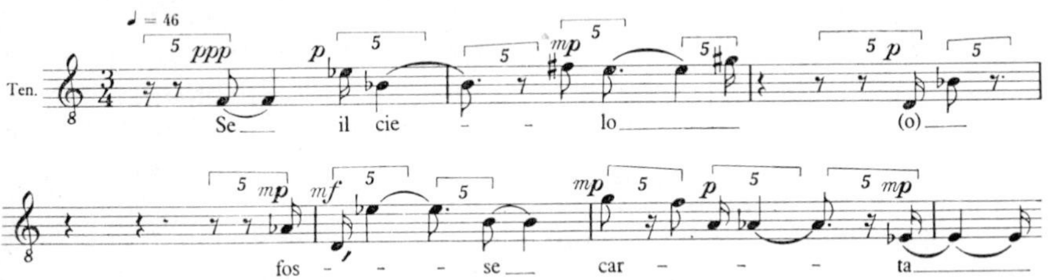

The most conspicuous landmarks in vocal writing have been the works written by Luciano Berio for Cathy Berberian, who has inspired a generation of composers (including Cage and Boulez), and has been the leader of a new school of singers. Cathy Berberian is not only a woman with a voice, but one with a vivid imagination and a strong stage personality. In collaboration with Berio, this has produced a highly flexible and decorative singing style, rich in novel effects, coupled with a stage 'presence' and theatricalism which are quite unique outside the opera house. The following example from Berio's *Circles* (1960) shows the free and florid style of his work, with typical coloratura passages, sounds of approximate pitch ( ), semi-spoken words 'on the breath' ( ), etc.:

Berio: ***Circles***

O ther or im) pos sib (ly as leep)

A considerably enlarged gamut of effects is found in Berio's *Sequenza III* (1966) for solo woman's voice, again specially written for Cathy Berberian. Only about one-fifth of this piece contains sounds of exact pitch; none of it contains notes of precise duration, or dynamics. The singer is given maximum freedom of invention in these more 'musical' parameters, while contrariwise details of 'effect' and interpretation (usually omitted by composers) are those written with most exactitude. In the following example taken from about the middle of this eight-minute piece, the vertical lines indicate divisions of ten seconds duration. Notes on five-line staves are sung at exact pitch, those on or between three lines are sung in the relative registers, while those printed around a single line are 'spoken' around the pitch shown. At the beginning of the second bar is an 'intonation contour' with tremolos. The remainder of the signs used are:

- - - - ● or σ——| = breathy tone, almost whispered.

♦ or ϕ = sung and whispered sounds as short as possible.

L = laughter.
←⊖ = breathing in, gasping.
ф = mouth click.
↑ = cough.
(hm) = hand(s) over the mouth.
(hd) = hands down.
+ = with mouth closed.

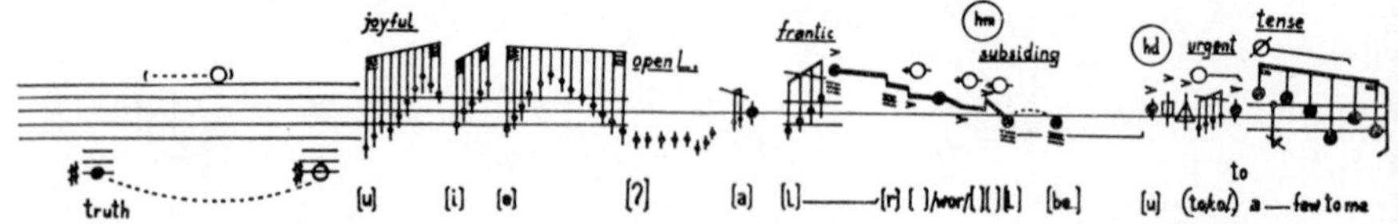

In the last few decades ensemble singing has become fairly rare, especially in music of a more advanced idiom. Perhaps this is because the difficulties are just too arduous to be surmounted without an enormous amount of preparation. For example, the following extract from Ligeti's *Aventures* (written as early as 1962) contains individual soprano, alto, and baritone parts. Though difficult, they are perfectly possible by themselves, but the real problems rear their heads when the three parts and the accompaniment (not shown) are put together:

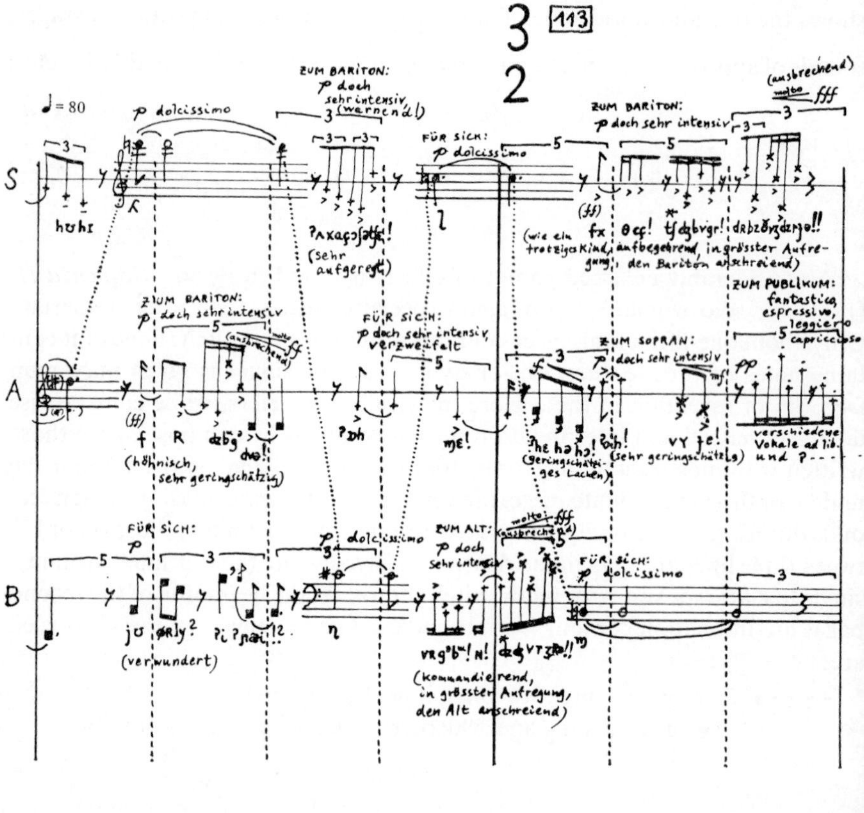

Fortunately, the extreme complications of such voice parts are less evident in choral music, though the general tendency is towards a complex sound produced by much subdivision of parts. As we shall see later with Berio's *Passaggio*, the individuality of parts can be so extreme that only a *total* sound can be heard, without any single part being clearly audible. This characteristic haze of sound may be created in what could otherwise be quite simple musical situations, transforming them into apparently dense sound-masses. For example, Ligeti's *Lux Aeterna* (1966), for sixteen-part mixed choir, is built on an essentially very sparse musical skeleton. The music begins as on page 168, with a unison F above middle C. Other sounds are gradually introduced to form clusters, and the note-span spreads almost imperceptibly upwards to cover an octave on the A above middle C. From this point the music then spreads downwards until it ends an octave lower than the first F. The whole of this movement occupies eight-and-a-half minutes—a considerable period for such an apparently elementary musical idea. But, of course, the music does not sound elementary at all. It seems to be suspended in time, fluctuating tenuously within small areas, the clusters gradually expanding and contracting almost imperceptibly. Note the metrical suspension, created by avoidance of the beat, and the subdivision of crochets into three, four, and five parts.

The multi-subdivision of voice parts is often designed to eliminate the old concept of 'choral melody on the top line', the prominent notes being so widely spaced and spread between the parts that no melody can emerge. In the same way, though a work may have harmonic and contrapuntal aspects, they may be so discontinuous as to be inaudible. Words are often broken up considerably. In fact, some composers subdue them almost completely, relying on the colour of vowels and consonants to produce an emotive 'landscape'. The colour of the sounds can entirely replace the intelligibility of the text. To put it the other way round—the text only serves as musical sound-material, material which by its own colour recreates the original emotive conception. The example on page 169 from Luigi Nono's *La Terra e la Compagna* (1958) is a typical example of this division of words, and the 'non-melodic' voice patternings (the accompaniment is omitted). The path of the words 'terra rossa terra nera' is shown by dotted lines. Note that the sounds which really emerge are those marked *mp*: top B flat, low C sharp, and top F sharp—all widely separated (this 8-part extract is actually a simple sample of this twenty-four part work, which at points reaches a considerable degree of aural complexity).

As an example of one of the most complex pages of choral music we quote on page 170 the entire second half of Sylvano Bussotti's *Siciliano* for twelve male voices. Knowing Bussotti's weakness for turning any page of music into a

Ligeti: *Lux Aetern*

Nono: *La terra e la Compagna*

graphic design (if at all possible), this page at first looks like just another extravagant flight of his imagination. But in actuality it is a much more practical and logical approach to notation than at first appears. Each voice part is quite clearly indicated, and if some are printed at odd angles this has not been done by caprice but so as to include a greater amount of musical material within each of the seven vertical time-spaces indicated by the dotted lines. Of course, the problems of pitch, co-ordination, and balance in this music are extreme if perfection is really aimed at. But as the composer indicates that this page should be 'chaotic and unrestrainable: *the stone which hides the ant-heap*', it is obvious that effect is much more important than precision. Too much rehearsal and attention to detail could produce a finesse which would be quite outside the real objectives of the composer and could destroy the real spirit of the music. The enigmatic aspects of the notation therefore have a purpose—to stimulate invention and avoid too much exactitude.

= approximate pitch.
= spoken.

= voiceless, without timbre.
\+ = breathed.

Free sounds:
= highest.
= medium.
= lowest.

Bussotti: *S ciliano*

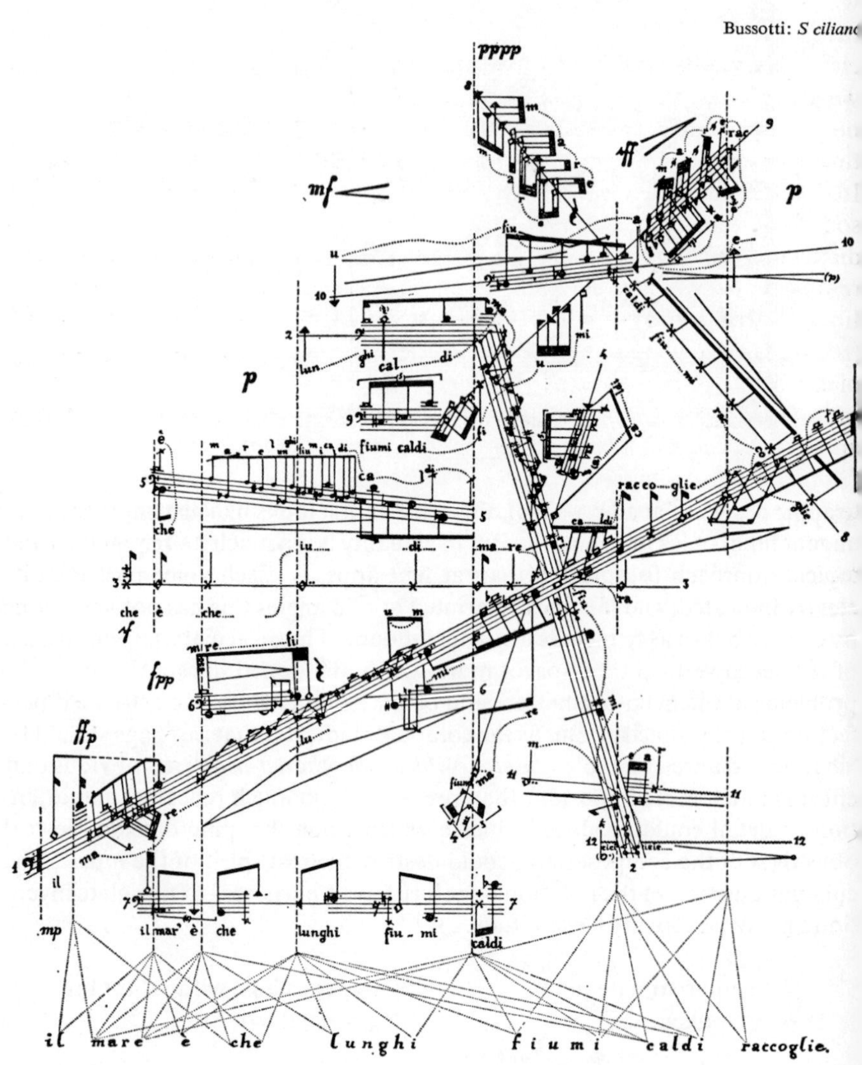

The spoken chorus is not unique to post-war music. Darius Milhaud's *La Mort d'un Tyran* exploited it as long ago as 1932; in fact, the virile sound of that work (with an accompaniment of percussion, piccolo, clarinet, and tuba) was rather raw meat for the audiences of that time. But in the last decade much choral music features spoken sounds with a whole gamut of effects such as whispering, consonant noises, unpitched sounds, shouting, murmuring, sibilant noises, etc. Sometimes speech is indicated with exact duration values in metrical time, sometimes different pitch zones are required (high, medium, low, etc.). In practice the difference between speaking in various pitch zones and sung sounds of approximate pitch is marginal, if the volume is the same. The real distinction lies in the fact that sung notes should be sustained in volume and remain at the chosen (approximate) pitch, whereas spoken sounds (unless deliberately held) tend to die away quickly and are more modulated in intonation. (It is notable that the old *Sprechgesang* or *Sprechstimme* has largely fallen out of use in vocal music, at least in its original form notated by Schoenberg, but the same general effect has been retained by a simple notation which indicates approximate sung and/or spoken pitches.) The following extract from Vinko Globokar's *Voie* for three choirs and orchestra shows a choral passage in sixteen parts where the difference between 'pitched' speech and singing in approximate intonation is negligible, the one merging into the other from moment to moment. (Sustained notes are shown ●⌒, short ejaculated sounds ɸ, and sounds sung with the mouth closed and undulating in pitch are indicated +∿):

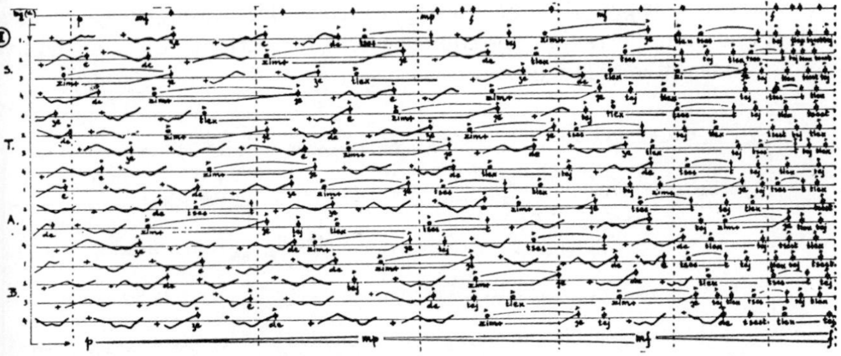

Probably the work with the greatest exploitation of choral effects so far written is Berio's *Passaggio* (1961–2),[1] written for soprano, two choirs, and

[1] Dedicated, significantly, to Milhaud.

orchestra; so much so that it is difficult to describe the wide variety of technique used without making a compendium of choral usages. Choir A is in the or chestra, while the soprano occupies the stage and acts out a sort of moder Passion of Persecution. Choir B is divided into five groups placed among th audience, and has several functions: commenting on the action and subjec matter in Italian, German, English, and French, taking a part in the Passio (often with passages in Latin), or identifying the audience with one aspect c society which is involved in this 'theatre'. The two choirs, in fact, represent tw opposing sections of society—the persecutors and the persecuted, the haves an have-nots, the violent and the meek, the revolutionaries and the reactionaries and we are left to identify ourselves with one side or the other, for or against th woman singer who acts out scenes of persecution, arrest, imprisonment, an social rejection, stumbling through a life of increasing degradation and aliena tion. *Passaggio* is a big canvas, painting the ills of our civilization, generating i us a feeling of confusion and bewilderment. The music is therefore deliberatel complex, and the choral parts especially so, becoming at times an immens babel of tongues in a great phalanx of sound. In one section, for example, th choirs are divided into over forty parts, each voice singing ad lib. a melody o motif from a different work (including 'God Bless America', 'O Sole Mio', 'G Down Moses'). The choirs begin separately and quietly, and then build up afte twenty seconds to a strident fortissimo for a further ten seconds. Of course, n single voice or melody is heard, or intended to be heard. The effect must be on of an immense sound mass in confused movement.

Sometimes each choir is given only a catalogue of words to speak or ejaculat over a certain time period. The following, for choir B in the audience, indicate spoken and sung parts (in approximate pitch) for various voices in the fiv groups, using different languages:

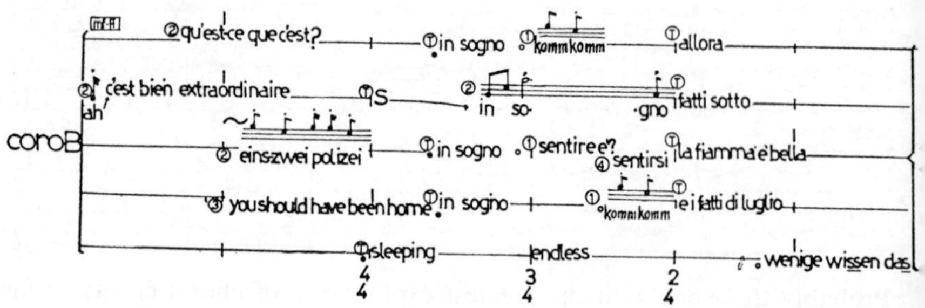

Sometimes an entire choir has only a graphic design, which indicates approxi- mate pitches and durations, and the outlines of various vocal 'gestures'. In the following example, while choir A sings fairly well defined music, with bars in both definite and indefinite pitch; choir B has a much more approximate score, ending in outlines representing vocal flourishes which are finally taken up also by choir A (orchestral parts are omitted, as is also the part for solo soprano):

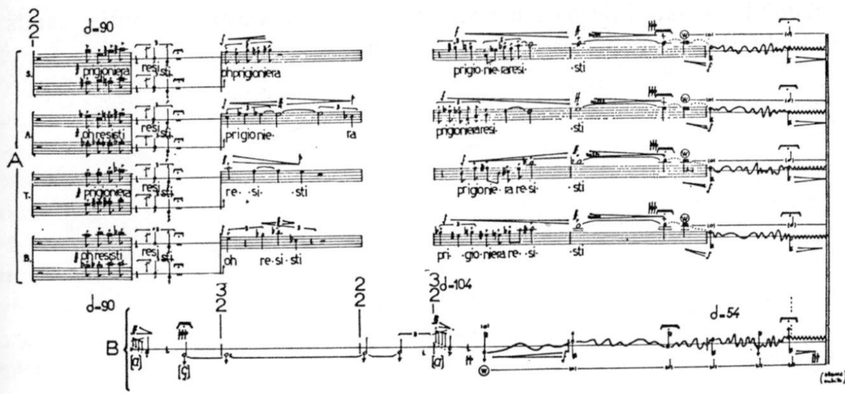

Much that Berio does looks deliberately irrational; some parts of the score are merely full of shouted numbers—'613000∼614000∼615000'. At another point a bleating young voice recites: 'I am a teenager and as most teenagers I dream about my future I dream of someday being a freshman in college . . . I dream human relations and I dream of getting married, etc.', while at the same time one section of choir B recites in Latin ('*quod ad hoc bellum . . .*') and other sections ejaculate a sequence of words which begins with 'biscuits' and ends with 'eight million coffins'. At last choir B shouts 'spasmodically' about megatons, coffins, and bombs for twenty seconds in response to a burst of laughter from choir A. This may all seem confusing. In fact it is deliberately so, intending to generate in us an overwhelming apprehension at the barbaric cruelties of our own civilization and its headlong course towards self-destruction. Could this have been done by more conventional musical means? Perhaps so. But this is beside the point. The real fact is that Berio's methods are efficient, their emotive impact is potent, and they are absolutely appropriate and well blended into the total musical structure.

In short, the new choral medium has become a highly powerful and expressive force with a whole armoury of new effects. Once again, it is 'effect' and 'colour' which are the key factors in the new choral exploitation. Composers are not so much interested in choralism for its age-old beauty of sound, as for the sensational vigour, stridency, and potency of some unconventional usages and the attractive colour and imagery of others. Add to this the use of electronics, with choral amplification or the colouration and distortion of sounds, and the panorama is vast. However, there are certain reservations to be recorded. Once these new effects have lost their novelty, their impact will be diminished and they may even become banal. They will then fall out of circulation and be replaced by yet other novelties. In short, we are on shifting sands, but that is the nature of this world and its music.

17

Notation

Notation has never been more than an approximate indication of composers' intentions. In the past, certain conventions in performance have compensated for the shortcomings of notation. But with modern music these conventions are no longer adequate. Composers have thus sought to set down their requirements ever more precisely. This has led to a proliferation of complexities which has certainly not helped performers, for a surfeit of symbols is an obstacle to good interpretation, however necessary they may be. Further, some music has changed its character in so many ways that it cannot be written down at all in conventional notation. Composers of such music have tended to invent their own systems, which may be ideal for one kind of music but useless for others. This has led to a profusion of different notational systems, as will already be evident from the great variety of musical examples quoted in previous chapters.

This is not a situation which can be properly summed up in one chapter—the subject is far too large. All we can do here is to summarize the cardinal points and indicate some new notations which, by their logic and growing use, seem to be emerging as relatively fitting and acceptable notations for much of today's music. Regrettably, we must ignore certain well evolved systems such as Klavarscribo and Equitone which have remained in obscurity, probably because they are so radically different from the old notation.

First, it must be said that conventional notation is still the most suitable way of setting down conventional music, to be played in a specific metre. Even here it would seem, however, that certain simplifications are necessary. Composers often resort to extremely complex subdivisions of time-units to obtain rhythms which can only be reproduced exactly by computer minds. If one accepts that precise performance of these rhythms is not strictly necessary, they can be written in other ways which are much easier to read and to play, and yet sound almost exactly like the composer's intentions. For example, the following part of the flute solo on the final page of Boulez's *Le Marteau sans Maître*, so irregular in metre and the subdivisions of beats, could be considerably simplified in notation in several ways which will become clear later. For the time being, the version shown at 'b' represents a rather rough and ready but much simplified way of writing the same sounds, without altering the character of the music to any significant extent:

Of course, Pierre Boulez would hardly agree with such simplistic solutions. Nevertheless, the question remains—is ultra-complex time notation really necessary and worthwhile?

A further simplification in conventionally notated music is resorted to by some composers where a rapid passage is required, but the exact notes used are not material. For example, in the following passage for string quartet Berio indicates the number of notes required within a given time space, and their general range. Even the fingering is shown, but actual notes are given only for the points of 'departure' and 'arrival'. This makes for a very brilliant effect, achieved with practical economy of effort:

Berio: *Sincronie*

Sometimes composers make a graphic design which indicates a certain kind of activity during a defined time period. If the design is unconventional and no proper explanation is given, the player will be worse off than ever. For instance, the following two bars for harp in Maderna's Oboe Concerto appear to indicate glissandos and expanding and contracting clusters. But these latter are not possible on the harp, and one can only assume that perhaps Maderna meant rapid activity within the shaded areas (strangely enough, the same two bars include two rapid piano parts which are notated in great detail):

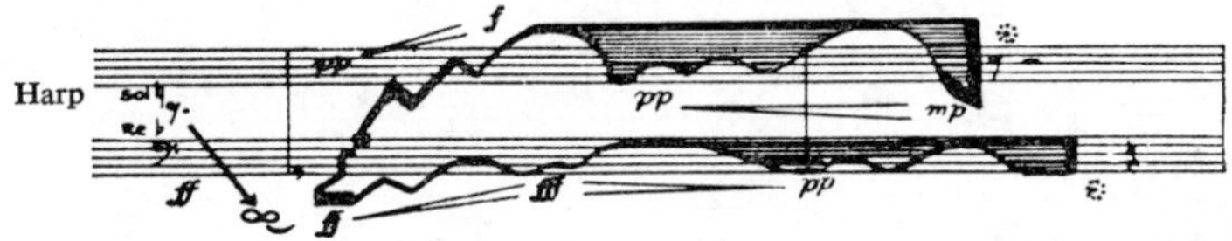

There are many instances in conventional notation, where composers go to great pains to score every note of a large number of parts, whereas a few simple, concise indications would be sufficient. For example, Ligeti's *Ramifications* for string orchestra or twelve solo strings begins with thirty bars filled with literally thousands of notes. Each of the twelve parts is fully written out using exactly the same note groups, but each with the beat subdivided differently (8, 7, 6, 5, 4, or 3 notes to each beat). In short, all instruments play the same notes but at different speeds. Ligeti really composed a close cluster of sounds which gradually spread over thirty bars to widely-spread chords, but as he wished to avoid a static effect and suggest an indistinct sense of movement, each instrument plays (more or less) the same note groups at a different pace. This could have been achieved by very simple means. The same note groups could have been indicated in a single part, valid for all players, with directions for each instrument to play at a different speed. Bar lines would be omitted, an overall duration for each different note group being sufficient. The actual sound would be the same as Ligeti's score, but without thousands of notes laboriously written by the composer or read by the players.

The real problem in notation occurs with musical situations which are not in metrical time. Sometimes this is called 'free tempo', but in reality there is no 'tempo' at all in the sense of metre (and its conventional subdivisions), but only an overall duration for each musical section. The problem is how to indicate the relative length of sounds. Sometimes conventional duration values, (quavers, crotchets, semibreves, etc.) can still be used to suggest notes of different length, as long as musical sections have specific overall timings. This usually entails performers playing from score so that they can co-ordinate with each other. Once players get used to the fact that normal note-values are only approximate indications, they play passages such as the following with great facility, and without any real need for a conductor:

Smith Brindle: *The Death of Antigon*

Such a passage can only be written in free time. To put it in the straitjacket of metre would not only make for a stilted interpretation but would create a degree of performance difficulty and reading effort which is out of all proportion to the end result.

Lukas Foss recommends a similar use of conventional signs—freed of their usual duration values—to indicate improvisation which has a defined overall pattern but is indeterminate as to pitch and real time. The stave is used only to show the pitch of the first and last notes:[1]

[1] Music example from an article on Lukas Foss in *Contemporary Composers on Contemporary Music* by Elliott Schwarz and Barney Childs (New York).

A 'time notation' initiated probably by Earle Brown in the Fifties uses a 'geometric representation of durations'. This is an excellent way of showing the relative duration of sounds, but there seem to be several disadvantages. When it is necessary to use accidentals these need space before each note, so that it is not clear whether this space represents silence or whether sounds are to be joined together (legato). It is not really clear when legato or staccato are required, unless such signs are included (sometimes they are, sometimes not). It is also difficult to judge just how rapidly the quickest note-successions should be played, for the amount of space any group of short notes occupies on paper cannot be smaller than legibility permits.

Earle Brown: *Available Forms 2*

'Proportional notation' is somewhat similar, but has developed into a more logical system. We have already noted Berio's use of this notation in a rudimentary form on page 64. Unfortunately Berio tried to associate the system with a 'beat' to some extent by indicating regular pulses with ictus strokes. The system as used in the Berio example also included a large number of conventional signs—dynamics, staccato dots, slurs, etc. Gradually these compromises with conventional notation have been reduced, so that all musical parameters are indicated by an absolute minimum of signs: see the example on page 180. The duration of sounds is indicated by the length of the horizontal line attached to the stem of each note, so that the 'rhythm' of a phrase is derived from the proportion of the spaces between notes. Obviously no metre is present. Where the horizontal line joins several note stems, this does not necessarily mean that the notes should be played legato. Slurs are used to show legato, and where they are omitted but the horizontal line is unbroken, notes should be bowed or tongued separately. Where the horizontal line is broken between notes, this indicates a silence in proportion to the length of the linear break. The volume of sounds is shown by the thickness of the horizontal line. A thin line is pianissimo, a very thick one fortissimo, and so on. Crescendos, diminuendos, and fluctuations of volume are shown by corresponding variations in the thickness of this line.

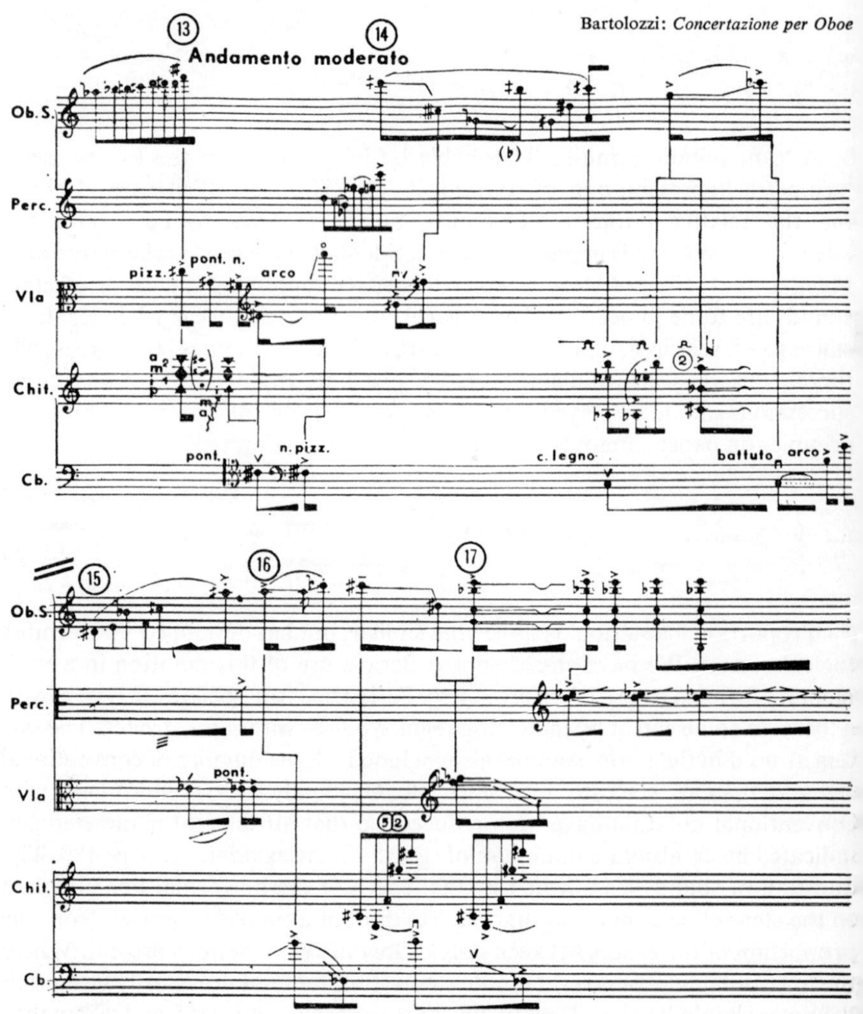

This system seems to be completely comprehensive and satisfactory for all but keyboard instruments, where the overlapping of many sounds of different length could not be clearly shown. One small disadvantage seems to be that while many conventional signs are no longer needed, certain indications such as staccato, accent, etc. are still indispensable. These interpretative symbols may always remain as part of any notation, however much we may prefer to simplify and economize.

Unfortunately, with non-metrical notation, instrumental parts cannot always be copied in the usual way. Sometimes it is necessary for performers either to play from score, or to have an abundance of cues in order to orientate themselves. In most cases, however, the music can be copied out in short timed sections, so that players can co-ordinate at frequent intervals.

In some musical situations, composers have found it convenient to indicate the dynamics of notes by their size:

Stockhausen: *Zyklus*

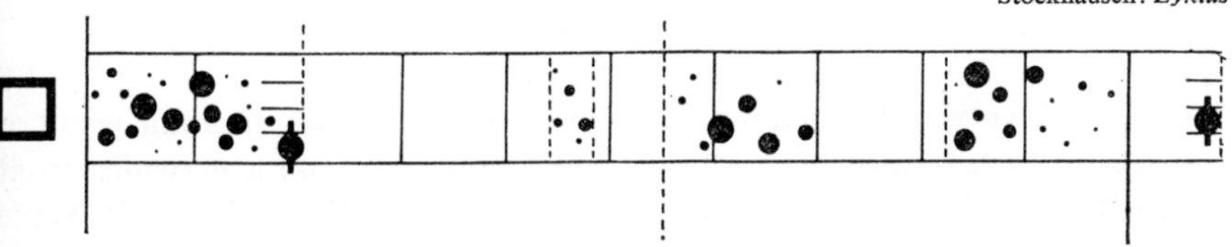

The rectangles represent time units, and the sounds are played according to their placing within the rectangle—an example of porportional notation adapted for percussion sounds.

So much for notations which have emerged as being generally suitable for much of today's music. There is no point in illustrating notations which are peculiar to one composer and have no universality of usage, and unfortunately every composer has his own bagful of symbols which are by no means the same as others use. For instance, Kagel's *Sonant* (*1960/ . . .*) is prefaced by a list of 202 symbols (for only four players!), at least 150 of which are not standard usage. If only a hundred composers were to do the same (which is not absolutely off the cards), we would then have 15,000 signs and symbols which are different! One is therefore discouraged from making a comprehensive list of signs and symbols which have come into recent usage. But it would seem useful to list a limited few which show signs of becoming standard,[1] and these may be found on pages 188-198.

[1] Unfortunately, this list is not completely selective, often showing several alternative symbols for the same effect. This is because it is quite impossible to select any one sign as being definitely preferable or more widely used. For further information the reader is referred to John Cage's book *Notation* (Bletchley, 1969) and Erhard Karkoschka's *Notation in New Music* (London, 1972). Cage's book, however, is only a collection of examples of scores, while though Karkoschka goes to great length in illustrating the symbols used by a limited selection of composers, he makes no suggestions as to which signs are most suitable. For an extensive discussion of percussion notation, the reader is referred to the author's book *Contemporary Percussion* (London, 1970).

18

The Avant-Garde and Society

As I have already said, much that has happened in music has been the result of outside pressures, music being the product of its environment (which itself comprises social, economic, and political factors and the philosophies these generate). Again, we are too near our own times to judge just how these multiple factors have had their consequences in music. But it is possible to make some generalizations.

One thing is certain, avant-gardism does not appear to be encouraged in the People's Republics of Eastern Europe and China, nor is any form of protest music or social comment. Avant-garde art only flourishes in the softer, sophisticated airs of the Western Democracies, or in socialist states where artistic individualism is tolerated (such as Poland or Yugoslavia). In the West, social comment is not only tolerated but allowed to run riot—to the extent of being antisocial. The musical avant-garde, however, has not shown itself to be particularly interested in politics and sociology. If one excludes certain works (such as Nono's *Intolleranza 1960*, Manzoni's *Atomtod*, Haubenstock-Ramati's *America*, and Bartolozzi's *Tutto ciò che accade*) one must record that the work of the avant-garde, particularly that of leaders such as Boulez, Stockhausen, and Cage, is singularly dissociated from this world. In choosing to ignore the starving millions, the destitute and war-ravaged, the nuclear holocaust which hangs eternally over our heads, we have perhaps been playing a selfish, idle game. But is not all artistic creation equally egocentric? What may seem so selfish and futile now may well prove a great blessing to later generations. It is an age-old paradox that music, the most sublime of man's creations, has no material value, but only a potential of spiritual therapy or intellectual appeal.

As regards 'committed' composers (those in the West who work closely with the Communist propaganda machine) there are some interesting paradoxes. While music in the main Communist countries remains conventional (and therefore stagnates), its purpose being to communicate easily with the masses in a spirit of good cheer and patriotic fervour, in the West the reverse is true. 'Committed' music is usually in an advanced language, incomprehensible to the masses. Far from instilling good cheer, it paints the grim picture of capitalist and imperialist oppression. Particularly notable is Nono's progress from the early anti-fascism of *Epitaph to García Lorca* and condemnation of Nazi atrocities in *Il Canto Sospeso* and *Ricorda quello che ti han fatto ad Auschwitz*, through the pro-Communist works such as *Intolleranza 1960* and *La Fabbrica Illuminata*, to the anti-Americanism of *A Floresta*. Notable too is the positive support given to committed composers by Communist parties in the West. For example, the region of Tuscany, being Communist, organized about three dozen provincial concerts of Nono's music in 1970, which were dutifully attended by the workers. Bussotti's opera *Lorenzaccio*, dedicated to the Communist party, was guaranteed performances at several provincial Italian opera theatres *before* it had ever been performed—a most unusual feat! (There is no need to mention the political colour of the provinces involved in this transaction.) Sometimes committed composers work in a curiously isolationist way —the retro-compositions of Donatoni for example, can hardly contribute much to the party spirit. (However, Donatoni's self-denying attitude, his insistence on artisanship, even the ironing out of his 'material' into impersonal, communal sound patterns, may be a manifestation of an inner willingness to conform with the anonymity of the masses.) Finally we must record the Maoist phenomenon of Cornelius Cardew's democratic 'Scratch Music', where in one class of activities—contrary to the Communist principle of all working together in a common cause—every individual component of the orchestra goes his own way on a journey of self-liberation. 'Music of the people', collective individualism, or revolutionary anarchy?

There can be some confusion if politicians' statements on art are taken as gospel. Chairman Mao says: 'In the world today, culture and art and literature are geared to definite political lines. There is in fact no such thing as art for art's sake, art that stands above classes, art that is detached from or independent of politics.' Is this really so in Red China? It is certainly not so in music of 'the world today' as we know it. And would one like music to be exclusively 'geared to definite political lines'?

Again—two rather similar statements. Chairman Mao says: 'Revolution is the main trend in the world today.' Cage also says: 'Our proper work now if we love mankind and the world we live in is revolution.'[1] But what do the Maoists think? 'Cage's line both in his writings and music helps to sow confusion and promote disunity, and in so doing definitely support (*sic*) the most oppressive class in the world's history—U.S. Imperialism . . . The outlook for Cage and the

[1] John Cage, *A Year from Monday* (London, 1968).

Imperialist Class reeling from one defeat to another both economically and politically is very dark.'[1] It is not my object to comment on such political observations, but merely to note the contrasting and confusing interpretations of the most fundamental words like 'revolution', 'imperialist', etc. Would not Cage throw a fit if he knew he was supporting the most oppressive class in the world's history? One could just as easily prove he seeks to undermine it. For example he says: 'U.S. citizens are six per cent of world's population consuming sixty per cent of world's resources. Had Americans been born pigs rather than men, it would not have been different.'[2] And so on. One could quote and requote without (as far as music is concerned) proving anything whatsoever.

In reality, music and politics are uneasy bedfellows, especially if the music is couched in an arduous language. A political message can only be put across effectively if it has absolute clarity, if it is not obscured by music of an impenetrable dialectic. Not that one expects political ideology to be so naïvely expressed as Mussolini's *Giovinezza*; but Nono's *A Floresta*, for example, is almost incomprehensible. The only way to get at its ideological message is to read the programme notes and ignore the music.

Finally, a curious offshoot of the political scene: if one can judge by the works of Ligeti and Penderecki, Eastern Europe is the last refuge of great religious music. While the new music of the West usually avoids religion like the plague, such works as Ligeti's *Requiem* and *Lux Aeterna* and Penderecki's *St. Luke Passion* are testimonies to the fact that where the Church is persecuted, it thrives most strongly.

In our world today there are those who are passionately involved in righting the wrongs of this world—hunger, famine, war, refugees, injustice, etc. Equally there are those who stand indifferently looking on. There are even those who regard society as something that owes them a debt, and therefore think anti-social behaviour a legitimate part of life. Though this may seem to have little to do with music, in reality it is precisely through these attitudes (concern, indifference, anarchism) that so much modern art is born.

Of the three attitudes, it is easy to recognize mildly anti-social behaviour in some of the more outrageous pranks of La Monte Young, and it is probably present in the deliberate eccentricities of many a lesser figure. Indifference is certainly reflected in the escapism of Feldman and Cage, the preciousness of Boulez and non-involvement of Stockhausen. And is the kind of collective anonymity to be perceived in some American theatre, many improvisatory works, and in much electronic and computer music, also a form of indifference,

[1] Keith Rowe, 'Cage Review' in *Microphone* (Greenwich, 1972).
[2] *A Year from Monday.*

just another way of avoiding involvement? Are some aspects of indeterminacy founded on an indifference (e.g. unconcern as to pitch, duration, performing means, etc.) which is both artistic and sociological? Certainly new music, and the avant-garde in general, has largely avoided real concern for the ills of this world. In mitigation, it may be said that it is by no means fashionable in artistic circles to be positively involved or concerned. It is certainly not fashionable to be patriotic. It is not even fashionable to be a rebel.

What remains? Only the art itself—which is not necessarily negative. After all, neither Haydn nor Schubert showed any direct involvement in the European tragedy they lived through. As for Rossini! We must remember, however, that sometimes an artist may be most concerned for the pains and injustices he sees around him, and yet this concern may not always show through in his work. For example, Van Gogh's early works do reflect the miseries of the peasant communities of the Brabant, but his last agonizing years in the asylum near Arles produced canvases which vibrate intensely with the heat and colour of the South but seem to ignore the tragedy around him—tragedy which in fact troubled him deeply. The truth is that we cannot expect an artist to crucify himself for ever for the sorrows of this world.

19

Conclusion

What impresses most in music since 1945 is the sheer pace of events. The rhythm of change has been frenetic. More has happened in music in these few years than in any previous five-hundred-year period. In this short book it has been impossible to give more than an outline sketch of the massive field which lies between the complete cerebralism of integral serialism and the almost total haphazardness of 'happenings'; or to paint in all the developments thrown up by electronic technology, colouristic expansions, the introduction of orientalisms, archaisms, improvisation, Cageian concepts, etc.

The period has been full of vivid experiences (mixed with disappointments), and challenges to our intellect and to the elasticity of our perception and sensibility. It has overflowed with new ideas and attitudes. But has everything been 'progress' and 'development'? Possibly not. We have certainly witnessed much destruction (of conventional values) and been bluffed by charlatans. Equally, we have seen the emergence of ample and highly expressive new musical resources, with a rich potential which may or may not form the basis of a more static musical situation for decades to come. But just what has been 'progress' is not for us to say: we are too near to judge, though the progress will be clear enough to our grandchildren, if they are fortunate enough to be around.

There have been many moments in the last decades when it seemed that music was reaching a dead end. The raw materials of music—intervals, melodic steps, harmony, etc.—appeared to lose all significance. The musical language itself seemed to be disintegrating, and every conventional value dissipated. Some musical events filled one with despondency. When Cage's Piano Concert was played at Venice with players up and down the stairs and corridors and in the piazza, it was mildly amusing. But when another concert featured a composer knocking nails into a board for a long, long time, it was neither funny nor interesting. It was tragic. It seemed to me that the nails were being knocked into music's coffin.

One leaves such events in despair. But fortunately hope is renewed. Now and then something happens which renews the conviction that the avant-garde is not after all the disintegration of an art, but its continuance and vital evolution. Such a renewal of hope came to me when I was invited to be a member of the International Jury of the Paris Biennale. This entailed listening to tapes of 120 works submitted by twenty-one radio corporations, representing the best of each country's younger composers. This could have been a terrible drudgery, for I detest listening to music in quantity. Instead, it was a vivid experience which taught me much. It taught me above all that music is still very alive. That young composers from locations as far apart as Lima, Budapest, Tokyo, and Cologne have great talents. That the international language which music has become is a worthy continuance of the age-old art.

Where do we go next? It would be presumptuous to hazard a guess. Perhaps from now on the pace will be much slower, with a broader exploration of existing idioms. Certainly there will be many processes of simplification now that the means, though so complex, are more under control. It could well be that our years of obsession with innovation may pass into an era, not of stagnation, but of quiet assimilation and fruitful creation. Looking back, we can see that some of man's greatest music was by no means wildly new, that in fact it was sometimes distinctly conservative.

Or musical change may continue at an even more vertiginous rate than before.

The truth is that we cannot see ahead at all. We can only hope and believe that, in whatever form, music will always continue as the most sublime of man's creations.

Some New Notation Symbols

For comments on some of these, see Chapter 17, pages 175–81

MICRO-INTERVALS

𝄲 quarter-tone sharp (or ♮↑)

𝄰 three quarter-tones sharp (or ♯♯, ♯↑)

𝄳 quarter-tone flat (or ♮↓)

three quarter-tones flat (or ♭↓)

CLUSTERS

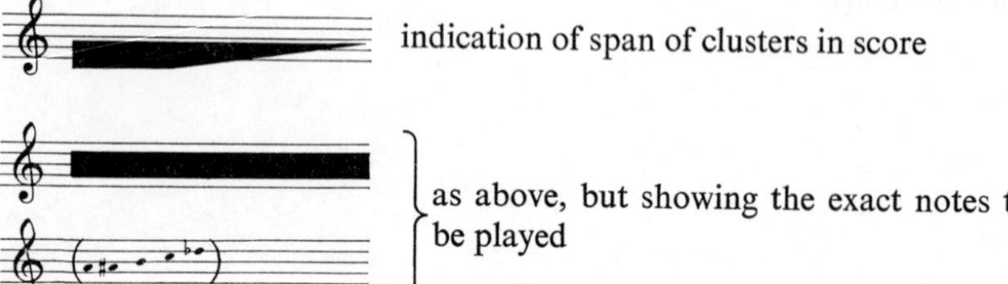

indication of span of clusters in score

as above, but showing the exact notes to be played

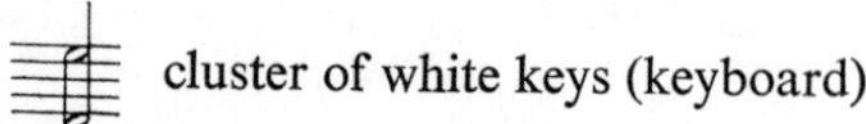

cluster of white keys (keyboard)

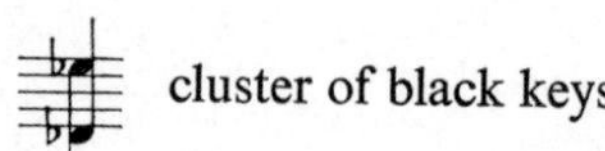

cluster of black keys

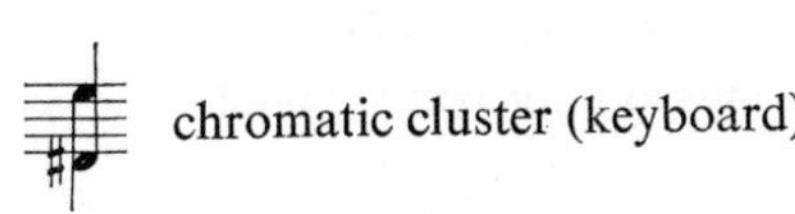
chromatic cluster (keyboard)

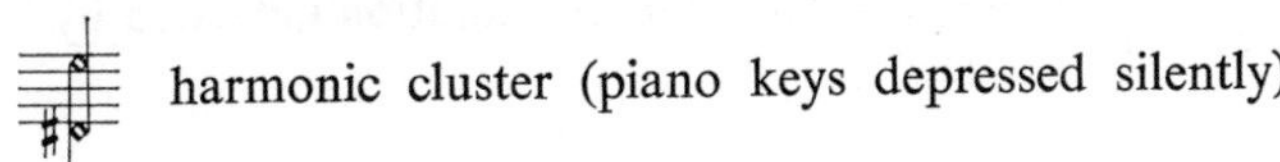
harmonic cluster (piano keys depressed silently)

VIBRATOS

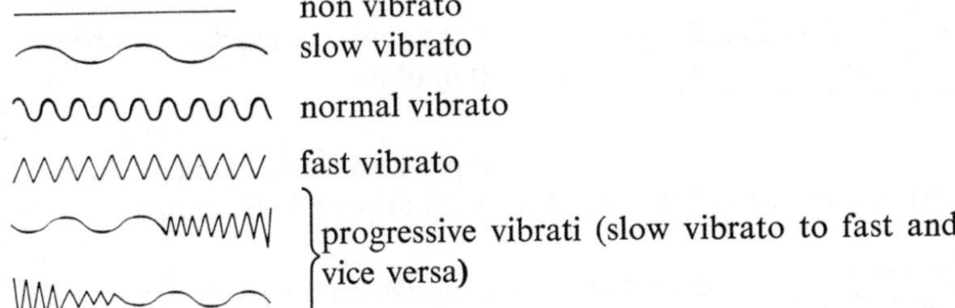
non vibrato
slow vibrato
normal vibrato
fast vibrato
progressive vibrati (slow vibrato to fast and vice versa)

OSCILLATIONS

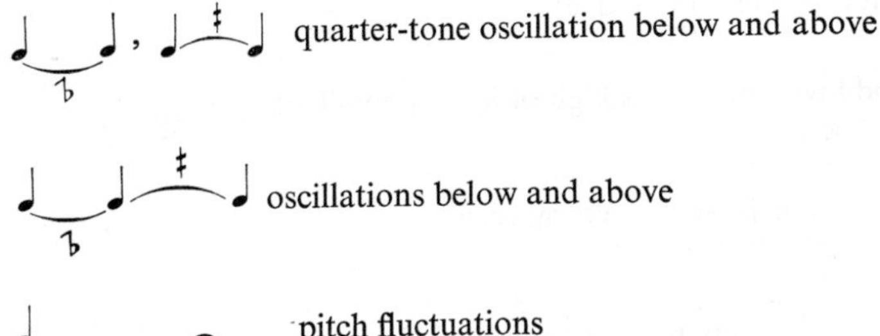
quarter-tone oscillation below and above

oscillations below and above

pitch fluctuations

NOTE GROUPS

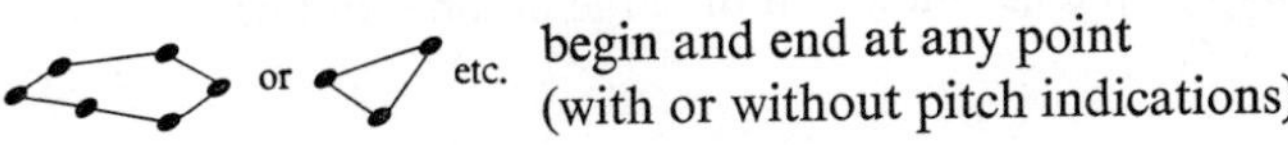
begin and end at any point (with or without pitch indications)

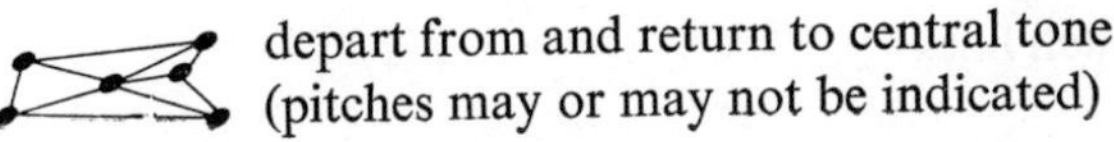
depart from and return to central tone (pitches may or may not be indicated)

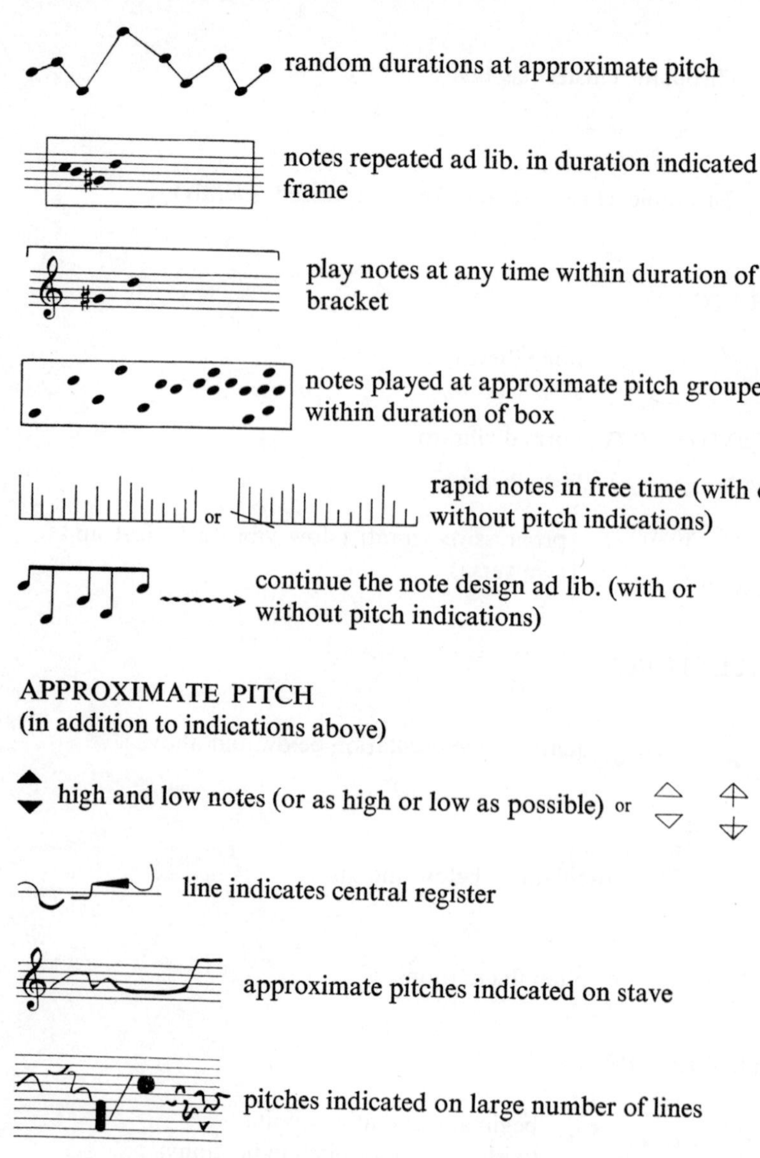
random durations at approximate pitch
notes repeated ad lib. in duration indicated by frame
play notes at any time within duration of bracket
notes played at approximate pitch grouped within duration of box
or
rapid notes in free time (with or without pitch indications)
continue the note design ad lib. (with or without pitch indications)
APPROXIMATE PITCH
(in addition to indications above)
high and low notes (or as high or low as possible)
or
line indicates central register
approximate pitches indicated on stave
pitches indicated on large number of lines
pitch lines

INTENSITY

accents

PAUSES AND EXPRESSIVE INDICATIONS

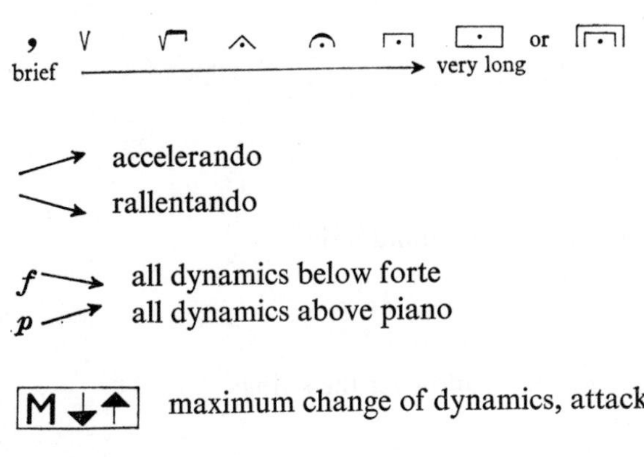

great activity

KEYBOARD SYMBOLS

, etc. staccato attack followed by silent depression of key

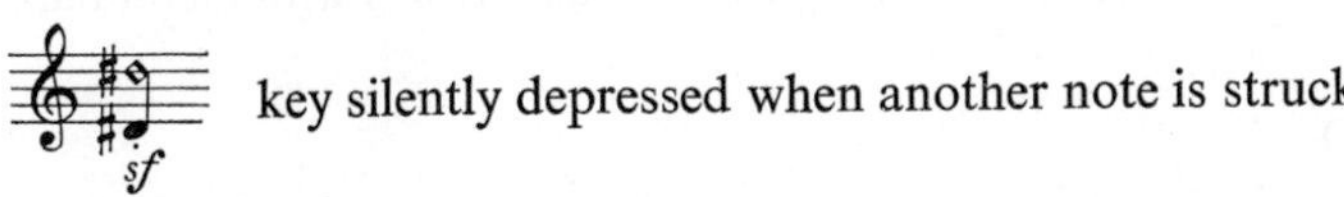

key silently depressed when another note is struck

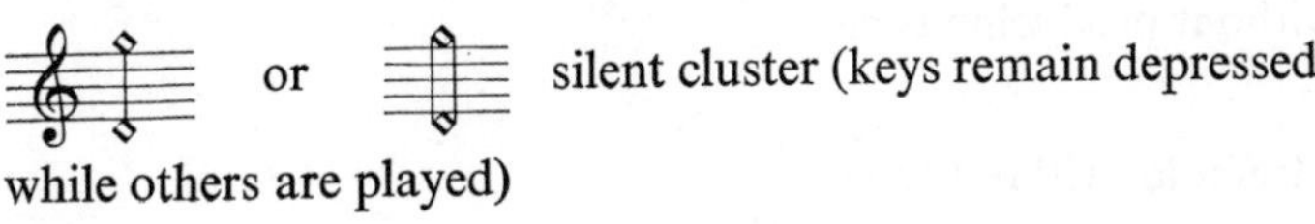

silent cluster (keys remain depressed while others are played)

chromatic cluster with arms, which are then removed and only one note held

Playing inside on strings

P , , , pizzicato

Mi, , , + damped with finger

Pu , × Pizz. with fingernail

glissando with fingernail along a wound string

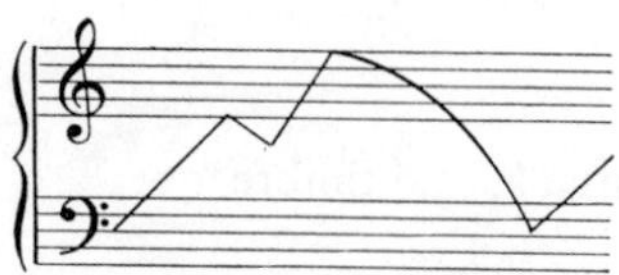

glissando over the strings

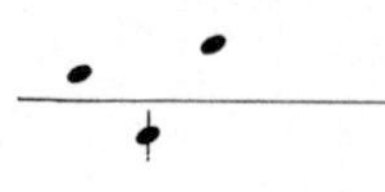

noises on wood or metal parts of piano (using hands, pieces of wood, metal, plastic, etc.)

strike keys or piano top with fingernails

scrape along bass strings with metal blade

WOODWIND

blow without producing tone

breath tremolo, without tone

, fluttertongue

+ key noise, without tone or + + + etc.

+ ___________ key noise, with tone held

+ .... key trill, without tone

harmonic sound

short glissandi

smorzato effect

BRASS AND HORNS

strike mouthpiece with flat of hand

strike tongue against mouthpiece

, blow without tone

vocal sounds at pitch given, while playing

, as short as possible

double or triple tongue

, fluttertongue

breathy sound

open (O) and closed (+) positions of plunger or other bell stopping

STRINGS

pizzicato rebounding against fingerboard (with two fingers for sforzandi)

or muted

or unmuted

, , or bow at the bridge

, , play between the bridge and tailpiece (on one, two or four strings, etc.)

bow on the tailpiece

bow on the bridge at right angles to strings

pizzicato behind bridge

left hand pizzicato

, , strike body of instrument with bow or fingertips

, exaggerated bow pressure producing distortion

fluctuating bow pressure

HARP

pedal positions

D C B E F G A all notes flat

all notes natural

all notes sharp

damp strings

'à la table'

or with fingernail

glissando with pedal

C♭ → C♯ pedal portato

C♭ pedal trill

or strike body of instrument with knuckles or finger(s)

or vertical glissando along one or more strings

(the above is only a small selection from a profuse number of new harp symbols, which have no universal usage)

VOICE

+ mouth closed, ○ mouth open

murmuring at high pitch, at low pitch

at various pitches

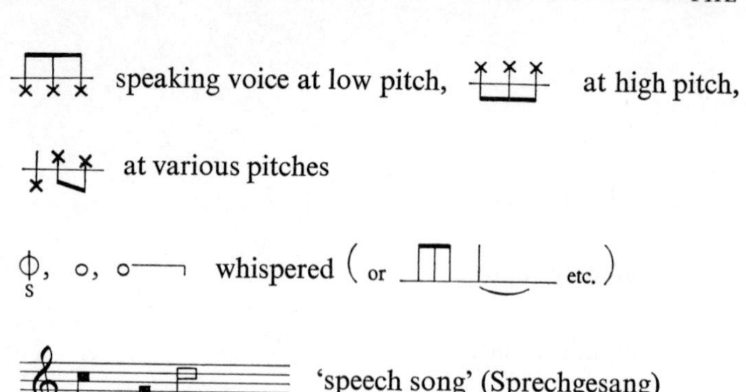

speaking voice at low pitch, at high pitch,

at various pitches

whispered (or etc.)

'speech song' (Sprechgesang)

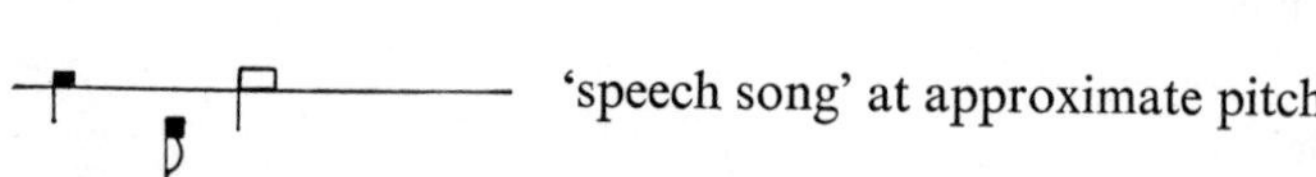

'speech song' at approximate pitch

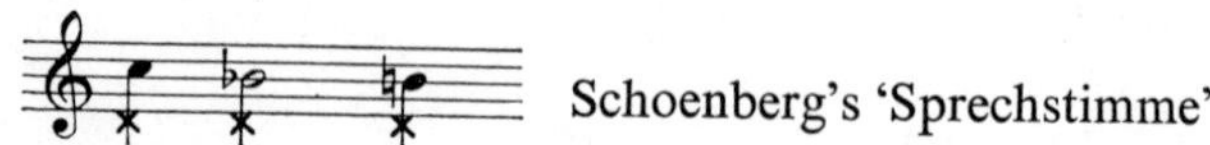

Schoenberg's 'Sprechstimme'

inhaling sound, exhaling sound

speak while inhaling

or mouth clicks

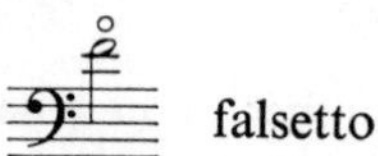

falsetto

toneless, without timbre

sung and whispered sounds, as short as possible

(The above are by no means standard, and represent only a small selection of a wide variety of vocal symbols.)

PERCUSSION

Metals

Crotales

Triangle

or Suspended cymbal

Pair of cymbals (clashed)

Pedal (high hat) cymbals

Cowbell

Sistrum

or Tamtam

Gong

or Sleigh bells

Vibraphone

Glockenspiel

Flexatone

Tubular bells

Woods

Claves

Wood block

Temple block

Log drum

Slit drum

Guiro

Maracas

Castanets

Wood (or glass) chimes

Marimba

Xylophone

Ratchet or rattle

Membranes

Bongos

Tambourine

Timbales

Tomtom

Wooden-headed tomtoms

Snare drum with snare

Snare drum without snare

Congas

Tenor drum

Bass drum (vertical)

Bass drum (laid flat)

Timpani

Indian tablas

Arabic tablas

Sticks or beaters may be indicated as follows:

Hard sticks (wood or plastic heads)

Medium sticks (rubber heads)

Soft sticks (lambswool or soft felt heads)

Metal sticks

Wire brushes

Bass drum stick

Heavy beater (for tamtam etc.)

Index